# BOSTON
# Red Sox
# FIRSTS

# BOSTON
# *Red Sox*
# FIRSTS

## The PLAYERS MOMENTS and RECORDS That Were FIRST in TEAM HISTORY

### BILL NOWLIN

LYONS
PRESS

*Essex, Connecticut*

An imprint of Globe Pequot, the trade division of
The Rowman & Littlefield Publishing Group, Inc.
4501 Forbes Blvd., Ste. 200
Lanham, MD 20706
www.rowman.com

Distributed by NATIONAL BOOK NETWORK

British Library Cataloguing in Publication Information available

**Library of Congress Cataloging-in-Publication Data**

Names: Nowlin, Bill, 1945- author.
Title: Boston Red Sox firsts : the players, moments, and records that were
  first in team history / Bill Nowlin.
Description: Essex, Connecticut : Lyons Press, [2023] | Includes
  bibliographical references. | Summary: "In Boston Red Sox Firsts, veteran Red Sox historian Bill
  Nowlin presents the stories behind the firsts in Red Sox history in question-and-answer format.
  More than a mere trivia book, Nowlin's collection includes substantive answers to the question of
  'who was the first...?' on a variety of topics, many of which will surprise even seasoned fans of the
  Sox"—Provided by publisher.
Identifiers: LCCN 2022056628 (print) | LCCN 2022056629 (ebook) | ISBN 9781493073382
  (paperback) | ISBN 9781493075645 (epub)
Subjects: LCSH: Boston Red Sox (Baseball team)—History.
Classification: LCC GV875.B62 N679 2023  (print) | LCC GV875.B62  (ebook) |
  DDC 796.357/640974461—dc23/eng/20221212
LC record available at https://lccn.loc.gov/2022056628
LC ebook record available at https://lccn.loc.gov/2022056629

# CONTENTS

# INTRODUCTION

THE VERY FIRST TEAM TO WIN THE VERY FIRST WORLD SERIES WAS THE team we now know as the Boston Red Sox. They were also, arguably, the first dynasty when it came to World Series wins. Come the current century, are they at it again? In the first 21 years of the twenty-first century, the Red Sox have won four more world championships, more than any other club.

Baseball is often described as a game in which numbers are of utmost importance—not just which team wins the most games. Baseball fans have always tended to enjoy looking at numbers. Trivia has always been prized by baseball aficionados, but many of the numbers are of real significance—which players hit the most home runs? Hit for the highest batting average? Which pitcher won 20 games in a season? Did a player set a team record for stolen bases? How many games in a row did a given team win? Does a player have a streak of some sort going?

Sometimes it's not just the aggregate numbers that matter, but there has always been a fascination with what comes first? What did a rookie do in his first at-bat? Who was the first player to hit a walk-off home run?

Having written (often working with others) a couple of dozen Red Sox–related books, from *Ted Williams: The Pursuit of Perfection*, to *Mr. Red Sox: The Johnny Pesky Story*, and the only biography of Tom Yawkey to anniversary books on Fenway Park and *Don't Let Us Win Tonight: An Oral History of the 2004 Boston Red Sox's Impossible Playoff Run*, and numerous other "team" books on the 1967 Sox, the 1975 team, the 1986 Red Sox, and so on, it seemed that a book on Red Sox "firsts" would fit right in.

This is just that—a book of firsts. Red Sox firsts. It goes back to the first games in team history, back in 1901. It looks at the first World Series ever played—won by Boston in 1903. It looks at the first Red Sox player to win this award or that. Who was the first Black player on the Red Sox? The first from the Dominican Republic? The first to throw a no-hitter?

It's another way of looking at a team's history, another way to appreciate the highlights (and a few lowlights) over the course of time.

The park the Red Sox plays in—Fenway Park—is the oldest park in major-league baseball. We'll look at some Fenway firsts, too.

Let's start with World Series play since that's the ultimate goal for any team. Then we can step back and look at the founding of the franchise, which started play in 1901. There's always an essential historical element to any look at "firsts," and this book will be no exception. The team has a rich history, and much of it will be explored here, moving forward through time to look at firsts in the categories of hitting, pitching, fielding, baserunning, and other elements of play on the field, as well as a number of things off the field as well.

# RED SOX POSTSEASON FIRSTS

BOSTON WAS INDEED THE FIRST TEAM TO WIN BASEBALL'S WORLD Series. The team was born in 1901 as a charter franchise in the American League. The team had a few names applied to it in its first several years. It was most often called the Boston Americans, distinguishing it from the National League's Boston Beaneaters.

**What was the team's first World Series game?**

The team finished in second place in 1901 and third in 1902, but in 1903, the Boston Americans finished first.

This was the third season for Boston's entry in the new American League. The Chicago White Sox had finished first in 1901 and the Philadelphia Athletics in 1902. Boston's team was populated by a number of players lured over from the National League, key among them the very popular third baseman/manager Jimmy Collins, who had played for the Boston Beaneaters from 1895 through 1900. The Beaneaters had won five NL pennants during the 10 years of the 1890s. Other Beaneaters who joined the 1901 Boston Americans were pitchers Bill Dinneen, Ted Lewis, and George Cuppy—and Cy Young, who had played with St. Louis. Position players from the Beaneaters included Buck Freeman and Chick Stahl. All but Lewis and Cuppy were still with the team in 1903.

The 1903 Americans finished 91–47, a full 14½ games ahead of the second-place Philadelphia Athletics. The 1903 season was the first time the NL and AL champions squared off against each other in what was called a "World's Series." The matchup was the Boston Americans against the National League champion Pittsburgh Pirates, who had finished 6½ games ahead of the New York Giants. The first game was played at Boston's home park, the Huntington Avenue Grounds, on October 1, 1903. Who won? See the next entry.

**Who was the first pitcher to throw a pitch in a World Series game?**

It was none other than Boston's Cy Young. He had led both leagues in wins, with 33 in 1901 and 32 in 1902. His 28–9 record was tops in the AL in 1903. His seven shutouts led both leagues. In Game One of the Series, he recorded outs from the first two batters he faced. Then he gave up a triple to Tommy Leach. Before the top of the first inning was over, he had given up (not in this order) the first single hit in a World Series, the triple from Leach, the first base on balls, seen the first three successfully stolen bases, suffered from the first three errors committed (two by his catcher, Lou Criger), seen the first runs scored (four of them before the inning was over), and was also the first pitcher to record four outs in an inning—after those first two outs, he struck out a batter but saw him reach on Criger's second error. He then struck out opposing pitcher Deacon Phillippe. The Pirates had batted around (another first) and led 4–0.

The first Boston batter to go to the plate in a World Series game was left fielder Patsy Dougherty. He struck out. So did the second batter, manager Jimmy Collins. Then came the first hit in franchise postseason history—by center fielder Chick Stahl, which was a single. Through the first six innings, Pittsburgh built a 6–0 lead. In the top of the seventh, Jimmy Sebring hit the first home run (and the first inside-the-park home run) in World Series history, and it was 7–0.

Finally, in the bottom of the seventh, Boston scored its first run. Right fielder Buck Freeman tripled to right. Shortstop Freddy Parent tripled to left and picked up the first-ever postseason RBI for the team. Perhaps of parochial interest, Pittsburgh's Kitty Bransfield (of Worcester, Massachusetts) was the first native of New England to get a hit in a World Series game. Boston's Hobe Ferris was the first native of old England to get one; Ferris was born in the United Kingdom and forever holds the distinction of being the first batter hit by a pitch in a World Series.

Pittsburgh won the game, 7–3.

4

**Who threw the first shutout in World Series history?**

The answer to this also serves as the answer to the question of when the Boston Americans won their first World Series game.

Game Two in 1903 was a 3–0 shutout at the Huntington Avenue Grounds thrown by Boston's Bill Dinneen. He allowed three Pittsburgh hits, walked one, and struck out 11. The Boston Americans scored two runs in the bottom of the first inning off Pittsburgh's Sam Leever. The righty had led the National League in 1903 with a 2.06 earned run average and posted a record of 25–7. He'd thrown three shutouts during the season, but any hope of doing that in Game Two evaporated when the very first batter homered. (See next entry.) Leever got the second batter, Jimmy Collins, to fly out to left, but Chick Stahl doubled to center field and Buck Freeman singled Stahl home. In the sixth inning, another home run provided the third run.

Dinneen also won two more games in the 1903 World Series: Game Six in Pittsburgh, and the final clinching game, Game Eight, back in Boston. That game was a shutout, too. In regular-season play, Dinneen (21–13) shut out the opposition six times in 1903 and 24 times overall in the 12 seasons he worked, 16 of them in his years pitching for the Americans.

**Who hit the first home run for Boston in World Series history?**

The Pirates' Jimmy Sebring snagged the honor of hitting the first home run in the history of the World Series, but who was the first batter to do so for Boston?

Left fielder Patsy Dougherty picked up the first postseason homer hit by a Boston batter, a leadoff inside-the-park home run in Game Two. Given that Dinneen pitched a shutout, the homer proved to be the only run his team needed. Dougherty was hit by a pitch his next time up, grounded out in his third at-bat, then homered to left field in the sixth, obviously thus earning a distinction that can never be taken from him: the first batter with multiple homers in a World Series game. With two RBI triples in Game Five, he drove in three more runs in Boston's 11–2 win. In the 1903 regular season, Dougherty had led the league in base hits with 195, but only four of them were home runs.

**What was the first win for Boston in the history of the World Series?**

It was indeed Game Two, as detailed in the previous entry, and was the hometown win on October 2, 1903. Through the 2022 season, the team has won 49 World Series games and has lost 29. There was one tie game in 1912. The team holds the odd record of winning the World Series every one of the first five times it competed in one, then losing the next four (each time taking it to Game Seven), and then winning its next four (so far).

**Which was the first baseball team to win a Game Eight in World Series play?**

That was Boston, in Boston, on October 13, 1903. Why was there a Game Eight? In 1903, it was a best-of-nine competition, and after seven games, Boston had won four games to Pittsburgh's three. Had it been a best-of-seven, Boston's 7–3 win in Pittsburgh on October 10 would have wrapped it up right then and there. Game Eight was another Bill Dinneen shutout; he allowed four base hits in that one. He walked two and struck out seven. The score in that one was the same as in Game Two: Boston 3, Pittsburgh 0. Boston's runs came on a two-run fourth-inning single by Hobe Ferris and an RBI single, also by Ferris, in the bottom of the sixth.

Dinneen became the first pitcher to throw two shutouts in a single postseason. He had lost Game Four, 5–4, and won Game Six just two days later, 6–3. With a 3–1 record, he had logged four decisions in one World Series. Each one was a complete game. He had thrown 35 innings and finished with an earned run average of 2.06.

Dinneen had been a 21-game winner in 1902, but he was also a 21-game loser that same year. He had been 21–13, with two saves in the 1903 regular season. In 1904, he had perhaps his best season, going 23–14 with a 2.20 ERA. But there was no World Series.

**Which was the first walk-off game in World Series play?**

That was Game Eight of the 1912 World Series. In 1912, the Series featured the Red Sox against the NL champion New York Giants. Boston won the first game behind the pitching of Smoky Joe Wood at New

York's Polo Grounds. The second game was at Fenway Park, an 11-inning tie at 6–6, in which both teams scored once in the 10th, but darkness resulted in the game being called. The Giants won Game Three, the Red Sox won Games Four and Five, and then the Giants won Game Six and Game Seven, the latter by 11–4, the only game that wasn't quite close. Game Eight was at Fenway, with Hugh Bedient pitching for Boston and Christy Mathewson for New York. The Giants scored once in the third; the Red Sox tied it with one in the seventh when pinch-hitter Olaf Henriksen batted for Bedient and doubled in Jake Stahl. Smoky Joe took over pitching for the Red Sox.

In the top of the 10th, left fielder Red Murray singled and first baseman Fred Merkle doubled him home, giving the Giants a 2–1 lead. Clyde Engle pinch-hit for Wood and lifted a fly to center field, which Fred Snodgrass muffed. Engle wound up on second. An out followed, then a base on balls to Steve Yerkes. Tris Speaker singled to right off Mathewson, tying the game again. He took second base on a futile throw to the plate. After an intentional walk, Larry Gardner hit a fly ball to right field deep enough for Yerkes to tag and score the winning run.

**When was the first time the Boston team won the pennant but did NOT play in the World Series?**

That came about in 1904. When Pittsburgh and Boston played in 1903, it was the first World Series. There was never any guarantee that it would become an annual tradition. The 1904 Boston Americans won the pennant again, but John McGraw's NL-pennant-winning New York Giants declined to play the AL winner. The public stance of McGraw and team owner John T. Brush was that the American League was really a "minor league," that the Giants were superior, and, essentially, did not want to lower themselves by playing a team from the lesser league. Boston thus remained the reigning world champions. It was only in 1905 and the seasons that followed that the World Series became an annual tradition.

**What was the first role that music may have played in a World Series championship?**

In 1903, Boston fandom included the fanatical Royal Rooters. This fervent booster club famously traveled to Pittsburgh where they sang, en masse, to a locally hired band, singing lyrics of their own to a Broadway song of the day, "Tessie"—with lyrics mocking some of the Pirates players: "Honus, why do you hit so badly. Take a back seat and sit down." Today, this may seem a bit juvenile, but it was really how persistently, aggressively, and incessantly they did it which appeared to rattle the Pirates. Pittsburgh baseman Tommy Leach said afterward, "I think those Boston fans won the series . . . we beat them three out of four games, and then they started signing that damn Tessie song . . . Sort of got on your nerves

Boston Rooters at Pittsburgh 1903 World Series. The Boston Rooters pose with Boston Americans players at the Pittsburgh Ball Grounds either before or after the game against the Pittsburgh Pirates on October 6, 1903. Players pictured in the front row: Cy Young, pitcher; Long Tom Hughes, pitcher; George Winters, pitcher; Fred Parent, shortstop; Patsy Dougherty, outfielder; Buck O'Brien, catcher; Jimmie Collins, manager and third baseman; Chick Stahl, outfielder; Buck Freeman, outfielder; Candy LaChance, first baseman; Hobe Ferris, second baseman. Michael T. McGreevy is seated behind Ferris to the right.
MICHAEL T. "NUF CED" MCGREEVY COLLECTION, BOSTON PUBLIC LIBRARY.

after a while." The story of "Tessie" and the relationship between the Red Sox and music is explored at length in the book *Love That Dirty Water!*

**Which team represented the first dynasty of World Series champions?**

Later in the twentieth century, the New York Yankees dominated, piling up world championships. In the first couple of decades, though, the only other team that could challenge the Red Sox (and they were the Red Sox from 1908 on) was the Philadelphia Athletics. The Athletics won the World Series in 1910, 1911, and 1913. But the Red Sox had won in 1912 and then went on to win in 1915, 1916, and 1918. With the notion that four tops three, one could argue that the Red Sox were the first dynasty. That after 1918 it took them 86 years to win again is another story entirely. For what it's worth, the Boston Braves won the World Series in 1914— and played their home games at the larger-capacity Fenway Park. That leads to another first—the first time a team won a World Series without ever winning (or even playing) a game in its own home park. The Braves swept the Series—from the Athletics.

The Red Sox win in 1912 was at Fenway Park and, once again, only ended with a Game Eight win, despite it being a best-of-seven series. How did that come to be? The Red Sox and Giants tied, 6–6, in Game Two at Fenway.

**When was the first time a Red Sox team won the World Series without ever playing a game in their own ballpark?**

The Red Sox weren't the first team to achieve this unlikely distinction. That team was the National League's Boston Braves, in 1914, the so-called Miracle Braves. The year before, they had finished 31½ games out of first place, behind the New York Giants. In the 1914 season itself, they were in eighth place—last place—as late as July 18. Then they started winning. They were 8–2 the rest of July and in fourth place as of July 31. They reached second place on August 10, and on August 25, they tied for first place, for one day. They dropped back to second, but on September 8, they were in first place and never lost their hard-fought top spot. They were 19–6 in August and 26–5 in September. When the season came to an end on October 6, they had won the pennant in 1914, a full 10½ games ahead of the second-place Giants.

The Braves played in the South End Grounds, which had a capacity of approximately 11,000. The demand for Braves tickets far exceeded capacity, and the Red Sox had Fenway Park not all that far away. Beginning on September 7 (Labor Day), the Braves played all remaining home games at Fenway Park thanks to an arrangement with Red Sox owner Joseph J. Lannin. On September 7 alone, they held a dual-admission doubleheader—a morning game and an afternoon game—drawing a reported 35,000 to the first game and 39,162 to the second game—or some 52,000 fans more than if they had played both games at the South End Grounds.

The 1914 Braves played Games One and Two against the AL champion Philadelphia Athletics at Shibe Park, winning the first game 7–1 and then the second 1–0, the lone run not scoring until the top of the ninth. (Charlie Deal doubled, stole third, and then—with two outs—scored on a single by Les Mann.) Both games are reported to have drawn precisely the same number: 20,562.

Returning to Boston and playing at Fenway Park, in front of 35,020, the Braves and Athletics battled for 12 innings. Game Three was tied 2–2 after four, and it went into extras. Philadelphia scored twice in the top of the 10th, but Boston matched that. In the 12th, a leadoff double, an intentional walk, and a throwing error charged to the pitcher on a sacrifice bunt led to the 5–4 win. Game Four was a 3–1 win, with a fifth-inning, two-out, two-run single by Johnny Evers providing the final runs. The Braves were world champions, and (most of) the crowd of 34,365 went wild—on the field at Fenway.

The very next year, it was Boston in the World Series again—but this time, it was the Red Sox. The Braves finished second, seven games behind the Phillies. So it was Boston versus Philadelphia again, but this time, it was with different teams.

When the Red Sox played the World Series in 1915 and 1916, they—like the Braves in 1914—played not one of their games in their own home park, even though Fenway was only three-plus years old. What was going on here that for three years in a row, each Boston team—regardless of league—only played its postseason home games in the other team's ballpark? Was this some new sort of Boston perversity? Not at all. The answer was revenue.

Brand-new Braves Field (which had been hastily constructed and opened on June 5) was even larger than Fenway and could field crowds of up to 7,000 additional paying patrons per game. By 1918, though, the Red Sox played at Fenway, and they won the final game at home—the last time that would happen for 95 years. They won the 2004 and 2007 World Series on the road. Only in 2013 did they again win at home.

In 1915, the Phillies won Game One, at Baker Bowl, 3–1. The Red Sox won Game Two, 2–1, with Rube Foster holding the Phils to just three hits—and drove in the winning run in the top of the ninth. Coming back to Boston, they won again—in front of 42,300 at Braves Field—but it was the same score, again scoring the second run in the ninth inning, though this time they were the home team, so when Duffy Lewis hit a single to drive in Harry Hooper from third base, it was all over. Game Three was—for the third game in a row—also a 2–1 Red Sox victory. There were 41,096 reported in attendance at Braves Field. Single runs in the third (driven in by Hooper) and sixth (driven in by Lewis) did the trick. The two teams traveled back to Philadelphia. The Phillies were up, 4–2, after four innings, but Lewis hit a two-run homer in the eighth inning to tie it, and Hooper hit a solo home run in the ninth to put the Red Sox ahead, 5–4. Foster got a strikeout and two groundouts, and the game was over.

The 1916 World Series saw the Red Sox repeat as champions. The first game at Braves Field didn't really draw all that many more than could have packed into Fenway—36,117—but they saw Boston beat the Brooklyn Robins, 6–5, limiting Brooklyn's ninth-inning rally (with the bases still loaded) to four runs. Game Two drew 5,000 more—41,373—and they saw a 1–1 tie after three innings not resolved until the bottom of the 14th. Both starters—Babe Ruth for Boston and Sherry Smith for the Robins—went the distance. The final 14th saw Dick Hoblitzell draw a walk. Duffy Lewis sacrificed to move him to second base. Mike McNally pinch-ran and scored on pinch-hitter Del Gainer's single to left.

At Ebbets Field, Brooklyn won Game Three, 4–3, then lost Game Four, 6–2.

Game Five was back at Braves Field (42,620), and Ernie Shore picked up his second win.

For three years in a row, a Boston team had won the World Series. In not one of the three years had they played a postseason home game in their own ballpark.

**What was the first World Series game ever attended by a sitting US president?**

On October 9, Game Two of the 1915 World Series was held at Philadelphia's Baker Bowl, with the National League champion Phillies hosting the Red Sox. The Phillies had won the first game, 3–1.

Erskine Mayer was to pitch for Philadelphia and Rube Foster for Boston. The game was held up for about 10 minutes, waiting for President Woodrow Wilson and his new bride to arrive. They were situated in a box near the Red Sox dugout, a box "festooned with flags and bunting." President Wilson threw out the ceremonial first pitch (a "bad throw," according to the *New York Times*).

Both contending pitchers threw very good games, though Foster only gave up three hits while Mayer gave up 10. The final score was 2–1. The Red Sox scored once in the top of the first and once in the top of the ninth (with Foster singling in the go-ahead, and winning, run). Foster was 3-for-4 at the plate. The Phillies scored only once, in the bottom of the fifth. The game took two hours and five minutes to play. All accounts indicated that the president was in exceptionally good spirits and enjoyed the game; he even kept his own scorecard. He was seen rooting for the home team Phillies but was visibly impressed by Foster in the ninth and was said to have rooted for Foster to seal his victory for the Red Sox.

"The Star-Spangled Banner" was played in the middle of the ninth inning, and the Associated Press characterized it as the "national anthem."

**Who was the first (and only) Red Sox player to play before both the President of the United States and the King of England and also had an audience with the Pope?**

Tris Speaker was 1-for-4 in the 1915 World Series Game Two that President Woodrow Wilson took in. He singled in the first inning, putting runners at first and third with one out. Then he and Harry Hooper tried a double steal. Speaker was thrown out at second base, and it looked like Hooper was out at the plate as well but for an error by Phillies catcher Ed Burns handling a difficult throw from second baseman Bert Niehoff on which Hooper scored.

Eighteen months earlier, on February 11, 1914, Speaker had been with a group of touring major-league ballplayers who were granted an audience at the Vatican before Pope Pius X. As has been noted elsewhere, this was particularly ironic in that Speaker was one of the Masons on a Red Sox team that bristled with division between Catholics and anti-Catholics. He was, at times, not on speaking terms with fellow outfielder Duffy Lewis, a Catholic.

Fifteen days after the Vatican visit, Speaker appeared in a baseball game at London's Stamford Bridge Grounds (home of the Chelsea soccer team). It was an 11-inning exhibition game between the New York Giants and Chicago White Sox, both teams populated in part by players from other major-league teams and taking part in a four-month postseason tour that took them to 13 countries on four continents. Speaker was on the Red Sox from late 1907 through 1915. He played on the "White Sox" during the world tour. The game was seen by King George V, who stayed for the full game. It was 1–1 after nine. The Giants scored twice in the top of the 10th but a two-run homer by Chicago's Sam Crawford tied it again. In the bottom of the 11th, White Sox batter Tom Daly (who later served as a Red Sox coach from 1933 through 1946) hit a game-winning home run deep into the crowd seated in left field to win it.

In the course of the tour, Speaker had also played before the last Khedive (Viceroy) of Egypt, Abbas II.

The world tour also brought Speaker to Australia, Hong Kong, The Philippines, Ceylon, and Japan. In a December 6, 1913, game against Tokyo's Keio University, he hit two home runs. Jim Elfers has written up the tour in his book *The Tour to End All Tours*.

## When was Babe Ruth's first World Series appearance?

Over the course of postseason play, Babe Ruth homered 15 times and drove in 33 runs. As a pitcher, he had been 18–8 with a 2.44 earned run average for the Red Sox in the 1915 season. The only two pitchers with better won/loss records were Rube Foster and Ernie Shore. Both of them were 19–8. The Babe had batted .315. Foster had hit .277, but Shore had hit just .101. How did Ruth do in this first World Series? Ruth didn't pitch to a single batter. He came to the plate once, as a pinch-hitter for Shore in the top of the ninth inning in Game One. Shore had been 1-for-3 in the game. The Phillies were leading 3–1. Ruth came up with a runner on first base and one out. He grounded out to first base, unassisted. The next batter made an out, and the Phillies had won. Boston won the next four games, though, all of them by just one run: 2–1, 2–1, 2–1, and 5–4.

**What was Babe Ruth's first turn on the mound in a World Series game?**
Ruth started Game Two of the 1916 World Series against the Brooklyn Robins. Henry Harrison "Hi" Myers hit an inside-the-park home run off him in the top of the first. He threw 13 scoreless innings and won, 2–1, in the 14th, when Del Gainer singled in the winning run. Ruth himself had driven in the lone Red Sox run back in the third inning, on a

Babe Ruth in his final year with the Red Sox, 1919.

groundout. As a batter, Ruth appeared in three World Series for Boston and was 1-for-11, the one hit being a two-run triple in 1918. In the 1918 World Series, Ruth threw a shutout to win Game One against the Cubs and won Game Four, 3–2.

### When was the first base hit by Babe Ruth in a World Series game for the Red Sox?

Babe Ruth played in 11 World Series games for Boston but never hit a homer. In fact, he only ever had one extra-base hit, a two-run triple in Game Four of the 1918 World Series. His first appearance in a World Series was in Game One in 1915. As noted, he pinch-hit in the ninth inning that grounded out to first base. It was his only appearance that year. The Red Sox returned to the World Series the very next year. He pitched Game Two and won it, 2–1, in 14 innings against the Phillies' Sherry Smith, who likewise went the distance but lost on a walk, sacrifice bunt, and single to left by Del Gainer. Ruth was 0-for-5 at the plate, but he had driven in the game's only run before extra innings, with a ground-out back in the third inning. As in 1915, Ruth only appeared in one game, though he likely would have pitched Game Five had the Red Sox not swept the Series in four.

In 1918, he pitched and won Game One, 1–0. He was 0-for-3 at the plate, with two strikeouts. He started Game Four and held the Cubs to two runs in a 3–2 win. In the fourth inning, Ruth hit a two-run triple to Fenway Park's right-center field, giving the Red Sox their first two runs. The Cubs tied it in the top of the eighth, but Boston scored a third run on a single, a passed ball, and then a throwing error by pitcher Phil Douglas on a sacrifice bunt that allowed the runner to score from second base.

For the Red Sox, Ruth had a total of 11 World Series at-bats and just the one quite significant base hit. He hit 15 homers in World Series play, all for the New York Yankees.

### When was the first time "The Star-Spangled Banner" was played ceremonially before a sporting event?

"The Star-Spangled Banner" wasn't officially designated the national anthem until 1931. But it was played during at least one of the games in

1903 (the final Game Eight). The first game of the 1918 Series played in Boston was Game Four. The First World War was on in earnest—the reason the World Series was played in September and not in October—and "The Star-Spangled Banner" was played prior to the game. There seems to be general acknowledgment that this was when the tradition began.

**When was the first time the Red Sox lost a World Series?**

It was 43 years after the team won their first World Series until the team lost their first one. After winning every one of the first five World Series in which they competed (1903 against the Pittsburgh Pirates, 1912 against the New York Giants, 1915 against the Philadelphia Phillies, 1916 against the Brooklyn Robins, and 1918 against the Chicago Cubs), the team went into some doldrums. They didn't even make the Series for the next 28 years. When they did, they lost it, in 1946, a Series that went the full seven games before the St. Louis Cardinals came out triumphant. As it happens, the Sox lost the next three Series in which they took part—1967 (losing to the Cardinals again), 1975 (losing to Cincinnati's Big Red Machine), and 1986 (losing to the New York Mets)—every one of them taking the full seven games to resolve but with the Red Sox coming up short each time. It was 86 years between World Series wins. They never won another one until after the next millennium began.

**Which was the first Red Sox team to go worst to first to worst?**

The first team to be worst in their division, win the World Series, then revert to worst once more was the Boston Red Sox. In 2012, the Red Sox finished in last place in the AL East, 26 games behind the New York Yankees. That team was 69–96 under manager Bobby Valentine. In 2013, they not only finished first in the division (97–65 under John Farrell), but they beat Tampa Bay, Detroit, and St. Louis to win all three rounds of the postseason, never once letting a series go to a final winner-take-all game. In 2014, they were 71–97 (still under Farrell) and finished last in the East, 25 games behind the first-place Orioles.

There has only been one other team that was a World Series winner the year after finishing in last place—the 1991 Minnesota Twins. They finished 29 games behind in 1990 but in 1992 only dropped to second place.

From 1918 to 2004 was more than a lifetime for many Red Sox fans.
BILL NOWLIN PHOTO

**Who was the first player to have played in only one game at Fenway Park—against the Red Sox—and to have earned and received a world championship ring as a member of the Red Sox?**

Admittedly, the notion seems strange. Someone who played against the Red Sox got a world championship ring from the Red Sox? They committed an error, allowing the Red Sox to win the deciding game? No, not at all. He was a pitcher. Okay, so he served up a gopher ball to a Red Sox batter to win a key game? Another clue—he pitched for the San Diego Padres. But the Red Sox have never faced the Padres in a postseason game. What year was it for which he earned this ring? It was 2004. Well, that was certainly a memorable year in Red Sox history—the first World Series win in 86 years. The team that year sometimes described themselves as "the idiots." So was this pitcher an idiot. "I think I could have been a great idiot," he said when the season was over.

He had joined the Padres in January, signing as a free agent after two seasons and throwing 68 games in relief for the Houston Astros. His record was 3–3. His name was Brandon Puffer.

When the Red Sox purchased his contract from the Padres on July 2, Puffer was 0–1, had appeared in 14 games for the Padres, and had an earned run average of 5.50. The game he had pitched at Fenway Park was on June 10, a Thursday night game. Curt Schilling—a more widely-known name on the 2004 Red Sox pitching staff—started for Boston. He gave up a run in the top of the first. Starting for the Padres was righty Ismael Valdéz. He pitched scoreless ball in the first and second innings, then gave up a run in the third on a Pokey Reese homer and two more in the fourth on a Manny Ramirez homer. After starting the fifth with a single, a walk, and an RBI double to Kevin Youkilis, Padres manager Bruce Bochy had Puffer relieve Valdéz. Puffer struck out David Ortiz.

There followed, though, an intentional walk, a double, a strikeout, and then another double. It was 8–1 Red Sox before the inning was over. Puffer retired the side in the sixth, then loaded the bases with nobody out in the seventh before retiring three batters in a row for another scoreless inning. The Red Sox won, 9–3, and three weeks later, they signed Puffer to a Red Sox contract.

That very same day, however, the Red Sox also acquired left-handed pitcher Jimmy Anderson from the Chicago Cubs. Puffer was told to report to Pawtucket. He pitched well there, appearing in 24 games with a 3–2 record, 21 of them as a closer, with a 3.26 ERA. Anderson only appeared in five games for the Red Sox, without a win or a loss.

After the major-league rosters expanded on September 1, Puffer was summoned to Boston. Ramiro Mendoza had a sore groin, and the bullpen had thrown 6⅓ innings on September 1. Puffer told the *Boston Globe*, "Even coming here as a visitor, the buzz around here was unbelievable. Being able to put this uniform on and play here is even a lot sweeter."

He did put the Red Sox uniform on and did some throwing, but he never got into a game for the team. Center fielder Johnny Damon got hurt in the September 2 game, and suddenly, the Red Sox needed a replacement outfielder. They called up Adam Hyzdu on September 3 and designated Puffer for assignment. Damon was out for four days.

Puffer had arrived on September 2, spent the evening of September 3 in uniform in the Red Sox bullpen, and then was gone the following day. The Red Sox beat the Rangers 2–0 on September 3, a Pedro Martínez start. Martínez went seven and, given such a tight game, was followed by the usual cast of bullpen supports—Timlin, Embree, and Foulke. Puffer had been with the team, ready to work if needed. He was part of the team, a reserve who could have been called upon. Perhaps he might have in a game like the 13–2 win in Seattle on September 13. But that is not how it panned out. Still, he was truly an official part of the team, and the Red Sox recognized everyone on the team with a ring.

In a December 2007 e-mail to this author, Puffer wrote, "The Red Sox were extremely gracious including me in the lucky group of people to receive such a special memento to 'The Nation.'"

## Who was the first (and still only) Red Sox player to have been on four World Series–winning Red Sox teams?

Right fielder Harry Hooper played for the Red Sox from 1909 to 1920. He was on four teams that won the World Series—1912, 1915, 1916, and 1918. He played in 24 Series games and batted overall at .293, with six RBIs and 13 runs scored. He was a key component, a leader on the four pennant-winning teams. Prized for his defense and skilled as a leadoff batter, he was never a team leader on offense but always among the leaders in runs scored during the regular season—ranking second in both 1912 and 1915 and tops in 1916 and 1918. There have been players such as David Ortiz on three Red Sox world championship teams, but none other than Harry Hooper has been on four.

## Who was the first Red Sox player to drive in four runs in successive clinching games that won both a League Championship Series and a World Series?

In Game Six of the 2013 ALCS, the Detroit Tigers threatened to tie the series at three wins apiece, setting up a winner-take-all Game Seven. Detroit held a 2–1 lead through the seventh-inning stretch. The Red Sox only had three base hits in the game. Jonny Gomes led off with a double, Boston's fourth hit. Max Scherzer struck out the next batter but then walked the third and was relieved by Drew Smyly. Jacoby Ellsbury reached on an error, loading the bases. José Veras replaced Smyly to pitch to Shane Victorino. Victorino, who was 2-for-23 (.087) in the ALCS. On an 0–2 count, Victorino hit a grand slam into the Red Sox bullpen in right field. The Red Sox won, 5–2, and clinched.

In Game Six of the 2013 World Series, the Red Sox held a three-games-to-two lead. There was no score until the bottom of the third. An Ellsbury single, intentional walk to David Ortiz, and Jonny Gomes being hit by a pitch brought up Victorino again with the bases loaded. This time, he doubled, clearing the bases. And in the very next inning, Victorino came up again with the bases loaded—three at-bats in a row this had happened (he had walked in the second). Victorino singled and drove in another run. The Red Sox won, 6–1, and clinched the World Series—at home for the first time since 1918.

Victorino was a Gold Glove right fielder in 2013 and hit .294 with 15 homers, 61 runs batted in, and 82 runs scored, but injuries prevented him from playing much in 2014 or 2015, when he was traded to the Angels in late July.

**Who was the first Red Sox player to hit a home run in his last at-bat in a major-league uniform, a home run that produced the winning run in the clinching game of a World Series?**

No prolonged guessing here—the answer is Bobby Kielty. He had played 579 major-league games before coming to Boston, and homered 52 times, in a career dating back to April 10, 2001. Kielty was a switch-hitting right-handed outfielder who had been released by the Oakland Athletics on July 31, 2007. On August 6, he signed with the Red Sox. He was 2-for-3 in his first game for Boston on August 19. With the Red Sox as a reserve outfielder, he got into 20 games, batting .231 with one homer and nine RBIs. Six of his RBIs and the homer had come in back-to-back lopsided games against the White Sox in Chicago, with Boston winning 14–2 and 11–1.

He was added to the Red Sox roster for the postseason, though not because of any demonstrated history in that particular department. He had previously played in nine postseason games for the 2002 Twins and the 2006 Oakland Athletics. He was 0-for-10 in the postseason, though in Game Five of the 2002 ACLS, he had walked and forced in the tying run in the top of the seventh, making it 3–3. The Angels scored 10 runs in the bottom of the seventh, though, and the Twins were eliminated.

In Game One of the 2007 ALCS, at Fenway Park against Cleveland, he was the starting right fielder and was 1-for-2 in the game with a two-run single in the fifth that boosted Boston's score to 7–1. He also started Game Five and was 1-for-3.

On October 28, in Game Four of the 2007 World Series, the Red Sox had won the first three games and held a 3–1 lead after seven innings at Coors Field. The game was being played under National League rules (pitchers were in the batting order), and so manager Terry Francona asked Kielty to pinch-hit for reliever Mike Timlin, who was due to lead off the top of the eighth. The Rockies' Brian Fuentes, a left-hander, came into the game and took his warmup pitches. Plate umpire Chuck Meriwether gave the sign to Fuentes to start the inning. Batting right-handed, Kielty swung at the first pitch the Rockies pitcher threw and knocked it several rows deep over the fence and into the seats in left field.

The homer made the score 4–3, and it proved to be the winning run since the Rockies' Garrett Atkins hit a two-run homer in the bottom of the eighth—and there was no more scoring. "Probably the greatest moment I'll ever have in baseball," he said after the game. "The game-winning home run in the World Series."

It was not just a game-winner. The victory gave the Red Sox the world championship; they had swept the Rockies. For Kielty, it was not the end of the road. He played five more years in the minor leagues and another in independent ball, but it was his last major-league at-bat. One swing, a ring, and a moment he could cherish forever.

### When was the first time the Red Sox won the World Series and then lowered ticket prices for the following season?

It was said that owner J. J. Lannin was a true fan of the game. Rather than sit in a sealed-off luxury suite, he preferred to sit in the bleachers, both for the enjoyment of it but also to learn what fans were truly thinking. In January 1916, after the team had won the 1915 World Series, they announced ticket prices for the 1916 season. Box seats were cut from $1.50 to $1.00, and grandstand seats were cut to 75 cents. They also offered 25-cent and 50-cent seats.

Less than three weeks after the Red Sox won the 1916 World Series, fatigued from constant disagreements with AL president Ban Johnson, Lannin preempted a move Johnson seemed to have in mind and sold the team to New York theater men Hugh Ward and Harry Frazee. Lannin was a native of Canada, and considerably more on him may be found in chapter 9 on foreign natives and the Red Sox.

# STANDINGS

AFTER THOSE FIRST FIVE WORLD SERIES WINS (AND WINNING THE PEN-
nant in 1904 without playing in the World Series), Red Sox fans experienced that lengthy 86-year-long drought between world championships.
Sometimes they finished first in the league, or their division, but they fell
short of the ultimate goal. Sometimes they finished last. After all, someone had to.

In the days since 1995, when the two leagues each had three divisions
and the Wild Card was first introduced, a team no longer needs to finish
first in its division to make the postseason—and potentially go all the way.
The Florida Marlins proved this in 1997.

**When was the first time the team finished in last place?**

For its first five years, the Boston Americans won more games than
they lost. In 1903, as we have seen, they won the first World Series ever
held. They won the pennant again in 1904, and the Giants declined to
take them on in what would have been the second Series. They finished
78–74 (third place) in 1905. To that point, the team had never suffered a
losing season.

Then they collapsed, losing 31 games more than any previous year.
They finished 49–105, solidly in last place (eighth place), 45½ games
behind the Chicago White Sox. There are no books devoted to chroni-
cling the 1906 team.

They hit last place, where they would stay, on May 2, after just 15
games, and remained in the cellar the rest of the season. They were only
marginally better at home than on the road (.364 to .342). Their best

month was April (6–7). There were 32 games that they lost by five or more runs.

Not even Cy Young seemed to be able to help. He was a 20-game loser, with a record of 13–21. Fellow right-hander Joe Harris had the worst record of all (2–21).

Jimmy Collins left as manager, succeeded for the final 40 games by Chick Stahl. And Stahl committed suicide less than six months later, near the end of spring training in 1907. The cause of death was never ascribed to the performance of the team or his own play—he hit quite well in 1906 (.286, second best), and the team played marginally better during those final 40 games. It was more likely due to depression and perhaps romantic situations.

The 1907 team was initially managed by Cy Young (3–3 in six games) and then two others before settling on Deacon McGuire. They finished in seventh place in 1907, fifth place in 1908, and third in 1909.

## When was the first time the team finished in last place two years in a row?

Those two years were 1922 and 1923. After winning the 1918 World Series, the team dropped all the way to sixth place in 1919 (66–71–1), bumped up a bit to fifth in 1920, and held there in 1921. But in 1922, they dropped to last place, winning just 61 games. Hugh Duffy managed in both 1921 and 1922. Frank Chance was the manager in 1923, and the team again won just 61 games and again finished last. Only a narrow escape in 1924 prevented a repeat. They finished seventh, 25 games out of first place—but a half-game ahead of the last-place Chicago White Sox. Had they lost one more game, it could have been more ignominy.

The 1920s weren't a happy decade for Red Sox fans. The 75 wins in 1921 were the most wins the team accomplished in any of the 10 years. With 595 wins and 938 losses, they averaged under 60 wins while losing more than 90.

## When was the first time the team finished last five years in a row?

It wasn't only five years in a row. It was six. And had they lost one more game in 1924, it could have been nine years in a row. The six years were: 1925, 1926, 1927, 1928, 1929, and 1930. The first three years, they lost over 100 games: 105 in 1925, 107 in 1926, and 103 in 1927.

Linked up with the back-to-back last-place finishes in 1922 and 1923, it was only by escaping by that half-game in 1924 that the optics were marginally better. In the stretch from 1925 to 1930, they never won as many as 60 games.

Why did 2,000 people come out to see the final Fenway Park game of the 1930 season? Maybe many were Washington Senators fans. Washington won 8–3. Why did 12,000 people come out to see the final Red Sox home game? It was at Braves Field on a Sunday, and the Red Sox couldn't play on Sundays at Fenway Park. It was a Yankees game, and Babe Ruth pitched for the Yankees. He won, giving him a record of 1–0 on the season. He didn't just pitch an inning. He threw a complete game win, 9–3. One of the runs was unearned. Ruth hadn't pitched in a major-league game since 1921. He was 2–0 that year. In fact, in his final four seasons pitching in the majors, Ruth was undefeated—1–0 in 1920, 2–0 in 1921, 1–0 in 1930, and 1–0 in 1933. He never lost a game pitching for the Yankees.

Why did any fans come out for Opening Day in 1931? Hope springs eternal? They had a new manager—John Francis "Shano" Collins—and it was a Yankees game. The Red Sox lost. They were 3–7 in April, but by year's end, they had won 62 games. And they finished sixth (the Tigers and the White Sox were even worse).

Perhaps this is enough wallowing in failure. Red Sox fans of a certain age are used to disappointment—first hope, but then what always seemed to be the inevitable letdown. But let's take a break. Let's go back in time and run through a number of firsts in franchise history.

**When was the first time the Red Sox took advantage of the Wild Card and did go all the way to win the World Series?**

The 2004 Red Sox finished second in the AL East standings, three games behind the New York Yankees. But they beat the Angels, beat the Yankees in the ALCS, and swept St. Louis in the World Series.

In 2005, they finished tied with the Yankees in division play, but as the Yankees had the better head-to-head record, the Red Sox played the White Sox in the ALDS—and were swept.

In 2007, they placed first in the AL East standings and held off the Angels in the Division Series, then beat Cleveland in the League Championship Series and swept the Colorado Rockies in the World Series.

They were second to the Tampa Bay Rays in the 2008 East standings and beat the Angels in the ALDS but lost to the Rays in the ALCS.

The Red Sox were second in the division in 2009 but were swept by the Angels in the Division Series.

They won the division in 2013 and went all the way.

After last-place finishes in 2014 and 2015, Boston won the division again in 2016. They were swept by Cleveland in the ALDS.

They repeated, winning the AL East again in 2017, but this time were eliminated by the Houston Astros, losing three of four in the Division Series.

In 2018, with 108 wins, they led the division and then won each of the three rounds of postseason play.

The 2021 Red Sox took advantage of the Wild Card once more, beating the New York Yankees, topped Tampa Bay in the ALDS, and came within two wins of reaching the World Series—but were beat out by the Astros, four games to two, in the ALCS.

As to the 2022 season, perhaps it's best to just pretend it never happened.

# FRANCHISE FIRSTS

Let's leave the World Series and—for now—concerns about where the team finished in the standings—and go way back to the very beginning. Naturally, most of any team's "firsts" are going to happen in the first game the team ever played. We'll look at that first game and many of the firsts that it spawned, sometimes with just a line or two, sometimes in a bit more depth. They may not have been the most memorable moments in team history, but they were the first and thus noteworthy. Given the lack of video coverage, we can't know the first time a batter stepped out of the box to call time, but we can present information about the first walk, the first wild pitch, and a few other firsts.

**What was the first game in franchise history?**

All these firsts happened in the very first game:

First franchise game: April 26, 1901 (Baltimore Orioles 10, Boston Americans 6), played at Oriole Park in Baltimore. Boston gave up three runs in the bottom of the first inning and never once held the lead nor drew even. Tommy Dowd, the team's left fielder, had four runs batted in.

Starting pitchers in the first game: The veteran (and future Hall of Famer) "Iron Man" Joe McGinnity (for Baltimore) versus Win Kellum (for Boston). Both pitched complete games. Over the course of their careers, McGinnity won 246 games and Kellum won 20, though only two were for the Red Sox. This was not one of them.

First player from Massachusetts to play in a franchise game: The leadoff batter in the top of the first inning was left fielder "Buttermilk" Tommy Dowd from Holyoke, Massachusetts. He grounded out to the Baltimore pitcher, McGinnity, 1–3.

First player born in Boston to play for the Boston Americans: Catcher Jack Slattery was the only man on the 1901 Boston Americans who was born in the city of Boston. He just barely made it, only getting into a game on the very last day of the franchise's first season. In the first game of the September 28 doubleheader, he was 1-for-3, picking up an RBI on a third-inning single. He also drew a base on balls but had to leave the game in the eighth inning due to a split thumb on a foul tip. Boston won the game, 8–3, and the day's second game as well. Ossee Schrecongost had taken over catching duties. Though Slattery later played in another 102 big-league games, none were for Boston.

First player to be a native of a country outside the United States: Boston starting pitcher Win Kellum, born in Waterford, Ontario, Canada. It was his major-league debut.

First pitch by a Boston pitcher: left-hander Win Kellum. Despite his nickname (short for Winford), Kellum lost the game.

First hit off Boston pitching: Leadoff batter John McGraw doubled off the fence in right field. McGraw played third base and also managed the Baltimore team.

First run scored off Boston pitching: "Turkey Mike" Donlin—the left fielder—followed McGraw's double with a triple over Chick Stahl's head in center field, and the score was 1–0, with nobody out and Donlin on third.

First base on balls issued by Boston pitching: Kellum walked second baseman Jimmy Williams, the third batter up in the first inning.

First strikeout: Win Kellum struck out right fielder Cy Seymour in the first, the first out recorded by the Boston team.

First wild pitch: It was thrown by Kellum but not until May 1 in Philadelphia.

First fielding out by a defensive player: Buck Freeman recorded the putout when Jim Jackson followed Seymour's strikeout with an out at first base.

First Boston batter to work a base on balls: Buck Freeman, in the second inning.

First manager of Boston's American League team: player/manager Jimmy Collins, who also played third base.

First Boston hit: Jimmy Collins, who doubled between short and third in the top of the fourth.

First Boston run scored: Jimmy Collins, from second base in the fourth inning.

First RBI: Buck Freeman, who swung at a 3-2 pitch and singled to left field, driving in Jimmy Collins in the fourth.

First multiple-hit game: Both Collins and catcher Lou Criger had two hits for three total bases apiece.

First double in team history: that two-base hit by Collins in the fourth inning.

First base hit by a Boston pitcher: Win Kellum, in the eighth inning on an infield single to third base.

First stolen base: the *Sun* of Baltimore box score shows Tommy Dowd with a stolen base in the very first game, though the Boston newspapers do not.

First Boston error: Jimmy Collins committed a fielding error in the bottom of the eighth inning.

Player-manager Jimmy Collins of the Boston Americans raises the first World Series championship flag on Opening Day of 1904 as members of the Boston Americans and Washington Nationals look on.
MICHAEL T. "NUF CED" MCGREEVY COLLECTION, BOSTON PUBLIC LIBRARY.

First Boston pinch-hitter: Larry McLean, who doubled to right field, batting for Kellum in the top of the ninth. Kellum thus became the first player removed for a pinch-hitter.

First futile Boston rally: Despite scoring two runs in the eighth and three more runs in the ninth, Boston still lost the game, 10–6.

First loss by a Boston pitcher: Win Kellum pitched a complete game but did suffer the 10–6 loss on April 26. In his next start, on May 1, he fared even worse, losing 14–1 in Philadelphia against the Athletics. He was tagged for 20 base hits. Six days later, he earned his first win, a 7–3 four-hitter in Washington. He lost his fourth start and won his fifth. Kellum wasn't long with Boston; though he is featured here in a number of firsts, he was released on June 25 with a record of 2–3 and a 6.38 earned run average.

### What notable firsts occurred in later games that first year, 1901?

First double play by Boston: Freddy Parent to first baseman Larry McLean, an inning-ending double play in the bottom of the first inning on April 27, in the season's second game. Baltimore won that game, 12–6.

First player to steal two bases in a game: Dowd walked and stole second in the first inning on April 29, then stole third and scored on a bad throw to third—all before the second batter completed his at-bat.

First Boston catcher to throw out a baserunner: unclear. It was either April 29 or 30, 1901. Criger got an assist on April 29, but contemporary news accounts don't make it clear how he earned it. He had three assists in the April 30 game, and two of them were throwing out runners. In the third inning, Criger threw out Phil Geier.

First home run: In the fourth game of the year, on April 30 in Philadelphia, Buck Freeman hit a two-run homer off Billy Milligan in the top of the ninth to send the game into extra innings. This was the game Boston won, 10–6, for the first win in team history. Freeman played for the team through 1906, with four April games in 1907. He hit 48 home runs over that stretch.

First win: After the team lost its first three games, the first win went to Cy Young, beating the Athletics, 8–6, in 10 innings on April 30, 1901, despite giving up 12 hits and walking one. Young won 33 games for the

1901 Boston Americans (he was 33–10) and led both leagues with an earned run average of 1.62. Five shutouts helped in that regard. The win was the first for the new team and the first of 192 wins that Cy Young had for the Americans/Red Sox. He's tied with Roger Clemens for the most wins in team history. Tim Wakefield is next, with 186.

First extra-inning game: that 8–6 win at Philadelphia on April 30, 1901. Young drove in two runs in the game. Boston was losing, 6–2, after three innings but added single runs in the sixth and seventh and then tied it with two more in the top of the ninth on Freeman's two-out, two-run homer. With one out in the top of the tenth, Charlie Hemphill singled to right for one run, then saw the baserunner on third score on Stahl's sacrifice fly. Young, who had struggled early on, only gave up three base hits over the final seven innings.

First extra-inning win at home: It might have seemed a long time coming. Boston lost three extra-inning games in July, all on the road. On August 13, the Philadelphia Athletics were in town. Facing Ted Lewis, they jumped out to a quick 2–0 lead in the top of the first inning. They added a third run in the top of the seventh. Lewis DeWitt "Snake" Wiltse had held Boston scoreless until the bottom of the eighth. It was Lewis who kicked things off with a leadoff double, but then Dowd flied out to center. Stahl hit one back to Wiltse, who threw out Lewis trying to get to third base. Two outs and Stahl on first base. Jimmy Collins tripled "to the ticket office," and Stahl scored. Freeman walked and then stole second. Hemphill singled into right field, and both runners scored. There the rally ended, but the score was 3–3.

There was no scoring in the 10th, 11th, or 12th, and Lewis held the Athletics scoreless in the top of the thirteenth. Jimmy Collins led off the bottom of the 13th with a triple to left field. Buck Freeman followed with a single to right field, and it was another Boston win.

First triple in franchise history: In the sixth game of the season, May 2, center fielder Chick Stahl tripled in the third inning. He wasn't the only one who tripled in the game. Boston's Freddy Parent and Lou Criger both tripled, too. Boston also hit seven doubles in the game, two of them by Parent. There were no home runs but 10 extra-base hits in the 23–12 win.

First extra-base hit by a Boston pitcher: Ted Lewis, a double, on May 2 in Philadelphia. In 39 appearances during the 1901 season—his last—he had three extra-base hits and a .174 batting average but won 16 games.

First truly high-scoring game: In the May 2 game, the final score was Boston 23, Philadelphia 12. Relief pitcher Bill Bernhard was tagged for 18 runs after starter Pete Loos gave up five in the first inning. Ted Lewis worked a complete game for Boston. Lewis later became the first Boston player to become a university president with his appointment to that post at the University of New Hampshire.

First postponement: in Washington on May 5, 1901, due to rain

First home game: After scoring 79 runs in its first 10 games (but only recording a 5–5 mark on the road), the team played its first home game on Huntington Avenue, on May 8, 1901. Cy Young won a 12–4 victory over the Philadelphia Athletics.

First player to hit two home runs in the same game: Buck Freeman (June 1, 1901, in Chicago)—Freeman was the first to do so in the American League. Boston won that game, 10–5.

First shutout win by Boston: May 25, when Ted Lewis threw a six-hit 5–0 shutout in Cleveland.

First ejection of a Boston ballplayer: Buck Freeman, on May 11, 1901, by umpire John Haskell. Nabbed off second base after doubling in the bottom of the second inning, Freeman "ran at the umpire and grabbed him by the two shoulders." His ejection may have spelled the difference in a 3–2 loss to Washington. Freeman was later fined $10. It was the 13th game in franchise history.

First shutout: a 4–0 loss to the Washington Senators, in Boston, on May 15, 1901. It capped the first sweep by an opponent in a series in Boston, as the Americans lost four games in a row to visiting Washington. Wyatt "Watty" Lee was the Washington pitcher; he held Boston to four hits and only walked one—opposing pitcher George Cuppy. Lee shut out Boston the next time he pitched against them, 2–0 in Boston on June 27, on seven hits. On July 7, Boston turned the tables on him, scoring seven runs in the first three innings and driving him from the game while Cy Young threw an eight-hit shutout for Boston.

First sweep of a homestand of more than two games: June 7–11, 1901. Boston swept all five games from the visiting Milwaukee team. Between June 17 and 20, Boston swept five games in a row from the visiting White Sox. In fact, Boston beat Chicago every one of the 10 games that the White Sox played in Boston in 1901. And beat Milwaukee every one of the 10 games the Brewers played in Boston. Chicago won the pennant, but Milwaukee came in last.

**What were some other first games before and after the regular season?**
First spring training game: April 5, 1901, at Charlottesville, Virginia: Boston 13, University of Virginia 0. It was one of only two preseason games they played against another opponent. The second was a 23–0 win over the University of Virginia on April 11. That's a total of 36–0 in the two games. One could hazard a guess that it wasn't the kind of competition to whip a team into top form. There were some intrasquad games, such as the 12-inning game they played on April 12—12 innings with the score Regulars 25, Subs 6. There was no tie after nine. They just played a few extra innings to get a little extra work in.

First midseason exhibition game: Such games were very common in the earlier years of team history. It was not infrequent for the team to play three or four such games. They played 10 of them in 1908, eight in 1919, 14 in 1921, and nine in 1934. The last year in which they played as many as four was 1951. The first was on April 28, 1901, at Weehawken, New Jersey: Boston 5, Weehawken 2.

First postseason game: an exhibition game held on September 30, 1901, at the Huntington Avenue Grounds: Boston Americans 7, Chicago White Sox 5.

**What was the first time the team basically killed time, playing post-season exhibition games while waiting for someone from the National League to play in the World Series?**
Let us allow a brief tangent while thinking about in-season and post-season exhibition games.

The last postseason exhibition game was in 1946. We're talking about games played after the regular season was over. There were three of them, on October 1, 2, and 3, and all at Fenway Park. The American League season had ended on September 29. The Red Sox had won the pennant by a full 12 games over the second-place Detroit Tigers. They had been in first place from April 25 on. Once they played their tenth game of the season, they were in first place and never once dropped back, even for 24 hours.

In the National League, it was different. When the season ended on September 29, the Brooklyn Dodgers and St. Louis Cardinals were both tied for first place with identical records of 96–58. Plans were made for them to play a best-of-three playoff series for the pennant. On October 1, the Cardinals won the first game, in Brooklyn, 4–2. The two teams traveled to St. Louis to play the second game, on October 3. The Cardinals won that one, too, 8–4. They won the pennant. But meanwhile, the Red Sox were in danger of losing whatever edge they might have had. They'd been able to cruise leading up to September 29 but now faced the prospect of sitting idle the next day and then the first five days of October as they awaited the World Series start on October 6.

Oddly enough, manager Joe Cronin had told several of his players to go on vacation in the waning weeks of the season. Realizing they really needed to try to keep as sharp as they could be to be ready to take on whichever team won the NL flag, arrangements were made to round up a number of "American League All-Stars" from other AL teams and play a series of games. Among the "All-Stars" were Joe DiMaggio from the Yankees (his brother Dom was a star with the Red Sox), Hal Newhouser from Detroit, Mickey Haefner and Stan Spence from the Washington Senators, and Luke Appling and Eddie Lopat from the White Sox. It might have been a good idea, but unforeseen was what came to pass. In the fifth inning, Dom DiMaggio singled, and Ted Williams came to bat.

Williams had hit .342 during the season, homered 38 times, and had driven in 123 runs. He ranked first on the team in average, topping Johnny Pesky's .335. His 38 homers were a full 20 more than second-place Bobby Doerr, who had 18. His 123 RBIs were four more than second-place Rudy York. There is a reason Ted Williams was the American League MVP in 1946.

Mickey Haefner was pitching for the All-Stars, and his pitch hit Williams on the right elbow. He had to leave the game. Though X-rays proved negative for bone chips and the like, the *Boston Herald* had observed that by the time he got into the clubhouse, his elbow was "puffed to the size of a tomato."

Though he was able to play in the World Series, he was sub-par throughout and only hit .200 with no homers and an RBI total of one. The rest of the team fought valiantly and took the Series to the full seven games but came up short.

The scores of the three very-costly postseason exhibition games were:

October 1 at Fenway Park: Boston Red Sox 2, All-Stars 0
October 2 at Fenway Park: All-Stars 4, Boston Red Sox 2
October 3 at Fenway Park: Boston Red Sox 4, All-Stars 1

### When were the first in-season exhibition games of the twenty-first century?

Since this is a book of firsts, we shouldn't really be talking about lasts—such as asking when the last in-season exhibition games were held. So, we've phrased the query differently.

As indicated, such in-season games were very common, particularly in the years before World War II. There were 237 of them. The team's overall in-season record is 142–86–9, with a tied intrasquad game at Coopers-town, New York, in 1989 when the Cincinnati team failed to show up.

The last two in-season exhibition games (or, let's say, the first of the twenty-first century) were in 2005 and 2008. What were these two games?

The 2005 game was held at Cooperstown on May 23. The Red Sox had won the 2004 World Series, ending the famous 86-year drought. There used to be an annual Hall of Fame game at Doubleday Field. In 2005, the Detroit Tigers took on the Red Sox, who drew thousands upon thousands who thronged the streets of Cooperstown to see the World Champions parade down Main Street in a series of open automobiles. Giving almost everyone a chance to play, Red Sox manager Terry Francona used 23 players in the game and four pitchers. The Tigers used 18 players and five pitchers.

With three runs in the seventh, the Red Sox overcame a 3–1 deficit to tie it, but a two-run homer in the bottom of the ninth by Single-A outfielder Derek Nicholson won it for the Tigers, 6–4.

**Back to 1901—what were the first transactions after the team's very first game?**

It didn't take long after the first game got underway for wheeling and dealing to begin. The very next day—on April 27—the team signed right-handed pitcher/outfielder Frank Foreman as a free agent. He'd been play-ing professional baseball since 1884 (and had actually been born during the Civil War—in Baltimore on May 1, 1863. His tenure with the Boston Americans was brief—21 days. Foreman was released on May 16. He took part in one game, on May 3 in Washington, a complete-game 9–4 loss. He was 0-for-4 at the plate. Foreman was both the team's first free agent signing after the games had begun and the first player released. He caught on with Baltimore and was 12–6 in 1901.

**What was the team's first player trade?**

The first trade occurred after the 1901 season, when Boston traded catcher and occasional first baseman Ossee Schrecongost to the Cleveland Blues for George "Candy" LaChance on November 16. Schrecongost had hit .304 for Boston, sharing catching duties with Lou Criger. After just 18 games with Cleveland, exclusively at first base, he was released and moved on to Philadelphia Athletics, hitting over .300 for both teams. Boston (and Cy Young) had preferred Criger as catcher, and ownership was willing to accept less production on offense for what they considered superior catching skills.

**How did the team finish in its first season?**

Boston's new American League team fared well in its first campaign, with a record of 79–57–2. They finished in second place, just four games behind the Chicago White Sox. Their longest winning streak had been nine games, from June 14–22. Their longest losing streak was already behind them at that point, the five games they lost from May 11–16.

They had been 49–20 when playing at home and were 30–37 on the road.

The only team that held a winning record against Boston was the Detroit Tigers, who took 11 of 20 games. The team they beat the most was the Milwaukee Brewers, against whom they were 15–5. June 1901 was by far their best month; the Bostons were 15–5 in June.

# THE TEAM'S FIRST BALLPARK

Every team has a home ballpark. They don't always play their home games in their home park—for any number of reasons. In earlier years, the Red Sox sometimes played at Braves Field, for its larger capacity. There might be renovations required, though the Fenway Park fire in early 1934 did not cause a closure. The most remarkable thing about the Red Sox is that they have played 122 seasons of major-league ball and only had two home parks—one that lasted 11 years and one that has, through 2022, been home for 111 years.

**What was the first home ballpark for the Boston Americans?**

It took about two months to construct. The first home of the Boston Americans (from 1908, known as the Red Sox) was the Huntington Avenue Grounds. Many ballparks of the era were simply known as "league park" or the "National League grounds," but the ballpark where the Red Sox first began was the Huntington Avenue American League Base Ball Grounds. It was constructed very quickly, on the former Huntington Carnival Lot, with groundbreaking on March 7, 1901. Superfan "Hi Hi" Dixwell turned the first shovelful of dirt. The first home game for Boston was played on May 8, just two months later. Dixwell threw out the first pitch.

Boston already had a major-league team—the National League's Boston Beaneaters. The competition between the Americans and the Nationals was accentuated by the proximity of the two parks. It was approximately 600 feet as the crow flies from home plate at the South End Grounds to home plate of the Huntington Avenue Grounds. It was even closer between the outside perimeters of the two parks. In between lay the tracks of the New York, New Haven, and Hartford Railroad and a couple of repair sheds used to service the trains.

When the Red Sox later moved to Fenway Park in 1912, they moved maybe a mile or so away from the Huntington Avenue Grounds, effectively just across the Muddy River and the Fens. The driving distance between addresses of the two parks is 1.6 miles, but the distance is much shorter "as the crow flies."

The Huntington Avenue Grounds had an initial capacity of 9,000, which was expanded by adding bleachers in left field before the 1905 season. Though this added only 14 new rows of seats, the new capacity was stated as 17,000. Five years later, adding more bleachers along the third-base side expanded capacity to offer room for another 500.

Fenway Park was reported to have an initial capacity of 24,000, though as many as another 8,000 gained entry during the 1912 World Series. An expansion in 1934 brought capacity up to 33,200. Various renovations and additions since have increased capacity to nearly 37,535 per the 2022 Red Sox Media Guide. For day games, the capacity is 37,085

The 1911 view of the infield and grandstands at the Huntington Avenue Grounds.
MICHAEL T. "NUF CED" MCGREEVY COLLECTION, BOSTON PUBLIC LIBRARY.

since a section of the center field bleachers is closed off to provide batters with a better backdrop.

On the site of the original ballpark, Northeastern University saw to the placement in 1993 of a statue of Cy Young on the site of the original pitching mound.

### A number of firsts before the home crowd

*What were some of the first achievements (or shortcomings) of the new team?*

First pitch: Cy Young in that first home game on May 8, 1901, the 12–4 win over the Athletics in front of some 11,000 fans. The team had played its first 10 games on the road and were 5–5 before Opening Day in Boston.

First out recorded: Philadelphia Athletics leadoff batter Jack Hayden, who grounded out to third base, Jimmy Collins to Buck Freeman.

First strikeout: Cy Young struck out the second batter in the inning, Phil Geier. There weren't many strikeouts in the game. Young struck out a total of two. Bill Bernhard didn't strike out any Boston batters.

First hit by either team in the franchise's first game: Left fielder Dave Fultz (a two-out single) off Cy Young in the first inning.

First Boston batter in a home game: Still batting leadoff as he had in the franchise's first game, "Buttermilk" Tommy Dowd was the first batter when Boston came to bat.

First Boston hit: Tommy Dowd, a first-inning leadoff single to left field

First Boston bunt: right fielder Charlie Hemphill, to sacrifice Dowd to second. Hemphill reached safely on a Philadelphia error, one of nine Athletics errors in the game.

First run scored: Tommy Dowd, in the bottom of the first

First RBI: Jimmy Collins, who drove in Dowd with a single

First home run: Buck Freeman, also in the bottom of the first inning, an inside-the-park homer that got by Geier in center field. Freeman also tripled and singled later in the game.

First rally at home: His teammates gave Cy Young four runs in the bottom of the first inning. They added one in the second inning and added

Jimmy Collins, third baseman; Freddy Parent, shortstop; Hobe Ferris, second baseman; and Buck Freeman, first baseman. Photograph 1901 by Rufus K. Holsinger.
MICHAEL T. "NUF CED" MCGREEVY COLLECTION, BOSTON PUBLIC LIBRARY.

another run in the third. In the fourth inning, they scored three more runs and added another two in the fifth.

First inning without Boston scoring a run: It was only when they got to the sixth inning that the Boston Americans played an inning at home without scoring at least one run. In the eighth, they scored the final run in what was a 12–4 win.

First triple: Charlie Hemphill in the fourth inning. In the same game (and the same inning), Buck Freeman tripled, while both Tommy Dowd and even pitcher Cy Young tripled in the fifth. It was an interesting phenomenon that the 1901 Bostons hit 104 triples and only 37 home runs.

42

Simply hitting the ball out of the park was much rarer in the earlier years of the twentieth century, and it was easier for a runner to make it to third base than all the way around the bases to home. Never once when the team played at the Huntington Avenue Grounds did they have as many homers as three-base hits. The first year in which Boston hit more homers than triples as a team was not until 1931.

First double: With Dowd's single and Freeman's home run in the first inning, and Hemphill's triple in the fourth, it's interesting that the first double in team history didn't come until the seventh inning, when Charlie Hemphill hit a two-base hit.

First hit by a Boston pitcher: Cy Young, singling to lead off the second inning after Boston had scored four runs in the first.

First extra-base hit by a Boston pitcher: Cy Young tripled into the crowd in the fifth.

First double play by Boston: shortstop Freddy Parent to second baseman Hobe Ferris to Buck Freeman at first base (6-4-3), in the second inning.

First stolen base: Charlie Hemphill (Freeman was caught stealing in the third).

First Boston catcher to throw out a baserunner: Lou Criger threw out Fultz trying to steal second base in the top of the first inning.

First Boston error: Buck Freeman, third inning.

First run scored off Boston pitching: an unearned run in the seventh inning off Cy Young, marring the 11–0 shutout he had going.

First base on balls issued by Boston pitching: Young issued no walks in the first home game, but George "Nig" Cuppy walked one batter in the May 9 game.

First hit batsman: Doc Powers hit by Cuppy on the same date—May 9, 1901.

First wild pitch in a franchise home game: Philadelphia pitcher Chick Fraser, also on May 9, 1901.

First Boston crowd to go home disappointed: May 11, 1901, in the third home game for the franchise, Washington beat Boston, 3–2.

First shutout borne: Washington pitcher Watty Lee shut out Boston, 4–0, on May 15, 1901, allowing just four base hits. Cuppy was the losing pitcher.

First shutout win for the home team: Cy Young on Saturday, July 6, 1901, shutting out Washington at the Huntington Avenue Grounds, 7–0. Young allowed eight base hits, walked one, and there were two Boston errors. The Senators left nine men on base. With the win, Young improved his record to 15–3. Senators starter Watty Lee had allowed seven runs through the first three innings, and then swapped positions with right fielder Dale Gear, who allowed no runs at all (and only three hits) in the final five innings. Gear had pitched in three games back in 1896 for the National League's Cleveland Spiders (0–2). With Washington, this was his twelfth appearance in 1901. He was 2–6. By season's end, he was 4–11 in 24 games.

First tie game in team history: The May 21 game at Detroit had to be postponed due to wet grounds. So the teams played two on August 31 at Detroit's Bennett Park. The Tigers scored four times in the bottom of the eighth and held on to win, 6–5. In the second game, the Bostons jumped out to a 4–0 lead in the fourth, but the Tigers got to Ted Lewis for one run in the fifth, one more in the eighth, and then tied it with two more runs in the bottom of the ninth. The game was then called due to darkness.

First grand slam in a franchise game: The first one hit at Huntington Avenue was hit on July 8, 1902, by Philadelphia first baseman Harry Davis, part of a 22–9 Athletics win. It was hit off none other than Cy Young, in the third inning, prompting his departure from the game.

First grand slam by the Boston Americans: It was later that same month, on July 25, 1902. Jimmy Collins hit a ball "to the clubhouse" for an inside-the-park four runs in the fourth off Jack Harper of the St. Louis Browns. The phrase appears not to refer to a particular clubhouse—the Huntington Avenue Grounds clubhouses were underneath the grandstand behind home plate—but to be a generic phrase of the day meaning a very long drive.

First balk by a Boston pitcher: Bert Husting, in the only game he pitched for Boston, on April 25, 1902, in Washington. He also gave up

15 base hits and walked eight. His teammates committed four errors. Unsurprisingly, Washington won the game, 15–4.

### *What was the first regular-season franchise game played at a non-major-league ballpark?*

On June 15, 1902, Boston played against Cleveland at Mahaffey Park, near Canton, Ohio. Appropriately, the *Boston Globe* that morning, under "American League Games Today," listed "Boston vs. Cleveland at Canton." The day before, Cy Young threw a three-hitter, beating the White Sox, 2–1. After that game, Boston took the train to Canton. The *Globe* noted that "Cleveland has thus far found the transferring of Sunday games to outside towns a successful proceeding." The Cleveland team found it could often draw large Sunday crowds in other venues.

## Some other firsts for the Boston Americans

### *Where were a couple of other places the team played regular-season games in its earliest years?*

Fort Wayne, Indiana: On August 31, 1902, at League Baseball Park, where they built on meadows once used for public hangings and known as Jailhouse Flats. Cy Young beat Addie Joss and Cleveland, 3–1.

Columbus, Ohio: The team played two games at Neil Park on July 23 and 24, 1905, against the Detroit Tigers, a "home game" for the Tigers. Cy Young won the first game, 6–1, and Bill Dinneen won the second, 7–1.

### *What was the first time the team lost 15 games in a row?*

It was in 1906—and they didn't just lose 15 in a row. They lost 20 in a row. They lost every game from May 1 through May 24, and they did almost all of that losing in front of the hometown fans. They'd actually been a mediocre 6–7 before the streak began. They lost on May 1 in New York and then every one of the next 19 games at home, a span of more than three weeks. They scored 50 runs in the 20 games, including four games in which they scored five or more runs. Then they won four of their next five and seven of 10. Surprisingly, they finished the season with 105 losses in a 154-game season. The 105 defeats was the same number they lost in 1925, only surpassed by 107 in 1926 and 111 in 1932.

In 1906, the team did boast a four-game winning streak at one point in the first half of August. In 1926, they managed one five-game winning streak (all at home), immediately followed by 17 consecutive losses, all but the last three also at Fenway Park. In 1932, they twice had meager three-game winning streaks, but none longer, and only four other times did they even win two in a row.

### When was the first time the team won 15 games in a row?

This is a happier outcome for Sox fans to contemplate. Again, it was early in the season. The first—and only—time they won 15 in a row was in 1946 when they won every game from April 25 through May 10. They won their first five games out of the gate, then lost three of four (including a notable game on April 23 when they gave up six runs in the top of the 11th inning and lost to the Washington Senators, 8–2). They lost 12–5 to the Yankees on April 24 but then reversed the score and beat New York, 12–5, on the following day. They then won the next 14, too, scoring 111 runs in the process. Three of the games were walk-off games, one of them winning on a Leon Culberson grand slam in the bottom of the 14th (the May 7 game). They later had an eight-game winning streak, a seven-game winning streak, and three six-game winning streaks. Two of the six-gamers were back-to-back, with a tie game in between but not a loss. They finished the season 104–50 but lost the World Series in seven games to the St. Louis Cardinals.

In 1948, the Red Sox had a 13-game winning streak, and they've enjoyed five that were each 12 games long—in the years 1937, 1939, 1988, 1995, and 2006. The 1946 streak noted as six wins and then six wins, with just a tie and not a loss in between, is worth recalling. It was an 8–8 tie that ran for 12 innings but was called due to darkness in the year before Fenway Park installed lighting for night games.

# FIRST TIME THE TEAM PLAYED AS THE RED SOX

THERE WAS A BRIEF STRETCH—FOUR YEARS—WHEN THE TEAM PLAYED as the Boston Red Sox and played at the Huntington Avenue Grounds. They were the years 1908 through 1911. They weren't particularly noteworthy years—the team finished fifth, third, fourth, and fifth. During those four years, though, two transitions occurred. They had never really had an official name their first seven years. From news accounts of the day, we find they were variously called the Pilgrims, the Puritans, the Collinsmen, Somersets, the Plymouth Rocks, the Americans—and if the context was clear enough to avoid confusion with the National League team—the "Bostons"—but they never had a formal name. Ever since 1908, they have been known as the Red Sox. And after 1911, the newly named team moved to a new ballpark.

**When did the team first take on the name Red Sox?**

John I. Taylor purchased the majority share in the Boston Americans team on April 19, 1904. As noted in *Red Sox Threads*, on December 18, 1907, shortly after Boston's National League team revealed that the new uniforms for 1908 eliminated their customary red stockings, Taylor pounced. He quickly decided that his team would adopt red hose and call themselves the Boston Red Sox. Taylor personally oversaw the uniform design, selecting red stockings because Boston's first professional baseball team—the Red Stockings—had worn them. Taylor appreciated the link with tradition. It was predicted that the name "Red Sox" would prove a popular choice.

Was Taylor imprudently putting the health, or even the lives of his players, in jeopardy? Historian Ellery Clark wrote that the owners of the

NL team, George and John Dovey, "decided the red dye in their club's stockings might well lead to blood infection and even worse if and when one or more of their players were cut in the leg by opposing spikes. The grand old color and the nickname were abandoned in the interests of health."

Rash though Taylor's decision may have been, generations of Red Sox players have come and gone with no documented case of red-dye disease. It wasn't until the 2004 postseason that blood on the stockings played any noteworthy role in Red Sox lore.

The actual red stockings were apparently first worn in Little Rock, Arkansas, during spring training on March 21, 1908. Tim Murnane wrote in the *Boston Globe* story datelined March 21 at Little Rock: "The new uniforms of gray and bright red stockings were very attractive this afternoon."

In an October 1908 article on baseball team names, the *Globe*'s Murnane noted that as early as 1875, there was a short-lived team known as the Red Sox in St. Louis, and that the Cincinnati team had originally been called the Red Stockings, which "set the style for naming clubs after the color of their stockings." The Chicago White Sox and St. Louis Browns were two other such teams. There was a Boston Red Stockings team from 1876 through the 1884 season and then in the year 1891. From that point forward, there's never been another Boston team using that particular name.

Murnane noted that "the Boston Americans took up the name Red Sox last winter, simply to have some trade mark that would be easy to write and have a baseball flavor." As a sportswriter, he was grateful: "The [use of] shorter names makes it much easier for those reporting the games or writing baseball."

Taylor's name stuck, and the team has been both beloved and bemoaned ever since: the Red Sox, the Sox, the Bosox, and, sometimes, "the Sawx."

### What was the first homer hit by a player in a Red Sox uniform?

We already know that Buck Freeman hit the first homer for the franchise and that Hugh Bradley hit the first home run ever hit at Fenway Park, but neither of them was wearing red stockings as part of their uniform. Who hit the first home run for the Boston Red Sox? Readers will recall that 1908 was the first season the team was known by that name.

The first homer hit by a ballplayer wearing a Red Sox uniform was hit by left fielder Gavvy Cravath, a "handsome drive" in the March 6, 1908, intrasquad game at the expense of Elmer Steele. Cravath was hitting for the Regulars, and Steele was pitching for the Yannigans.

The first homer hit against an opponent was third baseman Harry Lord's drive into the left-field corner in the fifth inning of the 6–0 defeat of the Little Rock Travelers, in Little Rock, on March 17, 1908. The two-run homer extended the Sox lead to 4–0.

Okay, that's nice, but what about in a regular-season game?

The first Sox homer hit in a regular-season game came on April 23 in Washington, with two outs in the top of the fourth inning when right fielder Doc Gessler "poled a low smash to center and crossed the plate before the ball was relayed in." It was the ninth game of the year. It was one of 14 homers hit that first year they were known as the Sox. The victim? Washington pitcher Bill Burns. The Senators won the game, 6–4. The homer was one of three Gessler hit in 1908. He hit a total of 14 home runs in 880 major-league games.

The first Red Sox homer hit at a home game was hit by left fielder Gavvy Cravath, on May 29 in a game against Washington. It was the first game of a doubleheader and the only run of the game for Boston, a solo home run in the bottom of the fourth, hit off Eli Cates. Washington won the game, 6–1.

## When was the first time the team moved to a new home ballpark?

It only happened once, in April 1912, when the Red Sox moved from the Huntington Avenue Grounds to the newly constructed Fenway Park. Even though the Huntington Avenue ballpark had only been used for 11 seasons, it was already the oldest park in use in the American League— only because the Tigers played their last 23 games of 1911 on the road, last playing at Bennett Park on September 10. The Red Sox played their last game on Huntington Avenue on October 7, 1911.

# FENWAY PARK FIRSTS

As any Red Sox fan worth his or her salt (and many who aren't even baseball fans) knows, Fenway Park is the oldest ballpark in major-league baseball. It's older than almost anyone likely to be reading this book—in April 2022, it had its 110th birthday. There have been several times that ownership had contemplated replacing the park, often when the team was not doing particularly well. Over the years, there have been thoughts of situating a park where there would be more ample parking for automobiles, or to build a domed stadium, a multi-sport stadium.

When current ownership took over—now more than 20 years ago—they saw the value of having the oldest park in baseball, and they invested tens of millions of dollars to renovate and expand it, even repouring much of the concrete base of the seating bowl over the offseasons. The park is set to last at least a few more decades, and maybe more. The team also had it placed on the National Register of Historic Places, for the recognition (and perhaps certain tax advantages). But let's go way back and look at some of the firsts.

**When was the first game at Fenway Park?**

It's been chronicled many places, of course. The game was on April 20, 1912: The Red Sox opened Fenway Park with an extra-innings win over New York, beating the New York Highlanders (already frequently being called the Yankees) in 11 innings, 7–6. The park had been built quickly—construction took six months, but it was built well enough that games are still being played there more than 110 years later. Before the Red Sox even got to bat in their new park, New York had scored three runs off Buck O'Brien. Boston scored one in the bottom of the first.

Fenway Park in September 1914
LIBRARY OF CONGRESS PRINTS AND PHOTOGRAPHS DIVISION.

Though down 5–1 after three innings, they drew even with three in the fourth and one in the sixth. Both teams scored once in the eighth, and the game went into extra innings—already, there was "free baseball" at Fenway. As skies began to darken, the 11th was virtually certain to be the final inning. New York didn't score. With two outs and nobody on base, shortstop Steve Yerkes (who had committed three errors in the game) had been 4-for-6 at the plate. He reached on a throwing error, then took second base on a passed ball. Hippo Vaughn was pitching for New York in relief. The count went to 3-2 on Tris Speaker. With first base open, there was some thought Vaughn would pitch around him and work to Jake Stahl but, the *Globe* wrote, at the last moment, he "tried to sneak one over." Speaker wasn't deceived and singled past the shortstop, driving in the winning run and letting the overflow crowd head home, most of them savoring a Red Sox victory.

**Who had the first Red Sox base hit in Fenway Park history?**

The first base hit by a Red Sox player in a game at Fenway Park was also the first double hit there, a two-base hit by second baseman Steve

Yerkes in the bottom of the first inning. It followed the first out (by right fielder Harry Hooper). It was followed by the second hit and the second double—hit by Tris Speaker, resulting in both the first run scored and the first run batted in by a Boston ballplayer.

**Which Red Sox player committed the first error at Fenway? Who committed the first balk? Who threw the first wild pitch?**

The first error happened even before the team got their first hit. It was in the top of the first inning. New York left fielder Guy Zinn was the first batter to step into the Fenway Park batter's box. He received the first base on balls in Fenway history and, thus, the first baserunner. The first hit by anyone at the new park was a single by Highlanders right fielder Harry Wolter, apparently reaching on an infield hit that Stahl did not field cleanly. Benny Kauff was the first out. The first sacrifice is credited to Hal Chase. The first RBI belongs to shortstop Roy Hartzell, a single that scored Zinn. That first error came next, when center fielder Bert Daniels tapped the ball back to Buck O'Brien on the mound. O'Brien threw to the plate, a "wild peg" that allowed Wolter to score. Next up was the third baseman Cozy Dolan, who O'Brien immortalized forever by making him the first batter hit by a pitch at Boston's new ballpark. (Hal Chase got hit by an O'Brien pitch in the fourth.) Earle Gardner singled, and it was 3–0, New York. This was not shaping up as the sort of game Red Sox fans had hoped for.

The first stolen base was by Hartzell in the third inning. The first balk was assessed by umpire Tommy Connolly, charged to O'Brien in the third inning, the Red Sox pitcher thus becoming the answer to the question as to who committed the first error and also who committed the first balk. Later in the same inning, with Gabby Street at the plate, O'Brien threw a wild pitch that allowed Dolan to take third base. Buck O'Brien is thus the answer to the third question, as well.

**Were the first three or four of the first home runs hit at Fenway not actually home runs?**

That's a trick question, and the answer is a debatable one. The crowd was large enough on Opening Day that about 1,000 fans stood in center field. The *Boston Herald* averred that "the ground rules robbed Speaker, Stahl, Hall and Yerkes of home runs." The *Globe* was more restrained, allowing that perhaps three of the hits "would have gone for three-base drives and possibly home runs." Whatever the hits might have been, Yerkes was the master of them in the first Fenway game, going 5-for-7; his day was also marked, though, by three errors.

**Who made the first Red Sox relief appearance in Fenway Park history (and who was the first Red Sox pitcher to get a hit at Fenway)?**

After four innings, Charley Hall took over for Boston. Buck O'Brien had given up five runs in the first four innings. Hall allowed only one run in seven innings of work. He also scored the tying run in the bottom of the sixth inning, when the Sox finally caught up with New York. His two-base hit in the bottom of the ninth inning established him as the first pitcher to hit safely at Fenway Park.

**Other firsts at Fenway**

One could go on and on. And we will, for a while.

*When was the first time the Red Sox committed seven errors in a home game and won?*

In their very first home game at Fenway, they committed seven errors but won, 7–6, in 11 innings. The opposing New Yorkers committed three errors.

*When was the first time each team had a player with the same surname in a game?*

Yankees second baseman Earle Gardner and Red Sox third baseman Larry Gardner (no relation), both played infield in that very first game. Larry had two hits; Earle only had one.

*When was the first time the Red Sox led in a Fenway Park game?*

It was not until the bottom of the 11th inning in that first game that they scored the winning run, 7–6.

### *Who hit the first triple in Fenway Park history?*

Would you believe Walter Johnson, the "Big Train," Washington's Hall of Fame pitcher? Let's hope so, as it appears to be fact. There were more or less 2,500 witnesses to this fact on Wednesday, April 24, in the fourth Fenway game. It didn't really contribute to the game; he never drove in a run nor scored from third base. He did, however, win the game, 5–2.

Johnson wasn't a bad-hitting pitcher, with a lifetime .235 batting average. He hit 41 triples in his time. This was one of four in 1912.

The first Red Sox player to triple was on the following day. Tris Speaker hit a two-out single in the bottom of the first inning against the visiting Senators, though he was left stranded. With the bases loaded and two outs in the bottom of the sixth, Harry Hooper tripled, a ball the *Herald* said was hit "over Germany Schaefer's head and started for the bleachers in West Somerville. Had the ground been dry, the hit must surely have gone for a homer." Had it, Hooper would have had the first grand slam at Fenway. Red Sox fans who wanted to see that first grand slam had to wait a long, long time.

### *Which Red Sox player hit the first home run at Fenway Park?*

When the park was first built, with its now-famous and very tall left-field wall (now dubbed the "Green Monster"), some said no one would ever hit a ball over the wall. In fact, Red Sox treasurer Bob McRoy had said, "the fence was made very high so that the ball could not be knocked over it." Hugh Bradley did so in Fenway's fifth home game. The date was April 26, 1912. The Red Sox took a 3–0 lead in the first inning but trailed 6–3 after six. They got one in the bottom of the seventh. Bradley came up with two out and two on and hit a homer fully seven feet over the wall. The *Boston Herald* wrote, "Few of the fans who have been out to Fenway Park believed it possible to knock a ball over the left field fence, but Hugh Bradley hit one that cleared not only the barrier but also the building— on the opposite side of the street," Bradley had driven in four of the seven runs in a 7–6 win against the Athletics.

He'd hit not only the first homer in Fenway Park history but also the first one over the Wall. It was his only home run of the year—home or away.

Hugh Bradley, 1912.
GEORGE GRANTHAM BAIN COLLECTION/LIBRARY OF CONGRESS

### *Who hit the first Red Sox grand slam at Fenway Park?*

As we have seen, the first Red Sox homer was hit by Hugh Bradley in the ballpark's fifth game. It was the first of 10 home runs the Red Sox hit at home in 1912.

In the 11 years that followed, the Red Sox hit 72 homers at home, but none of them were grand slams. One notes that the average number of homers was very low throughout baseball in the so-called Deadball Era.

Finally, though, the day arrived. It was on May 30, 1924—more than 12 years after the ballpark opened. A fan determined to see the first Red Sox grand slam at Fenway would already have attended more than 900 games.

Ike Boone had pinch-hit in two games for the 1922 Giants and appeared in five games for the 1923 Red Sox. In 1924, he became the team's regular right fielder. May 30 was Decoration Day (now known as Memorial Day), and the Red Sox hosted the Washington Senators for a Friday doubleheader. They drew a then-record overflow crowd, which was variously estimated at between 34,000 and 40,000, with at least a couple thousand on the field (in center and right field) behind ropes. Per ground rules, a ball hit into the crowd that day would count as a double.

Boone was having an excellent year. He was batting .385 coming into the day through his first 29 games. The score in the first game of the doubleheader was 1–1 after 3½ innings. In the bottom of the fourth, with righty John Martina on the mound, Red Sox batters singled, got hit by a pitch, and loaded the bases on a bunt single. Martina struck out the next two batters. But then he walked Bill Wambsganss, and left fielder Bobby Veach hit a ball into the crowd for a ground-rule double, driving in two more. First baseman Joe Harris walked, re-loading the bases. Boone was up.

At that point, "Boone poled a mighty homer into the centerfield bleachers." He hit a grand slam, a hard-hit ball that shot over the crowd in the outfield and into the bleachers. Whether it was in right-center, or center, or right, is the subject of differing accounts in several different newspapers. Indisputable was that it was no ground-rule double. It went over the crowd and into the seats, a grand slam. The first grand slam at Fenway Park.

The fans who had come to the game were rewarded. They saw Boone's slam and, in the top of the sixth inning, the Red Sox pulled off a triple play. Boston won the game, 9–4, but Washington took the second game, 10–5.

Boone hit 13 home runs in 1924, almost half of the total 30 hit by the entire team. He hit .337 and drove in 98 runs.

### When was the first time the Red Sox played an entire season at Fenway Park but only hit one home run all year long?

It was 1916, and this wasn't just any team. It was the reigning world champion team from 1915, which was on its way to another world championship in 1916. The only homer hit at home was one hit over the left-field fence by Sox center fielder Tillie Walker on June 20. That year's entire team only hit 14 homers all year long. Thirteen were on the road and one at home. It was Walker's third career home run at Fenway Park; he held the record at the time—in a park that was already in its fifth year.

*When was the first time a Red Sox player led both the American League and the National League in home runs for a full year but never hit even one in Boston?*

It was 1918. Babe Ruth's 11 home runs led both leagues. He was tied with, of all people, Tillie Walker, who had been sent to the Philadelphia Athletics as the player to be named later in a January trade. No one else in the league had more than six homers. Walker hit one of his at Fenway (as it happens, on the second anniversary of his June 20, 1916, home run featured in the previous entry) and two against the Red Sox when they were in Philadelphia. Ruth hit three in New York, three in Washington, three in Detroit, and one each in Cleveland and St. Louis. And the last one was on June 30. He didn't hit a single home run in July, August, or September.

*When was the first Sunday Red Sox game played in Boston?*

Playing sports of any kind on the "Lord's Day" used to be widely prohibited until some of the restrictions began to be loosened in the 20th century. Boston, Pittsburgh, and Philadelphia were the last three major-league cities to permit playing baseball on Sundays. There were efforts to open up possibilities in Boston, but it was only after the matter was put to a vote in a referendum in 1928 that it became possible.

Although the voters chose to permit Sunday baseball in Boston, there remained a restriction on playing within 1,000 feet of a house of worship. This prevented the Red Sox from playing at Fenway Park, due to a nearby church, so the team made arrangements to play Sunday home games at Braves Field from April 28, 1929, through May 29, 1932. That first Sunday game resulted in a 7–3 loss to the Philadelphia Athletics, a loss for Boston's Red Ruffing.

Their next Sunday game was on May 26, a 15–4 loss to the visiting New York Yankees. The first Sunday home win for the Red Sox was on June 2, a 12–3 win for Milt Gaston over the Cleveland Indians.

In all, the Red Sox played 50 Sunday "home away from home" games at Braves Field, with a record of 17–31 with two ties. Home-field advantage may not have been obtained, but then again, the team itself had winning percentages in those years (1929–1932) of .377, .338, .408, and .279.

### When was the first Sunday baseball game at Fenway Park?

The Lord may not have approved at first. The first Sunday home game for the Red Sox at Fenway Park was on July 3, 1932. The New Yankees won with ease, 13–2. They took a 4–0 lead in the first two innings, then added a nine-run inning in the top of the sixth. Ivy Andrews (who had been traded from the Yankees to the Red Sox on June 5) bore the defeat. One notes that the 1932 Red Sox were never a good bet to win: They finished 43–111, a gigantic 64 games behind the first-place Yankees.

### When was the first night game at Boston's American League park?

The first night game played at Boston's America League ballpark was not the June 13, 1947, game at Fenway Park. It was the September 11, 1907, game at the Huntington Avenue Grounds. Team president John I. Taylor arranged a game between the Cherokee Indian team and the Dorchesters. The notice in the *Globe* advised, "The Cherokees bring their own lighting arrangements . . . lights aggregating more than 50,000 candle power are placed about the field." The Indians had reportedly been active for many years, primarily playing in the Midwest. They mixed comedy and baseball, apparently excelling at both. The game was initially to have been played on September 2, but rain prevented that. Rain struck again on September 11, but they played nonetheless, getting in a full nine innings, with the Dorchesters overcoming a 3–0 Cherokees first-inning lead and winning 7–4. The *Boston Herald* said 1,500 fans braved the weather to take in the game.

### When was Fenway Park's first night game?

There were 35 years of day baseball at Fenway Park, from 1912 to 1946. It was not until 1947 that the Red Sox played their first night game at Fenway. The date was June 13, 1947. Though the team had played occasional night games on the road going back into the late 1930s, this was the first night game the Red Sox played at home, and it was a success: sold out with 34,510 fans in attendance. Boo Ferriss for Boston started and gave up 11 hits in 5⅓ innings, with a walk and a wild pitch, too. Bob Klinger relieved and held the White Sox to two hits in 3⅔ innings. The Red Sox only managed eight singles off Frank Papish, but three of them came in the fifth inning. Combined with two walks and a Chicago error, the Sox from Boston scored five times, enough to give them a 5–3 victory.

**When was the first radio broadcast from Fenway Park?**

It took a long time before the Red Sox got around to permitting the radio broadcast of a game. The first game broadcast was on August 5, 1921, by radio station KDKA of Pittsburgh of a game against the visiting Philadelphia Phillies. Harold Arlin was the voice. Other teams in other cities started allowing radio, but some owners were fearful that patrons wouldn't come to the park if they could sit home and listen to the game. More than three years later, radio station WBZ broadcast the first major-league game from Boston, but the game was the April 14, 1925, Opening Day game of the Boston Braves, hosting the Giants. It was almost to the day, one full year later, that the first Red Sox game went on air—Opening Day 1926, on April 13.

The station was WNAC, and the man on the air was Gus Rooney. Halfway through the game, no one could blame Red Sox fans for losing interest—those listening on the radio as well as those at the ballpark. The New York Yankees were leading 11–1. But then the Red Sox scored two runs in the bottom of the fifth and five more in the sixth. That made it 11–8, and they added a ninth run in the seventh inning and two more in the eighth. New York had added one in the top of the seventh, and that was ultimately the one that made the difference in the Yankees' 12–11 win.

Unfortunately, no recording was made of the game, so we cannot today hear Rooney and his description of the play-by-play. Worries that the availability of radio would undermine in-person attendance evaporated over time; the general conclusion came to be that many of those who first heard radio broadcasts of baseball made their way to the ballpark to see the games in real life.

**When was the first television broadcast in Boston of a Boston Red Sox game?**

The first television broadcast of a Red Sox game was a game at Yankee Stadium on April 23, 1948. Red Sox owner Tom Yawkey had seen some broadcasts in Detroit of the Tigers hosting the Red Sox in 1947. It was agreed that WBZ-TV (though it did not officially go on the air until June 1948) could participate in an experimental transmission of a Red Sox game, which Tom and Jean Yawkey, GM Joe Cronin, and a few hundred other invitees watched at Boston's Parker House hotel, following the broadcast of WABD in New York. They got to see the Red Sox win, with left-hander Mickey Harris shutting out the Yankees, 4–0. They got to see Ted Williams hit a home run.

The first television game from Boston was on June 15, 1948, with the Boston Braves beating the Chicago Cubs, 8–3. The first Red Sox game from Boston was on July 2. WBZ was the broadcasting station of that first from Fenway; the July 3 game was done by WNAC.

The Philadelphia Athletics won the July 2 game, 4–2. The Red Sox runs were driven in by Birdie Tebbetts in the second inning and Vern Stephens in the eighth. The next day's *Lowell Sun* reported, "Mom Tebbetts (Birdie's mother) got her first glimpse of her son in action via television . . . She didn't make the trip down from Nashua, N.H., but she did sit in on a telecast of the game and got a big kick out of it."

### When was the first time the Red Sox played a game at Fenway Park as the visiting team?

This had nothing to do with Sundays. Or the Braves. And it was a little confusing. They were supposed to play the Seattle Mariners, on the road, but on July 19, 1994, three 12-pound roof tiles from the Kingdome in Seattle came crashing down on the seats below. It wasn't during a game, and no one was injured. But repairs needed to be done, and the Mariners were in no position to host any teams. So they played in Boston—four games, from July 22–24. Each team won two. The Red Sox weren't really the visiting team; the Red Sox batted in the bottom of each inning (except for the two games in which they held the lead after 8½). They were responsible for the business arrangements and kept the home ballclub's share of the receipts.

TV cameraman working from the "high-first" position.
BILL NOWLIN PHOTO

*When was the first time that large crowds at Fenway Park—two days in a row—rooted for the Red Sox to lose?*

It was a doubleheader, on September 8, 1928. They'd lost both games of a doubleheader the day before to the Philadelphia Athletics. The Saturday twin bill on September 8 drew 28,000. They lost the first game, 7–6, in 10 innings and lost the second one, 7–4. Why would so many fans be cheering for the Athletics? The Red Sox weren't in the race; in fact, they were in last place—eighth place—and fully 40 games behind the leaders. The Athletics and the New York Yankees were tied for first. Aha—there's the clue. The Yankees were far from favored in Boston. Babe Ruth had hit 60 homers the year before and might still do it again in 1928. Massachusetts-born Connie Mack led the A's, which might have been a factor for some. He got a huge ovation at the end of the second game. Newspapers around the country noted that the "Bostonese" were applauding the visitors, though the *Boston Herald* dubbed it a "strange complex bothering the crowd." The paper wrote, "Undoubtedly the fans wanted to see the A's eventually win, but everything that the Red Sox did well all afternoon was applauded to the echo." At season's end, the Yankees prevailed by 2½ games.

*If Red Sox batters studied Yankees pitchers and could select the one they most wanted to face at Fenway, who would likely be their first choice?*

Andy Hawkins. He had a 10-year major-league career and spent three of those years with the Yankees, for whom he won 20 of his 84 games. He had three starts against the Red Sox at Fenway Park. On September 26, he lasted a third of an inning and gave up eight runs—with only one extra-base hit involved. On another Tuesday night, June 5, 1990, he again got one out before being removed. This time he was charged with five runs. On Saturday afternoon, September 1, 1990, he gave it another shot. Again, he got one out and only one. This time, two home runs powered in five runs. That's a total of three outs in three starts and 18 runs, all earned.

*When was the left-field wall first called the Green Monster?*

A newspaper archive search turns up the very occasional fleeting reference in the 1950s and 1960s. The first time it appeared with capital letters was in an AP story in October 1967. The first time we could find it in a headline was in 1971. It was a term gradually adopted, one that grew more or less organically over the latter decades of the twentieth century. In 2003, the Red Sox first opened the very popular "Monster Seats" on top of the left-field wall.

### *When was the first time Wally the Green Monster emerged from the left-field wall?*

The Red Sox mascot, Wally, first emerged from the left-field wall on April 13, 1997. Acknowledging the year is the reason he wears #97 on the back of his uniform. According to information provided on the MLB website, Wally's first game at Fenway was for its opening on April 20, 1912. He was a tremendous—really, unparalleled—fan and never missed a home game, but because he was covered with green fur, he had to attend in disguise. On a day in 1947, his mask fell off, and before he could retrieve it and mask up again, some workers came by, and he darted

A small Wally doll. Wally and his companion, Tessie, stroll the park at every Sox home game.
BILL NOWLIN PHOTO

inside the wall to hide. He decided to stay inside and make it his home. This certainly saved him a lot of money on ticket prices over the years. He saw exciting games, and he saw disappointing games, but Wally took them all in. Then one day, 50 years later, enticed by a whole bunch of happy children, he ventured out of the wall and was welcomed to great acclaim—even invited to throw out the ceremonial first pitch. He has not missed a game since and is always at the park—sometimes venturing to events in the region to help represent the Red Sox. For more about Wally, visit https://www.mlb.com/redsox/fans/mascots/about-wally.

### When was the first time there was a "Save Fenway Park!" movement launched?

On May 15, 1999, Red Sox CEO John Harrington announced that the Red Sox planned to replace Fenway Park—in effect, across the street to the other side of Jersey Street where Twins Enterprises has its souvenir shop. Rather than try to restore the original park, they would build a brand new one with modern amenities—and even larger grandstand seats. They would boost capacity to 44,130, add more luxury suites, and with additional revenue could be more competitive. A movement sprang up named "Save Fenway Park!" and was very active, liaising with community groups and effectively helping squelch the plan. New ownership of the team arrived in 2002 and saw benefits in retaining (while upgrading) the oldest part in the major leagues. This is not the place to go into how successful that effort has proven, but it is amply clear that the team has remained competitive in every way.

### Was there an earlier "Save Fenway Park!" movement?

The late 1990s were far from the first time there had been serious talk of replacing Fenway. Many other locations were discussed going back to the 1950s and 1960s. In the May 19, 1966, *Boston Globe*, there was an article about replacing the park with a domed multi-sport stadium. Columnist Bud Collins even used the exclamation point when he wrote, "Mossbacks, unite! Join the 'Save Fenway Park!' movement before it's too late. Perhaps you don't realize it but the dear old ball park is in danger of being classified 'obsolete' and phased out."

### *When was the first time the Red Sox played a game outside the United States?*

The first game the Red Sox played outside the United States was on March 27, 1911, when they played an exhibition game in Yuma. Arizona first became a state on February 14, 1912; it was the Arizona Territory in 1911, and the Red Sox played a game there as they made their way back from spring training in, of all places, Redondo Beach, California. The population of Yuma County in 1910 was just 7,733, and though a local booster club had invited them, Yuma could only find four local ballplayers ready to take on the Red Sox, so five Red Sox players were "loaned" to the other team. As one might expect, the Red Sox won handily, beating Yuma 17–5, despite those five Red Sox players augmenting the Yuma team. Hugh Bedient, Charley Hall, Red Kleinow, Duffy Lewis, and Billy Purtell all played for Yuma. Eddie Cicotte pitched for Boston. Each of the four local players did manage a base hit off him. Bedient was hammered for 31 base hits and 17 runs, though why he was hit so hard is not known.

Boston Red Sox at Spring Training, Yuma, Arizona, March 1911. Michael T. McGreevy (with mustache) poses with Boston Red Sox players in front of locomotive.
MICHAEL T. "NUF CED" MCGREEVY COLLECTION, BOSTON PUBLIC LIBRARY.

# FIRST GAMES IN FOREIGN LANDS

THE RED SOX HAVE PLAYED IN 42 OF THE 50 UNITED STATES—AND date back far enough that they played in Arizona before it even became a state. They played a spring training game in the Arizona Territory in 1911, the year before Arizona entered the union. See *The Great Red Sox Spring Training Tour of 1911*, also by the author of this book.

The states in which they have not yet played are Alaska, Hawaii, Idaho, Montana, North Dakota, Oregon, South Dakota, and Wyoming. Perhaps someday an enterprising PR maven will convince team owners to work up an exhibition tour of those eight states—and they can truly become "America's Team." In addition to the 42 states, they have also played in a number of other countries, most recently the United Kingdom in 2019.

**When was the first time the Red Sox played a game in a completely different country?**

It was an in-season exhibition game on July 24, 1916, played in Toronto, Ontario. The Red Sox had finished a lengthy 19-game homestand on Saturday, July 22, a doubleheader against the Detroit Tigers. The homestand had included six doubleheaders. Baseball was not permitted in Boston on Sundays. The next game on the schedule was Tuesday, July 25, in Cleveland. The team entrained to Toronto, where they were welcomed by Mayor Thomas Church, who hosted them on a "long motor boat trip around the bay." Manager Bill Carrigan had played for Toronto in 1907 and was presented with a gold watch.

The game drew 7,000 to see the Toronto Internationals take on the Red Sox. There was some scoring back and forth, but the game was 5–5 when Lena Blackburn of Toronto drove in two runs in the bottom of the eighth to tie it. Neither team scored in the ninth. In order to make their train to Cleveland, the Boston players had to stop after nine. Pitching for Boston was Weldon Wyckoff, who had two hits in the game, one of them a two-run triple. Babe Ruth pitched the next day, in the July 25 game, but lost, 5–4.

The next time they played in Canada was another in-season exhibition game on August 30, 1921, in London, Ontario, and the Red Sox lost, 5–3, to the London Champs. And then there was one in New Brunswick, played at St. John on August 26, 1930. That one was Boston 7, St. John 5.

Their first game in Quebec was on June 8, 1970. There was no interleague play yet. This was simply an in-season exhibition game but against the National League Montreal Expos, which had begun as a franchise the year before in 1969. Montreal Expos 8, Boston Red Sox 6. The Red Sox headed on to Chicago, but they did so without pitcher Jim Lonborg, who was trying to get in some work in coming back from arm problems (he hadn't pitched since May 28). He was hurt in the game and so returned to Boston to be looked at. He appeared in two July games, but his season was over.

**When was the first time the Red Sox played a game in Cuba?**
They played four of them at the end of March 1941; the first was against a picked team of Cuban ballplayers, in Havana on March 27. Then they played three games against the Cincinnati Reds. Led by manager Joe Cronin, they departed Sarasota for Miami and then Havana on the evening of March 25. They traveled by boat, departing on the *S.S. Florida* at 7:00 PM. Ted Williams, with an injured right ankle, was not among the party. The Red Sox stayed at Hotel Nacional de Cuba.

March 27 at Havana, Cuba: Cuban All-Stars 2, Boston 1
The games were played at La Tropical Stadium. The *Boston Herald* characterized the Cuba team as "an all white team picked from 17 A.A.U. clubs" and said they outplayed the Red Sox. Cuban pitcher Juan Decall (a telephone lineman by trade) held the Red Sox to five base hits and one run. Woody Rich pitched for Boston. Both teams scored once in the first inning, and the Cubans scored the winning run in the bottom of the

ninth. Boston's run came on a walk to Dom DiMaggio, a base hit by Lou Finney, and a sacrifice fly by Stan Spence. Some 2,000 to 4,500 came to see the game (accounts differ). The *Globe* reported that "The fans were so exultant at the finish they threw seat cushions onto the field, an old Havana custom."

March 28 at Havana, Cuba: Boston 9, Cincinnati 2
Red Sox batters pounded out 13 hits while rookie Earl Johnson (six innings) held the 1940 World Series champion Reds to just four hits, and Emerson Dickman (the final three innings) held them hitless. Cronin and third baseman Jim Tabor each had three hits. Two of Tabor's were doubles. Jimmie Foxx hit a 420-foot triple.

March 29 at Havana, Cuba: Cincinnati 6, Boston 3
Cincinnati's Johnny Vander Meer pitched better than Mickey Harris and Dick Newsome did for the Red Sox, holding Boston to seven hits (three by DiMaggio) while the Reds collected 13.

March 30 at Havana, Cuba: Cincinnati 2, Boston 1
Joe Dobson held the Reds to two runs, but the Boston team scored only once (on a fifth-inning double by Dobson, driving in Bobby Doerr, who had walked). The game drew the biggest crowd of the trip, reported as 10,000 in the *Boston Traveler*. The team returned to Florida that evening by boat from Havana harbor.

Both teams were said to have enjoyed the trip greatly. They came back with plenty of souvenirs from local shops.

**When was the first time the Red Sox played a game in Mexico?**
After playing the Angels in Scottsdale, Arizona, on March 25, 1965, the team traveled to Tucson, Arizona, to stay overnight before heading across the border to Nogales, Mexico, to play a spring training game there against the Cleveland Indians on Saturday, March 26. The team was held up for about a half an hour at the border because they had not supplied photographs that were necessary for temporary work permits. There were 2,212 in the ballpark and perhaps another 4,000 outside.

The *Boston Record American*'s story of the game began, "Not since Pancho Villa hung up his spikes has Mexico seen as many explosions as the Red Sox created yesterday in this border town seventy miles south of Tucson." The Red Sox hit 10 home runs in the game, and the Indians hit two. "Baseballs rattled through the narrow streets of Nogales and threatened to hit the barefoot Mexican boys chasing them." The final score was Boston 15, Cleveland 9. Carl Yastrzemski's mother in Long Island was ill, so he did not make the trip.

Each of the 10 Red Sox home runs was hit by a different player, in this order: Félix Mantilla, Bobby Guindon, Mike Ryan, Eddie Bressoud, Tony Conigliaro, Bill Schlesinger, Lenny Green, Chuck Schilling, Russ Nixon, and Dalton Jones. The major-league record to that point was said to be eight homers hit in a regular-season game, held by the New York Yankees.

The Cleveland starter was Jack Kralick, with the first five homers charged to him. The Red Sox collected 16 hits in all.

Dave Morehead had started for Boston, but he was wild, and Cleveland led, 4–0, through the first three innings. Then the bombardment began. Two Sox players were hurt, both by Max Alvis. A second-inning line drive hit Morehead in the pitching shoulder. Pete Charton took over from Morehead. In the sixth inning, Alvis collided with Mike Ryan at the plate, reinjuring a knee that had been hit in October 1964.

Managers Billy Herman of the Red Sox and Birdie Tebbetts of the Indians were given "handsome sombreros" before the game.

**When was the first time the Red Sox played a game in the Virgin Islands?**

They didn't play just one. They played two. On two different islands. Against the New York Yankees.

They flew to Saint Croix after beating the Baltimore Orioles in Miami on March 30, 1967.

On March 31, the U.S. Virgin Islands celebrated the 50th anniversary of Transfer Day, when the United States had purchased the islands from Denmark.

The score was Yankees 3, Red Sox 1 at Frederiksted, Saint Croix. The game was the first major-league baseball game on the islands and was played before 2,100 on a converted cricket field. The Yankees were staying at the Americana Hotel in San Juan and dressed there, flying into Saint Croix in uniform on a chartered flight.

Mel Stottlemyre held the Red Sox to four hits, though all four of them were two-base hits, including Don Demeter's eighth-inning RBI double, back-to-back after Dalton Jones had doubled. Reggie Smith and Rico Petrocelli both doubled, too. Jim Lonborg started for the Red Sox, giving up the first two of the Yankees' three runs, in his seven innings of work. Elston Howard doubled in the first one in the second inning, and Steve Whitaker hit a solo homer in the fourth. The Yankees' Horace Clarke was a native of the U.S. Virgin Islands and was presented with a new white Mustang before the game. The field was adjacent to a beach area where he had played semipro ball as a kid.

Jerry Stephenson also pitched for the Red Sox. The Yankees got six hits, two of them by their leadoff batter and second baseman Clarke.

After the game, a steel drum band serenaded them. Clarke gave the keys to the Mustang to his father, saying he wouldn't be back until the fall, and besides, he didn't drive.

The weekend Transfer Day celebrations continued at Charlotte Amalie, St. Thomas, the next day, April 1, 1967. The score was Boston 13, New York Yankees 4. Carl Yastrzemski had three hits, including a three-run homer, and drove in five of the runs. José Tartabull homered in the first inning for the first Red Sox run. Bill Landis started for Boston, relieved by Gary Waslewski, who gave up a go-ahead homer to Jake Gibbs in the sixth. That gave the Yankees a 3–2 lead. Joe Pepitone hit a solo homer later in the game. Mickey Mantle was 1-for-4.

Fred Talbot had started for New York. Stan Bahnsen took over in the bottom of the sixth, and the Red Sox jumped on him for six runs, the first two coming on a Petrocelli home run that put Boston back on top, 4–3. Bob Tillman doubled, Joe Foy singled him in, Yaz singled in Foy, and Tony Conigliaro doubled in Yaz. Thad Tillotson gave up five more runs later in the game. Waslewski got the win.

The Yankees then left for San Juan to play a game against the Pittsburgh Pirates on April 2. The Red Sox traveled to St. Petersburg, Florida, and played the Mets.

**When was the first time the Red Sox played a game in Puerto Rico?**

During spring training in 1966, the Red Sox played three games against the Minnesota Twins in Puerto Rico on March 25, 26, and 27.

The first game was a shutout in San Juan—Twins 9, Red Sox 0. The Red Sox had come into the game with a spring training record of 2–13. Perhaps leaving Winter Haven and playing in San Juan might prompt a better result? Instead, observed the Quincy, Massachusetts, *Patriot Ledger*, "The Boston Red Sox found a new place to lose." The Twins had beaten the Red Sox in 12 of 16 regular-season games played in 1965. Dave Morehead pitched the first five innings for Boston and gave up all nine runs scored by Sam Mele's Minnesota Twins. Trying to come back from arm surgery, Camilo Pascual pitched for Minnesota and allowed just one hit, a 190-foot double by Tony Conigliaro in the fourth inning. Tony Oliva and Don Mincher each had two-run homers for the Twins. Many players (and manager Billy Herman) were seen in San Juan casinos after the game.

In San Juan again, on Saturday, the Twins prevailed 3–1. Dave Boswell started for the Twins and let in the one run. Sox starter Earl Wilson gave up the three Minnesota runs. César Tovar led off with a single and went to third on a wild pitch. Oliva enabled him to come home with a sacrifice fly. They got two more in the fourth on a walk, single, stolen base, throwing error, and another single. In the bottom of the fourth, Carl Yastrzemski singled, and George Scott doubled to left-center field to bring him home.

The third game of the weekend visit saw the Red Sox beat the Twins, 5–1, in Ponce on March 27. The win broke what had become an eight-game losing streak. Dennis Bennett started for the Red Sox and gave up one run in the third. Dick Radatz took over and pitched the fourth through the sixth, becoming the beneficiary of a two-run homer by Conigliaro off reliever Jim Roland, knocking in George Thomas, who had reached on an infield hit. An error and a single by Joe Foy put two Sox on base, and Mike Andrews drove them in with a three-run homer. Radatz got the win.

The Red Sox returned to Puerto Rico 12 years later and played a game in Bayamon, beating the Pittsburgh Pirates 5–4 on March 21, 1978.

**When was the first time the Red Sox played a game in the Dominican Republic?**

The 2000 Red Sox team didn't have as many Dominican superstars as, say, the 2003 and 2004 Red Sox—with Pedro Martínez, David Ortiz, and Manny Ramirez. But they did have nine Dominicans who appeared in one or more games: Pedro, his brother Ramón Martínez, Israel Alcántara, Manny Alexander, Héctor Carrasco, José Offerman, Jesús Peña, Hipólito Pichardo, and Wilton Veras.

They also had a baseball academy, one they shared with the Hiroshima Carp. The Houston Astros and Red Sox had collaborated on a cooperative Dominican Summer League team back in 1996, both teams then organizing their own teams.

During spring training of the year 2000, the major-league Astros and Red Sox teams arranged to play each other in a pair of games at Quisqueya Stadium in Santo Domingo.

David Ortiz, Manny Ramirez, and Pedro Martínez with the 2013 World Championship trophy.
PHOTO COURTESY OF THE BOSTON RED SOX

73

The Dominican Republic was as "baseballic" a country as there was—more so, even, than the United States. As Pedro Martínez himself told *Globe* reporter Bob Ryan, "Obviously baseball is the No. 1 sport in the Dominican. There's almost nothing else." To be able to see two prime teams was a treat.

Both teams had played postseason ball in 1999. The Red Sox had made it all the way to the American League Championship Series, losing four out of five games to the New York Yankees, who went on to sweep the Atlanta Braves in the World Series. The Braves had beaten the Astros, three games to one, in the 1999 National League Division Series.

The Red Sox schedule was not that accommodating. It had them playing a night game against the Twins at Fort Myers and then catching a 6:45 AM flight the next morning to fly to the Dominican capital. They played a game that night, Saturday, March 11, and then a day game the next day, then hustled back to Florida for a Monday game.

And these were split-squad games, in that there was also a Red Sox game at St. Petersburg on March 11 (Tampa Bay 1, Boston 0), featuring players such as Rich Garces, Scott Hatteberg, Darren Lewis, Troy O'Leary, and John Valentin, among others. The Astros were also operating on a split-squad basis.

The reigning American League Cy Young Award winner was Pedro Martínez, but fans only got to see him work one inning, and brother Ramón likewise had only one inning. The Red Sox scored two runs in the first on RBI singles by Jason Varitek and Marty Cordova. The Astros got two off Jared Fernandez in the third. In the top of the fifth, Boston took the lead on a solo home run by Carl Everett, but Fernandez got touched up for two more runs in the bottom of the fifth. The final was 4–3, Houston.

The Astros also won the second game by one run, 3–2. Juan Peña started for the Red Sox and José Lima for the Astros. It was 0–0 after four innings. Once again, the Red Sox scored first, with one run in the fifth on an RBI single by Trot Nixon and another run in the sixth on a sacrifice fly by Red Sox left fielder Jermaine Allensworth (he had come to the team from the Mets but never played for the Red Sox, even in their minor-league system). The Astros scored once in the eighth and twice in the ninth, winning the game, 3–2, on Houston shortstop Julio Lugo's two-out, two-run homer in the top of the ninth off Boston's Rob Stanifer.

Ticket prices were high, particularly for split-squad games, and the stadium was not full either day, something lamented by Pedro. The prices were determined locally, not by MLB.

In Ft. Myers, the Sox lost there, too, beaten 9–8 in 11 innings by the Philadelphia Phillies. Boston manager Jimy Williams said, "We play the games. Four games in two days; that's all we can do. They told us to get on the plane to come down here. Now they're telling us to get on a plane and go back."

**When was the first time the Red Sox played a regular-season game in a completely different country?**

After the Toronto Blue Jays had been welcomed into the American League in 1977, Boston's first road trip there saw them play in Exhibition Stadium on the afternoon of Sunday, April 24. Bill Singer pitched for Toronto and yielded two runs in the top of the first inning, with Jim Rice driving in the first run and Carl Yastrzemski the second. The game was a 7–0 shutout for the Red Sox, whose starter went the distance. The starter was Fergie Jenkins, a native of Chatham, Ontario.

The teams played a doubleheader the next day, Toronto winning the first game, 4–3, and the Red Sox winning the second game, 6–5. When the Blue Jays made their first visit to Fenway Park, the Red Sox swept them in three early July games. The Sox won four out of five in Toronto in September and then three of four in Boston in late September.

It may be of interest to note that the Blue Jays won back-to-back World Series in 1992 and 1993. The Red Sox had to wait 27 more years after the 1977 game for their next title.

**When was the first time the Red Sox played a regular-season game more than 6,000 miles from Fenway Park?**

The team played two games against the Oakland Athletics to open the 2008 season. But Oakland is only about 2,700 miles from Boston. Yes, but the games were played in Tokyo, Japan—and Tokyo Dome is more or less 6,719 miles from Fenway Park. The Red Sox and Athletics split the two games, with Boston winning the first one, 6–5 in 10 innings, and losing the second, 5–1.

Before they took on Oakland, the Red Sox played two exhibition games at the Tokyo Dome.

March 22 at Tokyo, Japan: Boston Red Sox 6, Hanshin Tigers 5

March 23 at Tokyo, Japan: Boston Red Sox 9, Yomiuri Giants 2

## When was the first time the Red Sox played a game in Europe?

The Red Sox scored six runs in the very first inning of the first major-league baseball game ever played in Europe. The only problem was that the New York Yankees had already scored six runs in the top of the first and kept on scoring at a faster pace. One might have thought that London Stadium was in something like a "Two Mile High" stadium, the way baseballs were being hit around the facility.

Baseball's greatest rivalry was to be showcased in back-to-back games on June 29 and 30, 2019, in Olde England, in hopes of being able to spread the game's popularity. The game drew many American expatriates from around Europe, but what they saw that first evening was a game with an American football score.

The Red Sox were reigning world champions, and their starter was 2018 Cy Young Award winner Rick Porcello. He lasted one-third of an inning. By the time he was replaced by Colten Brewer, the Yankees already had five runs. Before the game was over, both teams had used eight pitchers.

The Yankees had a 6–0 lead after the first half-inning. Their starter was Masahiro Tanaka. He came into the game with a 3.21 ERA. Tanaka lasted longer than Porcello, but he only pitched two-thirds of an inning and gave up six runs. It was 6–6 after one.

The New Yorkers added two runs in the third and six more in the top of the fourth. Mike Sharawyn struck out three Yankees in one and a third innings but gave up eight earned runs. In the eighth relief appearance of his big-league career, he saw his career ERA more than double, from 3.18 to 8.36. It edged up a little higher when he worked in six more September games.

The Red Sox UK Supporters Club, from the United Kingdom, in the stands for the London Series, June 2019.
BILL NOWLIN PHOTO

The score was 17–6 in favor of the Yankees at mid-game. Red Sox relievers buckled down and allowed no more runs in the final four innings. Red Sox batters produced a few more runs. Jackie Bradley Jr. hit a solo home run in the sixth. Michael Chavis—who had hit a three-run homer in the first inning, hit another three-run homer in the seventh. His six RBIs were the most of anyone that day, one more than five RBIs by New York's DJ LeMahieu.

Neither team scored in the eighth or ninth. The final was Yankees 17, Red Sox 13. New York had out-hit Boston, 19–18. Fans of both teams were kind of shell-shocked. What had they just seen? Was there something mysterious about the ballpark? The baseballs? Did none of the pitchers get any sleep? Were they totally jetlagged? No one seemed to have an answer.

There was another game the next day. Both games drew more than 59,000. Whereas the first game had lasted 4 hours and 42 minutes, this one was played in 4 hours and 24 minutes. The Red Sox hit three runs in the first inning—Xander Bogaerts, J. D. Martinez, and Christian Vázquez—thanks to New York starter Stephen Tarpley. Boston's Eduardo Rodríguez actually worked a normal 5⅓ innings, allowing just two first-inning runs. It was Red Sox 4, Yankees 2, after the top of the second, and neither team scored again in the next four innings. In the top of the seventh, Marcus Walden (who had been 6–0 beforehand) earned both a blown save and a loss by facing four Yankees and giving up a double, a walk, a double, and a single. Matt Barnes came in and pitched to four batters. Josh Taylor replaced him and pitched to six more. The Yankees scored nine runs and took an 11–4 lead. The Red Sox couldn't recover. They did get three more runs in the bottom of the eighth, but it was 12–8 Yankees heading into the bottom of the ninth. Aroldis Chapman gave up a leadoff double but then struck out the next three batters, each one on a swinging third strike.

The New England Patriots had previously played two NFL games in England and won them both. With these two losses, the Red Sox had dropped to 1–7 against their baseball rivals. When the 2019 season was over, the Yankees were first in the AL East, and the Red Sox were third, 19 games behind New York. The Astros beat the Yankees in the ALCS, but the Washington Nationals beat the Astros in the World Series.

# ETHNICITIES

THE UNITED STATES IS KNOWN AS SOMETHING OF A MELTING POT. IN this section, we will look at some of the Red Sox players who came from varying backgrounds. Fans are well aware that a wealth of talent comes from the Dominican Republic—the 2004 Red Sox had Pedro Martínez, David Ortiz, and Manny Ramirez—not to mention a couple of other Martínezes on the team (cousins Sandy and Anastacio). In chapter 9, we will look at players who came from other countries. First, let us look at the first Red Sox players who came from a number of ethnic groups within the United States.

**Who was the first Black ballplayer on the Red Sox?**
The Red Sox have long been infamous as the last team in the 16 National League or American League teams to have fielded a Black ballplayer—Elijah "Pumpsie" Green in 1959, a full 12 years after Jackie Robinson had debuted for the Brooklyn Dodgers in 1947. The Red Sox had had first crack at signing Robinson and two other Negro Leaguers—Sam Jethroe and Marvin Williams—who came for a "tryout" at Fenway Park on April 16, 1945. The word "tryout" is placed in quotation marks because it has been almost universally seen as a sham, something the Red Sox agreed to only to avoid political pressure put on them by Boston city councilman Isadore Muchnick. The three never heard from the Red Sox again. Robinson became Rookie of the Year for the Dodgers in 1947, and Jethroe was National League Rookie of the Year in 1950 with the Boston Braves.

The story has been told many times, notably by Glenn Stout in "Tryout and Fallout: Race, Jackie Robinson, and the Red Sox," reprinted in Bill Nowlin, ed., *Pumpsie & Progress: The Red Sox, Race, and Redemption.*

There is a long, tortured history of other opportunities the Red Sox had—think of Willie Mays as another for whom the Red Sox had the inside track since he played for the 1948 Birmingham Black Barons, a team with whom the Red Sox had business ties given the Red Sox farm club in Birmingham.

Red Sox scout George Digby recommended that the Red Sox sign Mays. Digby spoke with the GM of the Black Barons and was told that the price for Mays's contract was $4,000. The team sent another scout to check out Mays—Larry Woodall—but, as Al Hirshberg wrote, "It rained all the time Woodall was there. Without ever watching him play, Woodall gave the front office a more accurate report on the weather than on Mays and, as I heard the story, when he came home he still hadn't seen Mays in action." Woodall reportedly advised that Mays "was not the 'Red Sox' type of player." Whatever the actual communication was, the Red Sox did not pursue Mays—who was the National League Rookie of the Year in 1951 and became a 24-time All-Star and two-time MVP, hitting 660 home runs and driving in 1,903 runs in the National League. The Red Sox could have had Ted Williams in left field and Willie Mays in center.

The Red Sox could have had Jackie Robinson, they could have had Sam Jethroe, they could have had Willie Mays. They could have had many, many other Black ballplayers had they decided to be first, or among the first, rather than the last, team to field a Black ballplayer.

When they did, the player they fielded was Pumpsie Green.

Green (who is also the first, and only, major-league player yet with the nickname Pumpsie) was born in Oklahoma but grew up in Oakland, California, and was a big fan of the Pacific Coast League Oakland Oaks. His favorite Oaks player was Piper Davis (featured elsewhere in this book). In 1955, the Red Sox organization signed Pumpsie, and both he and pitcher Earl Wilson progressed through the ranks. Green helped the Double-A Minneapolis Millers win the American Association playoffs. He was added to Boston's 40-man roster.

That was a first in itself, as was his joining the team for spring training in Scottsdale, Arizona, on February 25, 1959. The *Boston Globe* noted, "The Boston Red Sox—in spring training, at least—today broke the color line." But Scottsdale was a segregated city in 1959, and Green was unable to stay at the team hotel, needing to travel 17 miles to the Frontier Motel in Phoenix. The Red Sox team did not change hotels, and Green wound up finding a room in the Phoenix hotel used by the San Francisco Giants. Despite the indignity, he hit well in spring training, batting .327 with four homers and 10 RBIs. There were only four other players on the team with a higher average. Yet he was optioned to the Millers. This did not go over well, given that the Red Sox were already under fire for being the only major-league team not to have integrated—and that in Boston, which had been the cradle of the abolitionist movement 100 years earlier.

It was a public relations nightmare. There were hearings before the Massachusetts Commission Against Discrimination, looking at the club's hiring practices even in staffing Fenway Park. Meanwhile, Green was getting "more seasoning" with the Millers and was hitting .320.

On July 4, 1959, Pinky Higgins was replaced as manager. It was Higgins who had reportedly said, some years earlier, "There'll be no n-----s on this ballclub as long as I have anything to say about it." Billy Jurges became the new skipper.

Green's debut came against the White Sox, in Chicago, on July 21. The score was White Sox 2, Red Sox 1, after seven innings. In the top of the eighth, Vic Wertz pinch-hit for Boston shortstop Don Buddin and singled to center field. Green took over for Wertz as a pinch-runner. The batters behind him didn't produce, so he finished the inning still on first but then took over in the field as shortstop. Nothing was hit his way, and the game ended a 2–1 Chicago win.

He was welcomed by, among others, Ted Williams, who made it a point that year to have Pumpsie as his throwing partner before games, wordlessly demonstrating his welcome.

On July 22, still in Chicago, Green played his first full game, not getting a hit but making a couple of fielding plays and stealing his first base after a fifth-inning walk.

On July 28 in Cleveland, he got his first base hit (a single to left) and scored his first run in the second game of a doubleheader. Earl Wilson had meanwhile joined the Red Sox—the first Black pitcher for the team—and worked one inning of relief in the first game, retiring all three batters he faced.

After the 13-game road trip ended, Green and the Red Sox returned to Boston. August 4 was the date of his debut at Fenway Park. He played second base in both games of a doubleheader and was the leadoff batter in the Red Sox lineup. Fifty years later, Green later told a *San Francisco Chronicle* writer, "On my way up to home plate, the whole stands, blacks and whites, they stand up and gave me a standing ovation. A standing ovation, my first time up! And the umpire said, 'Good luck, Pumpsie,' something like that." In that first at-bat, he tripled off the wall in left field, scoring immediately afterward as number two hitter Pete Runnels grounded out to first base unassisted. The Red Sox won the game, beating the Kansas City Athletics, 4–1. Boston lost the second game; Pumpsie played second base. But on his first day at Fenway, Pumpsie Green had the triple, run scored, and a sacrifice bunt setting up the next two runs in the first game, and then a single, two walks, and reached on an error, then scoring another run in the second game. He handled eight chances without an error.

Batting in the bottom of the ninth on August 8, he drove in two runs to tie the Tigers in a game the Red Sox won in 10.

Green played with the Red Sox through the 1962 season, appearing in 327 games with an overall .244 batting average.

### Who was the first Black pitcher on the Red Sox?

As noted in the previous section on Pumpsie Green, Earl Wilson was the first Black pitcher for the Red Sox. He debuted seven days after Green, though he likely would have made the big leagues earlier but for a stretch in the Marine Corps. Wilson had been 10–2 with the Minneapolis Millers. The Boston team was in eighth place—last place—for much of June and July and had been last when Green was called up. The team was 41–55 the day Wilson was called up, still last, 15 games behind the league-leading White Sox. It was July 28, 1959, and the Red Sox were at Cleveland Stadium.

Thanks to five runs surrendered by starter Frank Sullivan in the bottom of the fourth inning, the Indians had taken a 5–2 lead. Wilson was the third pitcher of the day, asked to work the seventh inning. In the top of the seventh, Pumpsie Green had pinch-hit (fruitlessly) for pitcher Ike Delock, so Wilson was taking Pumpsie's place in the game. He got Minnie Minoso to fly out to left field, and then induced both Tito Francona and Rocky Colavito to pop up foul. Jackie Jensen pinch-hit for Wilson, but after the fourth, there was no more scoring in the game, and Cleveland won, 5–2.

In his second appearance, Wilson started, on July 31 in Detroit. He threw 3⅔ innings and walked nine batters in that short stretch. In the fourth, he walked the bases loaded for the second time in the still-young game (he'd walked the first three batters he faced in the first inning). He was replaced. Remarkably, he had not given up a hit, nor had any runs

Earl Wilson and Pumpsie Green on the dugout steps at Fenway Park, 1959.
COURTESY OF THE BOSTON PUBLIC LIBRARY, LESLIE JONES COLLECTION

scored off him. In his third outing, he gave up five earned runs in the first inning plus, and was replaced by Delock. Wilson was taken off the hook as Red Sox batters scored 17 runs in the game, winning 17–6. He got his first win working in relief on August 20. He finished the year 1–1, with an ERA of 6.08.

### Who was the first Black pitcher to throw a no-hitter for the Red Sox?

On Tuesday night, June 26, 1962, Earl Wilson took the mound against the visiting Los Angeles Angels. He walked four batters in the course of the game, including two in the top of the fifth inning, but he never let a single Angel get a base hit. Wilson struck out five, saw nine flyballs to the outfield all get caught, and saw solid defense by the infield as well. His was the twelfth no-hitter of 18 that have been thrown by Red Sox pitchers. It was the first no-hitter by a Red Sox right-hander in 39 years (since Howard Ehmke's in 1923). The only other no-no since Ehmke's was lefty Mel Parnell's on July 14, 1956.

Wilson was 12–8 for the Red Sox in 1962. He worked for Boston until mid-June 1966, when he was traded to the Detroit Tigers. Wilson's career record with the Red Sox was 56–58 (4.10). In five years with Detroit, he was 64–45 (3.18). He finished his career with a partial season with the Padres in 1970.

### Who was the first Red Sox pitcher to win his own no-hitter with a base hit?

The winning hit in the June 26 game was Wilson's solo home run off Bo Belinsky with one out in the bottom of the third inning. The home run was hit over the wall in left-center field. He was "the first player of his race to pitch a no-hit game in the American League" (*Boston Globe*). Oddly, plate umpire Harry Swartz had worked Belinsky's no-hitter (also 2–0) against the Baltimore Orioles at Dodger Stadium on May 5.

### Were there other Black ballplayers on the team before Pumpsie Green?

Attempting to assign racial identity is, of course, fraught with difficulty and often uncomfortable for all involved. For obvious reasons, and more so in the first half of the twentieth century, a Black ballplayer with lighter skin color would try to "pass for White" in order to have better occupations and other opportunities. There is every possibility that someone who could qualify as of at least partial African ancestry might instead have claimed to be of Spanish descent or some other less definable ethnic background. This is not a matter into which we plan to delve deeper here.

The story of race and the Red Sox may have dated back to at least 1912 and left-handed pitcher Doug Smith. He was recruited to the team by scout (and former manager) Patsy Donovan, who had seen him strike out 18 in a game at his hometown of Millers Falls, Massachusetts. Smith's first work in pro ball was when he pitched the final three innings of the July 10, 1912, game at Fenway Park against the visiting St. Louis Browns. After six innings, the Browns held an 8–2 lead gained off starter Hugh Bedient and relievers Larry Pape and Ray Collins. The 20-year-old Smith pitched a scoreless seventh and eighth, then gave up one run in the top of the ninth. It was the only major-league game in which he ever pitched. He worked the next five seasons pitching in minor-league and independent baseball—though he did travel to Fenway (not in uniform) to watch the final game of the 1912 World Series.

According to SABR biographer Michael Foster, someone wrote to the Red Sox in 1913 saying that Smith had "black blood." Family historians say he descended from "southern Connecticut river Indian tribes," ones that were "clearly tri-racial" (Indian/white/black). It is unknown whether this had anything to do with Smith's Red Sox career not continuing.

**Who was the first Black ballplayer to sign a contract with the Red Sox?**
The first signing of an acknowledged Black ballplayer by the Red Sox came when the team signed Lorenzo "Piper" Davis in September 1949 with a very substantial $15,000 payment to the Birmingham Black Barons, with $7,500 paid and the other half to be paid if he was still with the organization come May 15, 1950. He was not. Davis may have received $5,000 from the payment.

Red Sox manager Joe Cronin told the *Pittsburgh Courier* that December, "He's a fine kid. I'm going to try him out with the Scranton club. If he makes good, I'm going to waste no time in moving him to Boston."

When it came to spring training, in segregated Florida, though, things may have changed. Davis had to stay in other quarters than at the team hotel. It didn't appear this was particularly frustrating to team management at the site. Davis was not allowed to use the Red Sox clubhouse but told *Boston Globe* writer Larry Whiteside, "I had to dress in the visitors' clubhouse. I couldn't even dress with my own team at first. Then I went on the field and nobody would even play catch with me. I just stood there until finally a guy named Dale tapped me on the shoulder and said, 'Let's throw.'" He was ultimately placed with the Scranton Red Sox but was cut after 63 at-bats in 15 games, despite leading the team in hitting (.333), RBIs (10), and stolen bases at the time. He had three home runs.

He was told it was for economic reasons. Davis returned to Birmingham. It was almost 10 full years later that the Red Sox finally had a Black player appear in a major-league game.

**Who was the first former Negro Leaguer to play for the Red Sox?**

The common understanding for the past 60-plus years is that the Red Sox were the last team in either the National or American Leagues to sign a Black player. But perhaps they were one of the first. Perhaps the Red Sox had a Black ballplayer long before Pumpsie Green and 22 years before Jackie Robinson's 1947 debut with the Dodgers.

Havana's Ramón "Mike" Herrera played in 84 games for the Red Sox, 10 in September and early October 1925 and 74 throughout the full 1926 season while serving as a second baseman (and recording a .275 batting average). He also played for Negro League teams both before and after his stretch with Boston, one of a small number of players who played in both the Negro Leagues and what was then called the major leagues in the years before World War II.

Indeed, Herrera played in the Negro Leagues both before and after his couple of seasons. In the first year of the Negro National League's existence—1920—Herrera played 61 games (as many as anyone on the team) for Tinti Molina's Cuban Stars West, one of the eight constituent teams in the NNL. He primarily played third base. His .268 average ranked third on the team; he was fourth on the team in RBIs.

In 1921, he worked another full season in the NNL, for the same team (though it had changed its name to the Cincinnati Cuban Stars). He didn't rank as high in any of the offensive stats, but he held his own, and he was once again tied for first in the number of games played.

For the next four seasons, he played in "Organized Baseball" for the Springfield Ponies of Springfield, Massachusetts. The Boston Red Sox purchased his contract, and he debuted with a 2-for-5 game in the first game of a September 22 doubleheader at Fenway Park, against the visiting Detroit Tigers. He was 0-for-4 in the second game. The Red Sox lost both, as they did for most of the games they played in 1925. Herrera got into 10 games, with eight RBIs and a .385 batting average. As noted, he played the full 1926 season with the Red Sox, hitting a middling but solid .257 (the team batting average was .255 that year).

He was back with Springfield in 1927 and then with Mobile. He played winter ball in Cuba and, in 1928, returned to Negro League action, playing in the Eastern Colored League for the Cuban Stars East. Again, he played in as many games as anyone on the team. His .328 batting average ranked second.

Thus Herrera played in official Negro League baseball both before and after his time with Springfield and with the Boston Red Sox. Photographs seem to show that he could "pass" for White, and he clearly was never identified as a Black ballplayer, or he would have been prohibited. Did he have to "pass for Black" to play in the Negro Leagues? Particularly since he was playing for teams dubbed as Cuban Stars, he was simply another player on teams that routinely played together in Latin America without strict regard for skin color.

Herrera was not the only such player. Gary Ashwill of Seamheads.com notes that Cienfuegos-born pitcher Pedro Dibut played for the 1923 Cuban Stars West of the NNL, then for the Cincinnati Reds in 1924 and 1925. Both Dibut and Herrera were teammates on a "Red Sox" team in Cuba—the 1916–1917 Red Sox of the Cuban Winter League. In Herrera's case, he played in the Negro leagues both before and after his time in the majors.

**Who was the first acknowledged Black player from the American League to play in a game against the Red Sox?**

On July 19, 1947, just a little more than three months after Jackie Robinson debuted for the Brooklyn Dodgers, Willard Brown appeared in his first game in the American League, playing center field for the St. Louis Browns and batting fifth in the order. The Browns' opponent at Sportsman's Park was the visiting Boston Red Sox. Brown was 0-for-3 in the game, but most of the Browns were hitless that day—Boston's Earl Johnson threw a three-hit shutout, and the Red Sox won, 1–0, after Ted Williams singled in Johnny Pesky in the top of the sixth.

Willard Brown had nine years of experience with the Kansas City Monarchs to his credit and had led the Negro American League in RBIs for six of those seasons.

The Browns came to Fenway Park on July 25, and Brown played right field, batting sixth. He was 2-for-4 in the game with two doubles, one RBI, and one run scored in a game the Red Sox won, 7–6. It was 12 years later before the Red Sox fielded an acknowledged Black player of their own.

Brown played with St. Louis from July 19 through August 17, and then he returned to the Monarchs. Even missing nearly a full month in midseason, he once again led the Negro American League in RBIs in 1947 and again in 1948. Brown was inducted into the National Baseball Hall of Fame in 2006.

Needless to say, given that the Red Sox were the last team in the AL or NL to field a Black ballplayer, numerous other Black ballplayers played against them over the intervening years.

It is interesting to note that when Willard Brown played against the Red Sox in 1947, it wasn't the first time he had seen Fenway Park. He had played there, with Satchel Paige and the Monarchs, during a barnstorming visit in 1943, playing against the semipro Fore River Shipyard team.

**Who was the first Latino on the Red Sox?**

The first known Latino player for the Boston Red Sox was right-handed pitcher Frank Arellanes. Born in Santa Cruz, California, on January 28, 1882, his family was said to have come to California in the late 1700s from Puebla, Mexico. His Red Sox debut was a three-inning start in Boston on July 17, 1908 against the White Sox, departing after giving up three runs. The Red Sox ultimately came from behind, and Eddie Cicotte got the win. An article in the next day's *Cleveland Press* said, in part and apropos of what we do not know, "Senor Arellanes moocha caliente hombre, or in the language of the small boy, the Mexican is a 'hot number.'" Arellanes was 4–3 in the 1908 season.

In 1909, after Cy Young had been traded to Cleveland, Arellanes won 16 games (tops on the Red Sox) while losing 12, relieving in 17 games as well as starting 28, with a league-leading eight saves, while recording a 2.18 ERA.

In 1910, his only other year in the major leagues, he had a 2.88 ERA and was 4–7 in wins and losses before being traded in mid-August.

**Who were some other early Latinos on the team?**

Carlos Luis Hall joined the 1909 Red Sox in August, becoming the second Latino on the team's pitching staff. He was a Californian, too, born in Ventura to Arthur Hall and Elvira Mungari on July 27, 1884. His record that first year was 6–4 with a 2.56 ERA. In 1910, "Sea Lion" Hall was 12–9 (1.91 ERA), with Arellanes at 4–7 (2.88). Regarding his nickname, *The Sporting News* once said he possessed "a voice that could wake the echoes and scare little children out of their afternoon naps a mile away from the ball yard."

In Fred Lieb's obituary in the December 16, 1943 *Sporting News* said Hall was of "Mexican Indian stock" heritage and was "weened (sic) on hot tamales" and noted that he spoke Spanish.

Hall was the winning pitcher in the very first game ever played at Fenway Park, on April 20, 1912, taking over from starter Buck O'Brien after four innings. He worked seven full innings, winning it in 11. It was he who had scored the tying run in the sixth after getting on base with a walk. He was 15–8 that year with a 3.02 ERA.

The 1912 Red Sox made it to the World Series, against the New York Giants, and Hall relieved in two games: Game Two (which ended in a tie after he blew a save) and Game Seven. He threw 10⅔ innings, and he had a 3.38 ERA.

In 1913, Hall appeared in 35 games, all but four in relief. His record was 5–4 (3.43). He was released after the season, briefly returning for 10 games for the 1916 Cardinals and six for the 1918 Tigers.

### Harry Wolter—1909 Red Sox

Harry Meiggs Wolter was born in Monterey, California, on July 11, 1884. At first glance, one might not see him as Latino, but his father was Manuel Adolfo Wolter, who had, in turn, been born in 1847 on El Toro Rancho in Monterey to a German father, Charles Luis Wolter, and a California mother, Josefa Antonia Nepomucena Pascuala Estrada, in 1847. Harry's mother, Lucretia Catherine Little, was born in California to two parents from New York.

Wolter played in 528 major-league games for six different teams in a seven-year stretch, four of those years with the New York Highlanders/ Yankees. He was a left-hander and played most of the time either in the outfield or at first base but also pitched in 15 games, and 11 of the 15 were for the 1909 Red Sox, winning his first two starts, on April 17 and May 16. His record was 4–4 for Boston. He appeared in 54 games in all, batting .240 with 10 RBIs. He committed five errors in right field for a dismal .783 fielding percentage, faring better at first base (.978, with four errors in 185 chances).

### Ed Hearne—1910 Red Sox

Born Edmund Hearne on September 17, 1887, in Ventura, California, Ed's father, Nicholas, was a grocer at the time of the 1900 census, and both Nicholas Hearne and his wife Mary were native Californians. His mother, Maria Mary (Peralta) Hearne, was of "Mexican-Spanish" ancestry, daughter of Miguel and Maria Peralta, both from Alta California— generally from the area we now know as the state of California. Ed himself was a shortstop who played only two games for the Red Sox on back-to-back days.

On June 9, he played against the White Sox at South Side Park, Chicago. Irv Young threw a two-hit shutout against Boston's Frank Arellanes, who only allowed four hits. Hearne walked twice and was 0-for-1. He handled four chances without an error: two assists and two putouts.

The Red Sox traveled to Cleveland and played the next afternoon at League Park. Hearne was again at short, again batting eighth. The Red Sox got twice as many hits (four) off Cy Falkenberg, but none of them were Hearne's. A *Boston Globe* subhead suggests the following reason he was pulled from the game early: "Hearne Like a Sieve." Though not charged with an error, there were two runs that scored due to what were described as misplays. He only had one plate appearance, with two men on base, but struck out. Despite having a bad leg, Heinie Wagner replaced him before the fourth inning. Cleveland won, 3–1.

Hearne was kept on the roster for a few more weeks, but then his contract was sold to the team in Waterbury, Connecticut.

### Who was the first Latino in the National Baseball Hall of Fame?

This one's a bit controversial. It all depends on your definition. This author argues it was Ted Williams, a point elaborated on at length in the book titled *Ted Williams—First Latino in the Baseball Hall of Fame* (Rounder Books, 2018).

His surname was Williams, reflecting his father, Samuel S. Williams, but his mother was May Venzor, born as the daughter of two immigrants from Mexico, Natalia Hernadez and Pablo Venzor. Both came from Hidalgo del Parral, in the state of Chihuahua. Ted knew his grandmother Natalia, who came to live in Santa Barbara and who never became fluent in English. She once saw him hit a home run in Los Angeles, and he attended her funeral in 1954. May Venzor lived until after Ted Williams retired, dying in 1961. Her brothers and sisters were Pedro, Maria, Daniel, Saul, and Sarah. A lengthy interview with Sarah Venzor Diaz in May 1999 provided a great deal of valuable information. The full story of the family is detailed in the book, on the back cover of which is a color photograph of 33 members of Ted Williams's extended family taken by the author at the San Diego Hall of Champions in March 2003.

Ben Bradlee Jr., author of *The Kid: The Immortal Life of Ted Williams*, wrote, "No reporter . . . dug into [Ted Williams's] Mexican heritage until Bill Nowlin explored some of the Venzor family lineage in an article for the *Boston Globe Magazine* published in June of 2002, a month before Ted died." How is it that this remained more or less unknown for so long, with a figure as much in the limelight as Ted Williams had been? It was the way he wanted it. He was aware of the prejudices that obtained in the minds of many 100 years ago. Indeed, it was this sole unamplified line in his autobiography, *My Turn At Bat*, that triggered the curiosity and subsequent exploration: "If I had had my mother's name, there is no doubt I would have run into problems in those days, the prejudices people had in Southern California."

For more than one reason, Williams was very private about his family. But that awareness of prejudice may well have been reflected in his taking the occasion of his 1966 induction into the Hall of Fame to say, just after congratulating Willie Mays for passing him on the all-time home-run list: "I hope some day Satchel Paige and Josh Gibson will be voted into the Hall of Fame as symbols of the great Negro players who are not here only because they weren't given the chance."

That Williams was able to live as Anglo. He never experienced discrimination himself regarding his largely unknown ancestry. Scholar Adrian Burgos Jr. has argued that Williams "did not identify as Latino nor was he racialized as such during his legendary career." Furthermore, when he did have "the grandest platform he was provided"—his Hall of Fame induction speech—he did not take the occasion to talk about his own heritage. Essentially, Burgos argues, Williams did not live as Latino, and thus, it would be something of a disservice to retroactively define him as such. It is a legitimate argument. The counter is one of pure genealogy and an understanding that while Williams never denied he was Latino, he avoided that description for reasons of his own. One wonders how things might have been different had he been born 50-plus years later.

## Who was the first Native American ballplayer on the team?

What about the first Native American ballplayer? As with the question of who the first Latino in the Baseball Hall of Fame was, one needs to be clear about definitions. The first known Native American on the Red Sox was Louis Leroy, who played with the team in 1910.

Right-handed pitcher Louis Leroy hailed from Omro, Wisconsin, born there on February 18, 1879. He was a Stockbridge-Munsee Indian, a group of Mohicans who had relocated to Wisconsin at the beginning of the nineteenth century. He grew up attending reservation schools and then went to both the Haskell Institute of Kansas and the Carlisle Indian Industrial School, where he played for Carlisle coach "Pop" Warner for three years, 1899–1901. More than once, he ran away from school, hoping to play baseball elsewhere.

After four seasons of Eastern League ball, Leroy signed on with the New York Highlanders (later Yankees) and pitched in three late-September 1905 games, winning one and losing one. He was 2–0 in the first part of the 1906 season but returned to play for Montreal. He was known to have been of Native heritage, and newspapers of the day used some of the predictable and hackneyed phraseology—Leroy was "on the warpath" and a "heap good Injun."

From 1907 to 1913, he pitched for the St. Paul Saints, but when Red Sox scout Patsy Donovan became manager in 1910, he wanted Leroy on his team, and Leroy joined them for preseason work at Hot Springs. Leroy was a spitball pitcher, in times before the spitball was prohibited.

He only appeared in one game, on April 20, 1910, a home game at Boston's Huntington Avenue Grounds against the visiting Washington Senators. Starting for Boston was Charlie Smith, who gave up one run in the first, saw his teammates score twice, and then gave up two more runs in the top of the second. Leroy worked the third through sixth innings, yielding one run in the third, but three in the fifth and five more runs in the sixth inning. Five of the nine runs he gave up were earned; he walked two and gave up seven hits. The final score was Washington 12, Boston 4. Though he was with the team another couple of weeks, he returned to St. Paul in early May or, as the *Globe* put it, went "back to his old wigwam in the far west." He had no decision in his time with Boston. In his brief major-league career, he was 3–1, with a 3.22 ERA.

## Two other early players with Native American ancestry

There were two earlier players who had some Native American ancestry but were never enrolled with a particular tribe.

### Bert Husting—1902

The first was another right-handed pitcher, who also played in just one game, in 1902. In a 1948 obituary, Bert Husting was said by the *Milwaukee Journal* to be "proud of his Indian blood. He often pointed out that Mrs. Solomon Juneau was a granddaughter of the Menominee chief, Ah-ka-ne-no-way." His one outing was on April 25, 1902. He'd pitched in two games for Pittsburgh in 1900 and was 9–15 (4.27) for the American League's Milwaukee Brewers in 1901.

For Boston, he threw a complete eight-inning game in Washington and was 1-for-4 at the plate himself, with a run batted in. But he had given up 15 hits and walked eight Senators, tagged for 15 runs and a 15–4 loss. Four days later, he joined the Philadelphia Athletics, for whom he won 14 games and lost only five, helping the Athletics win the American League pennant. There was no World Series until 1903, so that ended his season. An eye accident later in the year ended his pitching career.

### Case Patten—1908

In his player questionnaire for the Hall of Fame, Patten declared his heritage as "Scotch, Irish, English, Dutch, and Indian," perhaps from his mother Mandana's side of the family. As was the case with both Leroy and Husting, Patten was a pitcher who only lasted one game. Patten was a left-hander, and he was the first known player to have claimed Native ancestry who pitched in a Red Sox uniform. His game was on June 18, 1908. He'd come to the Red Sox in a May 31 trade for Jesse Tannehill, after working from 1901 until that date for the Washington Senators, where he had won 106 major-league games. (He'd lost 127 but had a decent 3.34 ERA.)

The June 18 game in Chicago was his last in the big leagues. He worked the first three innings of the game with a scoreless first, then touched for one run in the second. After the Red Sox tied it 1–1 in the top of the third, Patten was hit for four runs in the bottom of the third. The team cut ties, and it proved to be his last outing in the majors.

### Who was the first Jewish player on the Red Sox?

The American Jewish Historical Society's baseball card set from several years ago, "Jewish Major Leaguers," lists Red Sox players Brian Bark,

Moe Berg, Lou Boudreau, Happy Foreman, Joe Ginsberg, Gabe Kapler, Buddy Myer, Jeff Newman, Al Richter, Sy Rosenthal, Adam Stern, and Kevin Youkilis. Al Schacht was a coach for the Red Sox in 1935 and 1936.

The first was born in Boston in 1903, Sy Rosenthal, an outfielder in 84 games in 1925 and 1926. He was a frequent left-handed pinch-hitter in those years as well, twice in 1925, but in 37 additional games in 1926. He hit .267, a bit better than the team's overall .255 batting average in 1926. In his total of 123 games, he drove in 44 runs and scored 40 times.

Sy's parents were immigrants: Philip Rosenthal from Russia and Anna Gottfried Rosenthal from Austria.

Hugh Duffy signed him to the Red Sox, and he tore up the Texas League with San Antonio, batting .331 with 21 homers before being called to Boston, where he debuted at Fenway Park, playing a double-header against the Yankees on September 8, 1925. He was 1-for-9 but had reached .264 over his 72 at-bats that season. His .267 the next year was pretty consistent for average. Sy's biggest day was in another doubleheader against the Yankees, on May 25, 1926. The Red Sox lost the first game (they did lose a lot of games in 1926, finishing in last place with a record of 46–107 with one tie), but Rosenthal hit a two-run homer in the bottom of the ninth, which produced a more respectable 5–3 final score. The Sox were losing again, by the same 5–1 score, in the second game heading into the bottom of the eighth. With one out and Phil Todt on first base, Rosenthal homered again, off future Hall of Famer Herb Pennock. That made it 5–3. The Red Sox added one more run but lost, 5–4. In the first game, Babe Ruth hit what was called at the time the "longest homer ever made at Fenway Park"—reportedly nearly leaving the right-field bleachers.

Rosenthal played in the minor leagues through 1935, averaging close to .333 in statistics available to us today. After coming home to Boston, he played semipro ball in the Boston Park League for a number of years. During World War II, both Sy and his son Buddy signed up—even though Sy was a little old and Buddy was a bit underage. Sy had to have knee surgery to pass the fitness tests. He joined the Navy in September 1942 and was assigned to a minesweeper. Buddy was killed in action around Christmas Day 1943 in the Solomon Islands during an attack to capture Japanese airfields on New Britain Island.

Sy Rosenthal was reportedly on board a ship as part of the D-Day invasion of Normandy and was himself seriously wounded by a German mine that sank the minesweeper he was on; 58 other crew members died. He was rendered paraplegic and wheelchair-bound for the rest of his life.

At Sy Rosenthal Day on September 13, 1947, the Red Sox helped raise money that purchased a house for him that had wheelchair ramps and other helpful fixtures. At an April 1960 testimonial dinner, the *Jewish Advocate* reported that "there is barely an hour when he is free from pain" but that he devoted his life to trying to help his fellow man. The account detailed the help he had given a boy afflicted with polio, a girl who was blind, and two sisters stricken with cerebral palsy. Three times he was elected president of the New England Chapter of Paralyzed Veterans of America and was involved in a number of other charitable works. Working with a Catholic priest who was also Black, he helped raise money in 1966 for a gym at the St. Augustine seminary at Bay St. Louis, Mississippi, which had been the first Roman Catholic seminary to accept African Americans, back in the 1920s.

He died at the VA Hospital in West Roxbury, Massachusetts, in April 1969, and his funeral was at Temple B'Nai Moshe, Brighton.

### Happy Foreman—1926

There was another Jew on the 1926 Red Sox, left-handed pitcher August "Happy" Foreman from Memphis. He only appeared in three June games. (He had previously worked in three September 1924 games for the Chicago White Sox.) He relieved in all three games, and the team lost all three games, but this was a year in which they lost 107 games. As it happens, it didn't come to pass that Rosenthal and Foreman were ever in the same game.

Foreman worked a total of 7⅔ innings, with a 3.52 earned run average, markedly better than the team's overall 4.72 ERA. His was the second-best ERA on the team of anyone working seven innings or more. Why he was not given more work is unknown.

### Buddy Myer—1927 and 1928

Let's look at two other players in this section—Buddy Myer and Moe Berg. Myer joined the Red Sox the year after Rosenthal and Foreman.

Buddy Myer had a career batting average of .303, built over 17 seasons, all but two of them with Washington. He started with them, then came to Boston for most of 1927 and all of 1928.

For the Red Sox, he played shortstop for most of 1927 and third base for most of 1928, batting .288 (second on the team) and .313, respectively (ranking first), leading the league with 30 stolen bases in 1928.

Washington wanted him back, badly, and traded five players—players who played, not just prospects, in December 1928. He became a two-time All-Star and the American League batting champion in 1935 (hitting .349). He hit .300 in the 1933 World Series.

## Which was the first game in which the Red Sox had three Jews play?

As noted, the Jewish Major Leaguers baseball card set listed 12 members of the Red Sox. There may well have been others—before and since. Ethnicity is not always known. But it is astonishing that during just one game—against the Texas Rangers at Fenway Park on August 8, 2015—the first-place Red Sox had three of the 12 Jewish players on their roster and ready to play. That's 25 percent of the total for the century-plus of Red Sox history.

None of the three started. It was 3–0 Rangers after the first half-inning, but the Red Sox bailed out Boston starter Wade Miller with four runs in the bottom of the first. The Rangers tied it in the second. The Red Sox took a one-run lead in the fourth, and the Rangers responded immediately with a tying run in the top of the fifth. A three-run homer gave the Red Sox an 8–5 lead in the bottom of the fifth.

In the seventh, still 8–5, the Red Sox had runners on first and second and nobody out. Terry Francona had Gabe Kapler pinch-hit. He grounded into a 1-6-3 double play. Boston did add three more runs before the inning was done. In the top of the eighth, Kapler went to play right field, and Kevin Youkilis was inserted in the game to play third base. With an 11–6 lead after eight, Kapler moved to left field to replace Manny Ramirez, and Adam Stern came off the bench to play right. There was a single to center but no scoring, and Boston won, 11–6.

By the end of the season, Youk had played in 44 games, batting .276. Stern had appeared in 36 games, batting .136. Kapler had also played in 36 games, hitting .247. None of the three made an appearance in that year's postseason; the Red Sox were swept in the Division Series by the Chicago White Sox. All three were on the team in 2006, Youkilis becoming the team's starting first baseman and later a three-time All-Star for the Red Sox.

# FIRST PLAYERS FROM OTHER COUNTRIES

MANY STUDIES OF BASEBALL HAVE ATTEMPTED TO PIN DOWN ITS ORI-gins. Did it derive from the English game of rounders? Might it even have been related to stick and ball games from ancient Egypt? Were there precursors in Native American games?

It's not something we're ever likely to be able to know, but it is clear that the game as we know it has very strong American roots and partic-ularly in the northeastern part of the country around the time just before the Civil War. One can document its spread to the South, to Canada, and overseas—to Caribbean countries and to Japan and beyond.

It's been known as the "National Pastime" in the United States, though other sports have become ascendant in recent years and, of course, e-sports have taken hold of younger generations.

Red Sox players (even on the 1901 Boston Americans) sometimes hailed from other countries.

In the past couple of decades, there has been a groundswell of talent from many other lands, such that sometimes a majority of the nine players on the field during any given inning might well be from countries other than the United States. If one counts Puerto Rico as another land, and treats Scotland, England, and Wales as different lands, through the 2022 season, the Red Sox have had natives of 26 different lands represented as players.

Let's look at some of the first.

## Who was the first team player born outside North America?

The first Boston player not originally from North America was Edward Morgan "Ted" Lewis. He debuted in the May 2, 1901, game, starting the game and benefiting from some run support from his team-mates—it was 21–2, Boston, after 2½ innings. The *Boston Globe* noted that Lewis "did not pitch gilt-edge ball by any means." He went the distance but gave up 12 runs. He still got the win.

Lewis was born on Christmas Day 1872 in Machynlleth, Wales. Mach (as it is called locally) is a small market town, population slightly over 2,000, set in the lower Dyfi Valley about 10 miles in from the coast. It's also known as the Ancient Capital of Wales. Lewis is—so far—the only Boston player to come from Machynlleth.

The Lewis family came to America while Ted was young, and he grew up in poverty in Utica, New York. Never allowed to play much baseball at home, his parents wanted him to be a minister and packed him off to college at Marietta—where he got himself on the baseball team. After receiving a scholarship offer in 1893, he transferred to Williams College and was signed to a contract with the Boston Nationals immediately after graduation. His contract specified that he would be exempt from having to play baseball on Sundays—not that this happened in Boston until nearly 40 years later—reflecting a pious outlook that saw him nicknamed "Parson" Lewis.

Lewis kept at his studies and earned a master's degree from Williams in June 1899. Promptly upon completing his 1901 season pitching for the Boston Americans, he started teaching at Columbia. For nine years, he taught elocution and oratory at Williams, later moving to become an English professor as dean of students at Massachusetts Agricultural College. In 1917, Lewis came to know New England poet Robert Frost when they met in the home of University president Meiklejohn at Amherst.

Frost had a lifelong interest in baseball (he'd been the best pitcher on his high school team in Salem, New Hampshire) and dreamed that he'd pitch in the major leagues, so it was perhaps a foregone conclusion that the two would become friendly. Frost asked Lewis to show him how to throw a curveball and recalled, "He let me into the secret of how he could make a ball behave when his arm was just right. It may sound superstitious to the uninitiated, but he could push a cushion of air ahead of it for it to slide off from, any way it pleased." On several occasions, the two enjoyed playing catch. In 1927, Lewis became president of the University of New Hampshire.

Information on Lewis and Frost can be found in Lawrence Thompson's book, *The Years of Triumph*. The preceding paragraphs on Lewis come from the book *Red Sox Threads*.

## Who was the team's first foreign-born manager?

The first foreign-born manager of the Red Sox was Fred Lake. He managed the team during the first year it was named the Red Sox in 1908 and again in 1909. Lake was born October 16, 1866, in Cornwallis, Nova Scotia, Canada. Coincidentally, the only other Sox skipper born outside the United States in the twentieth century was the man who succeeded Lake: Patsy Donovan, born March 16, 1865, in Queenstown, County Cork, Ireland.

In 2018, Puerto Rico–born Alex Cora managed the team to a World Series win in his first season at the helm. He managed again in 2019, 2021, and 2022. Cora was born in Caguas on October 18, 1975, between Games Five and Six of that year's World Series. He had played briefly for Boston in the 2007 World Series.

## Who was the team's first foreign-born owner?

The first (and last) foreign-born owner of the Red Sox was Joseph J. Lannin, who was born on April 23, 1866, in Lac Beauport, Quebec, Canada, and is said to have sought his fortune, walking all the way from Quebec to Boston. Lannin owned the team from 1914 to 1916, thus presiding over two World Series wins, in back-to-back years 1915 and 1916.

His first work was as a bellhop and then a waiter at a Boston hotel, but he clearly had a winning personality, ambition, and a talent for entrepreneurship. He was promoted and became manager of the hotel. He met a number of influential men over time and began to invest in real estate, rather quickly developing it into a sizable enterprise. He had become a baseball fan and, in 1912, bought some shares in the Boston Braves. In December 1913, he became president of the Red Sox (which required him to dispose of his Braves shares). He became sole owner in May 1914.

Two months later, he bought the contracts of Ernie Shore and George Herman "Babe" Ruth from Baltimore's International League club.

He maintained good relations with the Braves and, in 1914, helped make arrangements for them to play World Series home games at Fenway Park, a larger facility than their home park. When Braves Field opened in 1915, it had a larger capacity than Fenway, so the Red Sox played home games in both the 1915 and 1916 World Series at Braves Field. It was a true oddity that for three years in a row, a Boston team was in the World Series but never once played a home game in its own home ballpark.

Red Sox owner J. J. Lannin and manager Bill Carrigan, 1916.
GEORGE GRANTHAM BAIN COLLECTION / LIBRARY OF CONGRESS

In some regards, as far as baseball went, he may have been more of a fan than a magnate, and the actual ownership of the team was sometimes an aggravation, in particular in his relations with league president Ban Johnson. Johnson had boosted him for the position but perhaps only to serve his own purposes at the time, and the two appear to have often been at odds, with Lannin finding Johnson meddlesome. Lannin even told the *Boston Herald*, "I am too much of a fan to own a ballclub." He sold the club to theatre men Harry Frazee and Hugh Lord before Ban Johnson could begin to orchestrate a sale to new owners of his own choosing.

Lannin moved on to other interests, owning county clubs and hotels along the Eastern seaboard and even becoming involved in sponsoring competitive checkers tournaments and taking up primary residence on Long Island. In 1927, he either jumped, fell, or was pushed out of a hotel window in Brooklyn, one he had under renovation, plunging to his death.

## Who was the first foreign-born Latino on the Red Sox?

Shortstop Eusebio González was a member of the 1918 world champion Boston Red Sox. Born in Havana in 1892, he played several years of Cuban baseball but debuted with Boston on July 26, 1918—more than three decades before the date became a Cuban revolutionary holiday. He hit .400 for the 1918 team, albeit in limited time with them.

The Red Sox were on the road, in Comiskey Park, for a series with the Chicago White Sox. Halfway through the game, with Chicago holding a 7–1 lead over Boston, manager Ed Barrow had González substitute in for shortstop Everett Scott, batting sixth in the order. The first ball hit went right to González, who threw to first for an out. He took a throw from catcher Wally Mayer in the sixth inning and tagged out Ray Schalk on an attempted steal. When his first time to bat came, he led off the top of the eighth with a triple to left center and scored moments later when Jack Stansbury singled. "Gonzy" was batting .400; White Sox pitcher Eddie Cicotte had held Babe Ruth to 0-for-4.

Two days later, he was 0-for-1, pinch-hitting in another game at Comiskey.

On August 3, he played a full game, all 10 innings, in Detroit against the Tigers. He was 1-for-3, a single, and was walked once as well. That base on balls came when he led off in the top of the 10th. He came around to score the run that put the Red Sox ahead. They added two more and won the game, 7–5.

Those three games represented the entirety of his major-league career—but he's in the record books as a .400 hitter on a world-champion team.

González played error-free ball throughout his days with the Red Sox, both at shortstop and at third base. He had three chances at each position. Never once did he mishandle a ball.

After his brief time with the Red Sox, he played five seasons in Toronto and four other minor-league clubs, including back-to-back seasons in San Antonio in 1925 and 1926, before his final year in 1927.

**Who are some of the other Cubans who have played for the Red Sox?**

Well before we would get to Luis Tiant, there were two other natives of Havana who played for the Red Sox in the 1950s. Mike Guerra caught 10 games for the 1951 Red Sox before he was dealt to the Washington Senators, with whom he had first broken in back in 1937. Though he only hit .156 in his brief time with Boston, with two RBIs, the team won each of the first six games in which he played and 7 of 10 overall.

Right-hander Mike Fornieles broke in with the Senators in 1952, joining the Red Sox in mid-June 1957. He played parts of seven years with Boston, into 1963. Overall, he was 39–35 (4.08) in 286 games for the Red Sox, 90 percent of them in relief. His 70 appearances in 1960 led the league, a year in which he was 10–5.

**Who was the first Mexican native on the Red Sox?**

Mel Almada played for the Red Sox from 1933 to 1937. He was not only the first native of Mexico to play for Boston but also the first to play in the American or National Leagues.

Baldomero Melo Almada Quirós was born on February 7, 1913, in Huatabampo, Sonora, Mexico. His father was appointed governor of Baja California, but this was during the Mexican Revolution, and he was unable to assume the position. He wound up becoming the consul in Los Angeles. Melo had lived in California since he was one year old. His older brother, Louis Almada, played for Seattle in the Pacific Coast League, and during a visit, Mel was spotted by Seattle manager Ernie Johnson, signed to the Red Sox by Eddie Collins. He hit over .300 for Seattle in 1932 and 1933.

Almada debuted with Boston on September 8, 1933, and was 1-for-4 in both games of the day's doubleheader against the visiting Detroit Tigers. For the seventh-place Red Sox, he played in 15 games before season's end and finished with a flourish, collecting three hits in three of his last four games. His batting average at the end of the year was .341 (15-for-44), with 11 runs scored and three RBIs. He had a .473 on-base percentage.

After hitting .328 in 135 games for the 1934 Double-A Kansas City Blues, he returned to the Red Sox the following September and got into another 38 games, hitting .233. In 1935, though, he played in 151 of the team's 154 games, all but three of the games as an outfielder. With Native American Roy Johnson playing left field and Almada in right, the

Boston Red Sox outfielder Mel Almada and Boston Red Sox first baseman Babe Dahlgren, 1935.
COURTESY OF THE BOSTON PUBLIC LIBRARY, LESLIE JONES COLLECTION

September 24 *Boston Globe* declared, in a way that would not be deemed appropriate decades later: "An Indian in left field and a Mexican in right. 'Tomahawks' and 'Hot Tamales,' what a combination." Almada hit .290, fifth-best on the team. In his five years with the Red Sox, he hit. 272.

In mid-June 1937, Almada was traded to the Washington Senators, along with brothers Wes and Rick Ferrell, and later played for the St. Louis Browns and Brooklyn Dodgers, wrapping up his career in 1939.

### Who was the first native of Puerto Rico on the Red Sox?

In 1968 and 1969, Juan Pizarro had 11 years of major-league experience before the Red Sox purchased his contract from the Pittsburgh Pirates near the end of June in 1968. A native of Santurce, Puerto Rico, born there in 1937, he was a left-handed pitcher who had already worked for the Milwaukee Braves, Chicago White Sox, and the Pirates. In 1963 and 1964, he'd been an All-Star while with the White Sox. His 1964 season (19–9, 2.56) was his best. After Boston, he went on to play for four other clubs and then saw a final seven games for Pittsburgh.

Because of injuries, he had begun to work more as a reliever before coming to the Red Sox, but in the remainder of the 1968 season, he was assigned 12 starts (6–8, 3.59). He appeared in six early April 1969 relief stints before being part of a six-player trade that sent him to Cleveland. In all, he was 6–9, with two saves and a 3.78 ERA for the Red Sox. Pizarro had 131 major-league wins in his career, with a 3.43 earned run average. Puerto Rico baseball historian Jorge Colón Delgado has written, "Juan Pizarro is the best Puerto Rico pitcher of all time."

### Who was the first native of Venezuela on the Red Sox?

Hall of Fame shortstop Luis Aparicio, born in Maracaibo in 1935, spent the last three years of his 18 years in the majors with the Boston Red Sox, 1971–1973. He'd been Rookie of the Year for the Chicago White Sox in 1956, among his accomplishments leading the league with 21 stolen bases (he led the league for every one of his first nine seasons) and in assists at short (as he did for each of his first six years.) He was named to 13 All-Star squads, the last two times as a member of the Red Sox.

After his first seven years with Chicago, he was traded to Baltimore as part of a six-player deal in January 1963. He hit .308 in the 1959 World Series, playing for the White Sox, and won a world championship ring with the Baltimore Orioles in 1966 with one RBI in each of the team's first two World Series wins. The White Sox reacquired him after the 1967 season, again as part of a six-man trade. He also earned nine Gold Gloves for his work at shortstop.

In December 1970, he was traded to the Red Sox for Mike Andrews and Luis Alvarado. He hit kind of a low point in 1971, batting only .232, but rebounded the next two seasons, hitting .257 and then .271.

## Who was the first native of the Dominican Republic on the Red Sox?

The Red Sox have benefitted greatly in the first couple of decades of the twenty-first century by virtue of the number of Dominicans on their teams. Pedro Martínez, David Ortiz, and Manny Ramirez were important parts of the 2004 world champions, as were the latter two in 2007. All three are in the Red Sox Hall of Fame, and both Martínez and Ortiz have been inducted into the National Baseball Hall of Fame.

The first Dominican on the Red Sox was Santo Domingo–born shortstop and second baseman Mario Guerrero. Born in 1949, he was first signed by the New York Yankees but came to the Red Sox as the player to be named later in the June 1972 Sparky Lyle trade. His first major-league action was with Boston. In his first game—April 8, 1973—he was 2-for-3 with one run scored against the Yankees in a 4–3 win. The winning run was a homer off Lyle by Orlando Cepeda in the bottom of the ninth.

The Red Sox had Luis Aparicio and Doug Griffin as middle infielders and then Rick Burleson at short. Guerrero nonetheless got into 66 games in 1973, batting .233, which he bumped up to .246 in 93 games the following year. Fellow Dominican and future Hall of Famer Juan Marichal joined him for one year on the 1974 Red Sox team. Just before the 1975 season got underway, Guerrero was traded to the St. Louis Cardinals for Jim Willoughby. In 1976 and 1977, he played for the Angels and, in 1978 through 1980, for the Oakland A's.

## First Natives of Other Nations
### *Aruba*

The first native of Aruba on the Red Sox has two world champion-ship rings. Shortstop Xander Bogaerts was born in Oranjestad, the capital of Aruba, on October 1, 1992. Aruba is in the Caribbean, a large island off the northern coast of Venezuela and home to just over 100,000 inhab-itants. Politically, it is described as a "constituent country of the King-dom of the Netherlands." Aside from the Netherlands itself, the other two "constituent countries" are Curaçao and Sint Maarten. Bogaerts was signed by the Red Sox and first made the big-league team in August 2013. He appeared in 18 games, splitting his time between third base and shortstop. Added to the postseason roster, he appeared in a couple of Division Series games but was in all six of the ALCS games (scoring four runs) and every one of the World Series games against the Cardinals.

By 2014, Bogaerts became installed as the team's regular shortstop, and in 2022, he overtook Everett Scott for a team record that had stood for 100 years—most games played by a shortstop in Red Sox history. Scott had played 1,093 games.

Bogaerts was part of the 2018 world champion team as well, driving in 103 runs in the regular season and driving in another seven in the postseason.

Through 2022, he has won four Silver Slugger awards and been a four-time All-Star.

### *China*

#### *Hong Kong*

China, of course, presents a bit of a complicated question politically in that there are two Chinas—the Beijing-led People's Republic of China. Then there is Taiwan, known officially as the Republic of China.

Austin Brice was born in Hong Kong on June 19, 1992. That adds yet another level of complexity. On July 1, 1997, after Hong Kong had been under British rule for 156 years, there was a "transfer of sovereignty" that put it under the control of Beijing. It is now known as the Hong Kong Special Administrative Region of the People's Republic of China. Brice, a right-handed pitcher who graduated high school in Pittsboro,

North Carolina, was thus born in an area under British rule. Hong Kong is generally considered "China" now, and we have listed the Republic of China here as Taiwan.

Brice first joined the Red Sox pitching in 13 home games—never once with any fans in the stands at Fenway Park. When he won his first game, on August 19, not a single fan cheered. It was during the pandemic year of 2020. In all, he pitched in 21 games for Boston that year, all but one in relief. His record was 1–0 (5.95) in 19⅔ innings. That one start was an odd one. It was at Yankee Stadium on August 2. He worked one inning and no more. He struck out three batters, though he had also walked two and seen one Yankee reach on an error. Matt Hall replaced him to pitch the second.

Brice relieved in 13 games for Boston in 2021, without a decision but a 6.59 ERA. He spent most of the year with the Triple-A Worcester Red Sox, where he was 3–0. In March 2022, he signed with the Pittsburgh Pirates organization.

### Colombia

The first Colombian to play for the Red Sox was Jackie Gutiérrez from Cartagena, who broke in with Boston with five games late in the 1983 season (hitting safely in 10 at-bats). The only two of his countrymen to precede him to the majors were Lou Castro in 1902 and Orlando Ramírez in 1974. Jackie's sister, Alma Rosa Gutiérrez, was married to Ramírez. He was the starting shortstop on the 1984 Red Sox and played in 151 games, batting .263. That year, in August, Gutiérrez became one of only 14 franchise players who have ever executed the hidden-ball trick. It happened at Fenway Park on August 17, in the seventh inning, catching Tim Teufel off second base. A fan favorite, the Boston Baseball Writers voted Gutiérrez rookie of the year.

Though considered a superb defender, he was hampered by a knee tendon injury, and his productivity at bat fell off in 1985 when he hit just .218 in 103 games. At the end of the year, he was traded to the Orioles for pitcher Sammy Stewart.

The only other Colombians to play for the Red Sox have been Orlando Cabrera in 2004, Édgar Rentería in 2005, and Jeter Downs in 2022.

### Denmark

Olaf Henriksen became a Red Sox hero in the final, deciding, victorious Game Eight of the 1912 World Series. So proclaimed the *Boston Globe* in a subhead: "Pinch hit hero mobbed by rabid Red Sox enthusiasts." His family emigrated to the United States before Henriksen was a year old. He had been born in 1888 in Kirkerup (now part of the town of Roskilde).

He spent most of his childhood in the Boston suburb of Canton and joined the Red Sox in 1911, serving primarily as a pinch-hitter and reserve outfielder. He hit well, batting .355 over his first three seasons with the Red Sox (67 hits in 189 at-bats). He also drew 35 walks. Though he played seven seasons (through 1917) for the Red Sox, he finished with an overall .269 batting average.

In 1916, he once batted for Babe Ruth, largely a result of manager Bill Carrigan pulling Ruth after a dispute. Henriksen walked, forcing in the tying run in a game the Red Sox won, 2–1.

In that final game of the 1912 Series, the New York Giants led the Red Sox 1–0 heading into the bottom of the seventh inning. Christy Mathewson had only given up four base hits. A single and a walk put two runners on, and manager Jake Stahl (he made the call from second base since it was he who had singled) had Henriksen bat for pitcher Hugh Bedient. Henriksen doubled down the left-field line at Fenway, driving in Stahl with the tying run. The Giants re-took the lead in the top of the 10th, but the Red Sox came back with two and won it on an error, walk, Tris Speaker single to tie, and a sacrifice fly from Larry Gardner.

He remains the only native of Denmark to make it to the major leagues. To our knowledge, there has been no statue yet erected in his hometown.

### Germany

As the German version of Wikipedia informs us, "Wasseralfingen ist mit knapp 12.000 Einwohnern der zweitgrößte Stadtbezirk von Aalen in Baden-Württemberg und eine ehemalige Stadt." Wasseralfingen is the second largest district of Aalen in Baden-Württemberg and a former city, with almost 12,000 inhabitants. That's where Otto "Pep" Deininger hailed from, about an hour's drive from Baden-Württemberg's state capital, Stuttgart. His family emigrated to the United States when he was in his sixth year, in 1883. He grew up in the Jamaica Plain neighborhood of Boston.

Deininger appeared in two games for the 1902 Boston Americans. He both doubled and tripled in his first game on April 26 in Washington. The only other game in which he appeared was more than a month later, on May 30 in the first game of a doubleheader in Boston against the visiting Detroit Tigers. He was 0-for-2 in that game. His career stats for Boston were .333 at bat (2-for-6) but a 9.75 earned run average. Yes, he pitched in both games, seven innings in relief of Bill Dinneen in the first game, giving up 11 runs in a game Boston lost, 15–7. Dinneen was assigned the loss. Deininger started the May game but was given the loss in that one as Detroit won, 10–5. He had been described as "very nervous" playing in front of friends at home. A few days later, he was in the minors.

Pep did make the majors again, but not until 1908, with the Philadelphia Phillies. His pitching days were behind him, but he got into 56 games, mostly in center field, and hit a respectable .260. He continued to play baseball, though not in the majors, through 1917.

### Ireland

With Boston having been a major beneficiary of Irish immigration in the nineteenth century, one might think there would have been a lot of Irish natives on the Red Sox. There have not been. The first was manager Patsy Donovan, who hailed from Queenstown. He's been credited as the one who convinced the Red Sox to sign Babe Ruth.

Donovan had a lengthy playing career, mostly as a right fielder, starting with the Boston Beaneaters in 1890. He played 15 years in the National League, one in the American Association, and for Washington in 1904 in the American League, for whom he managed during the latter part of the season. His career batting average was .301.

In all, Donovan managed for five different teams for a total of 11 seasons. His last such work was with the Red Sox in 1910 and 1911. He managed the team to winning records both years (81–72 in 1910 and 78–75 in 1911). After he was replaced by Jake Stahl as Red Sox skipper,

Donovan continued to work scouting for the team, and it was in that capacity that he spotted Ruth playing for Baltimore.

The only Red Sox player to hail from Ireland was Jimmy Walsh, an outfielder born in Rathroe who played in 1916 and 1917, appearing in 71 games and batting .257. He was a member of the 1916 world champion Red Sox team (and had played in the 1914 Series against the Boston Braves two years earlier, in 1914). With the Athletics against the Braves, he was 3-for-9 in the World Series; with the Red Sox, he was 0-for-3 as a late-inning replacement in Game Two. He hit one ball back to the pitcher and then hit two foul popups.

### Jamaica

The Red Sox have had two Jamaicans on the team. When right-handed pitcher Justin Masterson first joined the team in 2008, he was the first. He'd been born in Kingston on March 22, 1985. His father, Mark, was dean of students at Jamaica Theological Seminary. The family moved back to the United States when Masterson was very young. A second-round draft pick out of San Diego State in 2006, he made it rather quickly to the big leagues, starting his first game on April 24. He limited the visiting Angels to one run over six innings and left with a 3–1 lead, but the first seven Angels to bat in the seventh (off a series of three different Red Sox relievers) all reached base and five of them scored before the fire was put out. The Sox lost the game, but it hadn't been on Masterson's watch.

He won his next three starts, one in May and two in June. He was transitioned to the bullpen and appeared in 36 games, finishing the season with a win/loss record of 6–5 and a 3.16 ERA. He had an exceptional postseason, pitching in nine games in the ALDS and ALCS for a total of 9⅔ innings, allowing just one run in each round. He was 1–0 with a win in Game Five of the ALCS against Tampa Bay.

Through July 29 in 2009, Masterson had a spate of starts (six) at the beginning of the season, then worked out of the pen. He was 3–3 (4.50) when traded to Cleveland. He had a rough start with them but then worked four-plus seasons, mostly as a starter, ending his career back with the Red Sox as a free agent signing in 2015. He was 4–2 in 18 games (nine starts) but with an ERA of 5.61 and was released in August.

Another Red Sox player from Jamaica was Chili Davis, the team's hitting coach for three years, from 2015 through 2017.

In 2019, Masterson traveled to Jamaica for a three-day goodwill baseball visit.

### Japan

*First Japanese-born pitcher to work a game for the Red Sox*

Tomo Ohka was the first pitcher from Japan to appear for the Red Sox. He was a native of Kyoto, which has been designated a Sister City of Boston since 1959. Ohka was born there on March 18, 1976. After a few years with the Yokohama Bay Stars, Ohka signed with the Boston Red Sox and put together a remarkable first season in 1999—he was 15–0 in the minors. He was 8–0 with Double-A Trenton and 7–0 (and a 3.00 earned run average) with the Triple-A Pawtucket Red Sox (with a 1.58 ERA). His first two starts in the majors, though, were disappointing. He lasted one inning (plus two batters) in his July 19, 1999, debut and was charged with five runs and a loss. Four days later, in Detroit, he lost another game, giving up seven earned runs in 4⅔ innings. He was sent back to the minors and picked up a few more of the above-mentioned wins there. When he was recalled to Boston, he pitched in six more games—all in relief—and never gave up another run. He also picked up a win in his final game, on October 1, being in the right place at the right time, working three innings of scoreless ball as the Red Sox beat the Orioles, 6–2.

Ohka was up and down in 2000 and 2001 as well (3–6, 3.12 in 2000, and 2–5, 6.19 in 2001) before being traded to the Montreal Expos as part of a deal to acquire Ugueth Urbina.

*First pitcher born outside the United States to throw a no-hitter for the Red Sox*

There is a Japanese connection here, too. The first pitcher to do so was Hideo Nomo—and he threw his no-hitter in the first game he pitched for the Red Sox. Nomo came from Osaka and pitched five seasons (1990–1994) in the Japan Pacific League for the Kintetsu Buffaloes of Osaka.

Water buffaloes are indeed known in Japan, though on Honshu, they would typically be in zoos.

Nomo signed with the Los Angeles Dodgers in 1995 and became NL Rookie of the Year, with a 13–6 record and a 2.54 ERA. On September 17, 1996, Nomo threw a no-hitter against the Colorado Rockies at Coors Field, Denver.

Over the course of his career, he signed nine different times—often for just one year—as a free agent. The Red Sox became the fifth team of seven major-league teams with which he signed. He pitched for Boston in the year 2001. For the Red Sox, with 100 years of franchise history behind them, he did something that had never been done before. As noted, he threw a no-hitter (a Nomo no-no) in his first game with a new team.

It was April 4 at Oriole Park at Camden Yards, the third game of the 2001 season. Both Baltimore and Boston were 1–1. He walked a batter in the first inning and saw another reach in the second. In the top of the third inning, the Red Sox scored two runs on Brian Daubach's two-run homer off Sidney Ponson. He walked a batter in the fourth and another in the seventh. Both pitchers were striking out the opposition; Ponson struck out the side in the fourth, and Nomo did in the sixth. Daubach was perhaps the only one who truly had Ponson's number; he hit another home run, a solo homer leading off the eighth. Ponson struck out 10, and Nomo struck out 11. Most importantly, Nomo didn't allow a base hit (a key element of any no-hitter), while Daubach's two homers gave the Red Sox all the runs they needed.

He had now thrown a no-hitter in each league, one of only five pitchers to have done so: Cy Young, Jim Bunning, Nolan Ryan, and Randy Johnson are the others.

On May 25, Nomo threw a one-hit complete-game shutout against the Blue Jays. He finished year with 14 wins and 10 losses and a 4.50 ERA. And then moved on to another team—actually returning to the Dodgers, where he settled in for the next three seasons.

*First Japanese native to start a game for the Red Sox in Japan*

Daisuke Matsuzaka's major-league debut was in Kansas City on April 5, 2007. He not only started the game but won it as well. Dice-K, as he was known, threw seven innings, holding the Royals to one run. The Red Sox won the game, 4–1. The Tokyo-born Matsuzaka finished the year 15–12, third to Josh Beckett (20) and Tim Wakefield (17) for wins on the team and working more innings than any other pitcher. He won the final Game Seven of the 2007 American League Championship Series, working the first five innings and beating Cleveland 11–2. He then won Game Three of the World Series against the Colorado Rockies. His third-inning single to left field drove in the third run of six the Red Sox scored on their way to a 10–5 victory.

Dice-K then established another first. When he pitched on Opening Day in the 2008 season, he became the first foreign-born player in American League history to start on Opening Day in his native land. Matsuzaka pitched against the Oakland Athletics in the Tokyo Dome on March 25, 2008. He worked the first five innings, giving up two runs, and left with a 3–2 lead after his teammates scored three runs in the top of the sixth. The lead didn't hold, but the game was won by the Red Sox in extra innings.

*First Japanese-born relief pitcher to win a game for the Red Sox in Japan*

Hideki Okajima won that March 25, 2008, in Tokyo. Brandon Moss tied the game against Oakland, 4–4, with a solo home run in the top of the ninth. Okajima—who had pitched 11 seasons for the Tokyo-based Yomiuri Giants—entered the game in relief. He had joined the Red Sox in 2007 and was, like starting pitcher Matsuzaka, a member of the 2007 world champion team. Matsuzaka struck out the first of the Athletics he faced—Kurt Suzuki—then walked the next. The third batter flied out, and the fourth grounded the ball back to Okajima, who threw to first for the third out. Manny Ramirez hit a double in the top of the 10th driving in both Julio Lugo (who had singled) and David Ortiz (walk) to give Boston a 6–4 lead. Jonathan Papelbon, though giving up one run and leaving two batters on the basepaths, closed out the game for the Red Sox. Okajima pitched for Boston through the 2011 season, working in 261 games with a record of 17–8 and a 3.09 ERA.

*First Japanese-born player to help kick off what was almost indisputably the most important comeback postseason victory for the Red Sox*

Dave Roberts, stealing second base and then scoring to tie the Yankees in the bottom of the ninth inning in Game Four of the 2004 American League Championship Series. The Sox had lost the first three games and were about to be swept by the Yankees and knocked out of the postseason by New York for the second year in succession. Down by a run, losing 4–3, the Red Sox came to bat in the bottom of the ninth. Kevin Millar walked. Roberts—a native of Naha, Okinawa, Japan—pinch-ran for Millar. Everyone at Fenway Park and watching on television knew that Roberts's mission was to steal second base and get into scoring position. Those knowing included future Hall of Fame reliever Mariano Rivera and catcher Jorge Posada. On Rivera's very first pitch, Roberts stole the bag. On his third pitch to Bill Mueller, the reigning AL batting champion singled to center, driving in Roberts with the tying run. With a sacrifice and error, Mueller wound up on third with just one out, but neither Orlando Cabrera, Manny Ramirez, nor David Ortiz could bring him home. The game went into extra innings. In the bottom of the 12th, Ramirez singled, and Ortiz homered to give Boston a 7–6 win. As almost everyone reading this book will know, the Red Sox won the next three games and then swept St. Louis in the 2004 World Series to capture their first world championship in 86 years.

### Korea

Cho Jin-ho broke into major-league ball at age 22. A native of Jeonju of the Republic of Korea (South Korea), a right-handed pitcher, he never played in KBO baseball until after five years in the Red Sox organization. He had, though, played on Korea's Olympic baseball team. His first game—his debut—was his best game. It was on Saturday, the Fourth of July, 1998, at Fenway Park. The Red Sox were in second place, already 10 games behind the Yankees, hosting the Chicago White Sox. He threw four scoreless innings, then gave up a leadoff home run to Mike Cameron with his first pitch in the fifth inning. It was the only run scored off him in the six full innings he worked. After he gave up a leadoff single to Magglio Ordóñez in the top of the sixth, Derek Lowe relieved him.

Ordóñez was caught stealing, and Lowe struck out the next two batters. The Red Sox never scored in the game and lost, 3–0. Cho took the loss. He lost his second start, too, eight days later in Baltimore, but that was because he gave up seven runs in 4⅓ innings. On July 19, he lost again, to the Tigers, tagged for five runs in 5⅓. They were his only three decisions that year. Another start saw the Sox win, but after Cho had left.

The following June, he was recalled to Boston and won his first two decisions but then lost three. For his 13 major-league games, all for the Red Sox, he was 2–6 (6.52).

Cho played the next three seasons in the Red Sox minor-league system and then returned to Korea, where he played his first professional games there in 2003, with a 5.20 ERA. Wikipedia says that in 2004 he was "caught in a scheme to dodge military service. He spent several years in prison and non-combat military service before returning to the mound for the Samsung Lions in 2007." He appeared in 15 games in 2007 and 2008 but with an overall ERA of 5.99 in his time in Korea.

### Netherlands

It's one thing to be born in, say, Denmark but raised in the United States. It's another to learn baseball in another land, particularly one without the sort of baseball culture that we know in countries such as the Dominican Republic. Wilhelmus Abraham Remmerswaal was born in the Netherlands, in the Dutch capital of The Hague, on March 8, 1954. He became, as his SABR biography notes, "the first European-trained major leaguer." A right-handed pitcher, he was known as "Win." He did win—one game in his first year with the Red Sox (1979) and two more in 1980.

In his big-league debut, Remmerswaal worked three innings of relief, allowing just one run, on August 3, in Milwaukee. Two days later, he got the win in the second game of a doubleheader, also against the Brewers. Dick Drago started but left after three innings. The Red Sox had an 8–0 lead when Remmerswaal entered the game to pitch the fourth. He worked three innings and gave up three runs, but Boston held a 15–3 lead heading into the bottom of the seventh. Tom Burgmeier took over, and then Bill Campbell. The final was 19–5, and Win was the beneficiary of all the early scoring. He appeared in six more games without another decision, finishing 1979 with an ERA of 7.08.

In 1980, Remmerswaal pitched for Pawtucket but was called up to Boston on June 21. He also appeared briefly in three late-season games—14 games in all, all in relief, with a couple of strong efforts (six innings of two-hit relief in Baltimore on July 3) giving him two more wins while losing one. He finished the season 1–2 (3.86). After another season in Pawtucket, he played five years of pro ball in Italy. As noted in his SABR bio, he was a victim of alcohol abuse, confined to a Dutch nursing home for close to 25 years before his death in July 2022.

### Nicaragua

The son of a lobster fisherman and baker from Pearl Lagoon, Nicaragua, on the Central American country's Caribbean (and largely English-speaking) coast (the Miskito Coast), Devern Hansack threw—in this author's opinion, if not that of Major League Baseball—a no-hitter on the final day of the 2006 season. It was just his second start. He'd lost his debut, 5–3, in Toronto on September 23.

That the October 1 game got underway at all—after a three-hour, 23-minute rain delay—was due to a window in the weather that opened for a little more than an hour and a half.

Major League Baseball is entitled to make its own rules, but right-hander Hansack's Fenway Park game on October 1 saw Mike Lowell hit a three-run homer in the bottom of the first and the team to add six more runs over the first five innings. Hansack allowed no hits in those five innings, the only baserunner coming when he walked Fernando Tatis with one out in the top of the second (a double play took Tatis off the basepaths). After five, the rains resumed, and the game was called.

It's in the books as a win. It's in the books as a complete game. It's in the books as a shutout. Hansack allowed no hits. But a rules change in 1991 (after more than a century of major-league ball) required that to be deemed a "no-hitter," a game had to last nine innings. Hansack was, of course, nonetheless glad to get the win.

He was briefly part of the 2007 world champion team, working in two May games and one in September, with a record of 0–1. In 2008, he got into four September games, the only decision a win over the Yankees in the 10th inning of the second game on September 28. His major-league career was 2–2, with a 3.70 ERA. Subsequent shoulder surgery prevented him from continuing a pitching career.

### Panama

The country of Panama boasts two Hall of Famers—Rod Carew and Mariano Rivera. The first to play for the Red Sox was left-handed left fielder Ben Oglivie, drafted out of Roosevelt High School in The Bronx in 1968. He was born in Colon in 1949. He joined the big-league team in September 1971. In his debut on September 4, he pinch-hit for pitcher Jim Lonborg and grounded out to first base but picked up an RBI in the process. His first full game was two days later, and he was 2-for-4 against the Yankees.

Though he played 16 years in the majors and hit for a career average of .273, with 235 home runs and 901 runs batted in, his first three seasons with the Red Sox were relatively anemic. Though he played in 166 games, he hit .235, with his average progressively declining in each of the three years. It was a tough challenge he faced—trying to break into an outfield of Carl Yastrzemski, Reggie Smith, and Dwight Evans.

One source described him as an "intelligent, bookish man who read philosophy, he attended four colleges and studied Zen Buddhism." Bill Lee noted that a lot of people assumed Oglivie only spoke Spanish because he was from Panama but said he himself marveled at Oglivie's "ability to complete the *New York Times* crossword puzzle in about five minutes."

When able to get more playing time, Oglivie blossomed, and in his final nine seasons with Milwaukee, he was three times an All-Star.

### Poland

Later in life, Johnny Reder became chief engineer at the J. J. Corrugated Box Company in Fall River, Massachusetts. Before that, he was an all-American soccer player and then a major-league baseball player.

Clearly an accomplished man, he was born in Lublin, Poland, on September 24, 1909. His family emigrated to the United States in 1912.

Before he joined the Red Sox, he had been a goalie with the New York Yankees. That was not a typo. His Fall River soccer team had won the Eastern final of National Challenge Cup play of the United States Football Association on March 16, 1930. In the national finals, his team became U.S. champion. In 1931, Reder joined the American Soccer League's New York Yankees, which won the national soccer championship on April 19 in Chicago. After his death in 1990, an obituary in the *Fall River Herald News* states that he "was also considered one of the top professional soccer players in the country and was named a soccer All-American."

As noted in his biography for SABR, Reder continued playing soccer right into 1932, winning yet another American Soccer League championship on January 3 with another team (the New York Giants). Reder then joined the New Bedford Whalers and beat the Giants in the Eastern finals of the National Challenge Cup, yet again in New York. Three weeks later, Reder was in Savannah, Georgia, playing for the Boston Red Sox and trying to win an infield job.

He made the team and debuted as a pinch-hitter against baseball's New York Yankees on April 16 at Fenway Park. He played first base in five other April games, getting his first hit—a double—on April 23. He didn't get many hits. Reder appeared in 17 games, the last on June 12. He batted .135 in 37 at-bats, with that one double and drove in three runs. He played one game at third base but otherwise played first and pinch-hit. His final appearance was as a pinch-runner. He spent the rest of 1931 at Boston's Class-B team in Hazleton, Pennsylvania, and spent the next five years in the minors as well but never got another call to the major leagues.

### Saudi Arabia

Right-handed reliever Alex Wilson worked in 26 games for the 2013 Red Sox, a total of 27⅔ innings. He had been a second-round draft pick of the Red Sox in 2009 (out of Texas A&M) and rose reasonably quickly through the minors, converted from starting to relieving during the 2012 season at Pawtucket. He was born on November 3, 1986, in Dhahran, on the Persian Gulf in northeastern Saudi Arabia. The city was a hub for oil production and also home for a while to a U.S. Air Force base. Wilson's father, Jim, was a geologist who worked in the oil business. After he was about a year old, the family moved home, and he mainly grew up in West Virginia. Asked about his time in Saudi Arabia, he told the *Globe*, "I don't remember anything about it. It just looks cool on paper."

When John Lackey had to go on the disabled list, Wilson got the call to Boston, first appearing on April 11. Opponents did not score a run in any of his first six appearances. His first decision was a win on May 17, when a Jonny Gomes sacrifice fly in the top of the 10th inning gave the Red Sox a win in the Twin Cities. He was sent down after July 8, 1–1 with a 4.88 ERA.

In 2014, Wilson appeared in 18 games, all but two of them in August and September. In 28⅓ innings, he was 1–0 with a 1.91 ERA. That December, he was part of a trade to acquire starting pitcher Rick Porcello.

He pitched another five years in the majors, appearing in 290 games in all with a record of 14–14 (3.23).

### Scotland

In 1923 in Glasgow, Scotland, Bobby Thomson was born. His father had left five days beforehand to seek better opportunities in the United States, and the family later followed, settling in Staten Island, New York. Bobby played some minor-league ball in the New York Giants' system and spent most of World War II in the U.S. Army Air Corps. In September 1946, he made the big leagues and was a full-time starter for the Giants for the next seven seasons, primarily playing the outfield. He made his first of three All-Star teams in 1948, and in four of his seasons with the Giants, he drove in more than 100 runs.

Thomson's greatest fame came thanks to his "Shot Heard 'Round the World"—in the deciding game of the three-game playoff between the Brooklyn Dodgers and the New York Giants for the 1951 National League pennant. With one out in the bottom of the ninth at the Polo Grounds, the Dodgers leading 4–2, Thomson hit a Ralph Branca pitch for a three-run walk-off home run that won the pennant for the Giants.

He hit 189 home runs in all for the Giants, with a .277 average. Thomson played for a couple of other teams—the Milwaukee Braves and the Chicago Cubs. Near the tail end of his career, the Cubs traded him to the Red Sox for pitcher Al Schroll. He appeared in 40 games for the 1960 Red Sox, homering five times and driving in 20, with a .263 average. He helped win a couple of games, but almost all his RBIs came in Red Sox losses. The Red Sox released him on July 1. He signed on with the Orioles but only for three final weeks.

### Slovakia (Austria-Hungary at the time)

Jack Quinn pitched for the Red Sox from 1922 until July 10, 1925, when he was claimed off waivers by the Philadelphia Athletics. During those exceptionally difficult Red Sox seasons, Quinn won 45 games and lost 54, with a 3.65 ERA. In all, the right-hander worked for seven different major-league teams with a 247–218 (3.29) record.

He was born on July 1, 1883, in Stefurov, part of Austria-Hungary at the time; his birth name was Johannes Pajkos. He came to America when he was just under one year old, his family settling in Western Pennsylvania. By the age of 12, he was working as a breaker boy in coal mines. Baseball offered a way out, and it is understood that he took on the name Quinn to avoid ethnic discrimination.

Quinn was the starting pitcher on April 12, 1922, Opening Day at Fenway Park. He threw a complete game, allowing just three runs—only one of them earned—but his team could only produce two runs (one of the RBIs was his) and lost to the Philadelphia Athletics, 3–2.

For the Red Sox, he threw 53 complete games in the years he turned 38 through 41. He pitched until he was 50 years old, his last game coming six days after his fiftieth birthday. SABR member Steve Steinberg visited Stefurov in April 2022 and was welcomed by the mayor, Jana Riskova, to the town with a population of 117. Steve and Lyle Spatz collaborated on an award-winning book, *Comeback Pitchers: The Remarkable Careers of Howard Ehmke and Jack Quinn.*

### Taiwan

Che-Hsuan Lin was born on September 21, 1988, in Hualien on the eastern coast of Taiwan, about 100 miles south of Taipei. An outfielder, he was three times a member of the Chinese Taipei baseball team in the

World Baseball Classic in 2009, 2013, and 2017. In 2008, he played for Taiwan in the Olympic Games and was the MVP of the Futures Games World Team. The Red Sox had signed him as a free agent in 2007, and he spent six years in the Red Sox system, pretty much progressing one level each season and reaching Triple-A Pawtucket in 2011. Though he never hit for a high average, he had a good eye and got on base. In his minor-league years, he hit .254 but had a .349 on-base percentage. He was rated a solid defensive outfielder with a strong arm.

After an injury to Jacoby Ellsbury at the beginning of the 2012 season, Lin was brought to the majors and debuted for the Red Sox on April 14. After eight innings against the Tampa Bay Rays, with Boston leading 13–5, he was sent to play Fenway Park's center field. Three batters later, the game was over, and he had not been involved. It was almost a month later before he got another shot, when other injuries provided an opening. On May 20, he had the distinction of replacing David Ortiz in the lineup late in the game against the Phillies. The following day, in Baltimore, he cracked the starting lineup, playing right field and batting ninth. In his first at-bats, he grounded out twice, then struck out, but in the top of the eighth, he singled to left field. Two batters later, he scored on a Dustin Pedroia single, making the score 8–5, Boston.

He appeared in nine games, going 2-for-3 against the Yankees on October 1 in his final game, both hits off CC Sabathia. That brought his average to .250, three singles in 12 at-bats. After the season, the Red Sox let him go.

Lin played in Triple-A for the Houston Astros in 2013, then began play in the Chinese Professional Baseball League. He spent two seasons with the EDA Rhinos and was the Series MVP when the team won it all in 2016. The team changed its name to the Fubon Guardians, and he played another six years with them. As of this writing in 2022, he is still active and playing in Taipei. In his eight seasons of CPBL play, he has hit .294 with a .373 OBP, through his first 26 games of the 2022 season.

### Virgin Islands
Outfielder Joe Christopher's time with the Red Sox was brief and disappointing. It came after seven years in the major leagues, including

one quite good year in 1964 for the New York Mets. Two milestones in his career include being a member of the 1960 world champion Pittsburgh Pirates and a charter member of the 1962 "Amazin' Mets."

Christopher was born in Frederiksted, St. Croix, U.S. Virgin Islands, on December 13, 1935. Signed by Pirates scout Howie Haak, he spent four-plus years in the team's minor-league system before being summoned to Pittsburgh to work in 15 games in May–July 1959. He appeared in 15 games, drawing one walk and executing one sacrifice, but failed to get a hit in 12 at-bats, though he appeared as a pinch-runner and did score six runs. In 1960, he got into 50 games, hitting .232 (including a 5-for-7 game in late September) and scoring 21 times. He had three pinch appearances in the 1960 World Series, hit by a pitch and scoring as a pinch-hitter in Game Two, and scoring the final run in the Game Five win as a pinch-runner.

With the 1962 Mets, in 119 games, he hit .244, but his best year was 1964 when the outfielder played in 154 games, batting exactly .300, with 76 RBIs and hitting 15 of his career 29 home runs. He slipped to .249 in 1965 and was traded after the season to the Red Sox for Eddie Bressoud.

With the 1966 Red Sox, Christopher was only used sparingly, appearing in just 12 games through June 9, only once as other than a pinch-hitter. The only hit he had was in the one game he played the field, a single in a 15–5 loss to the Yankees. On June 14, he was part of a trade that also sent Earl Wilson to the Tigers. He never played for Detroit but kicked around the minors for a couple of years before leaving the game.

### Wales

See a brief sketch of Ted Lewis in the section on the first team player born outside of North America.

# RELATIVES WHO PLAYED FOR THE TEAM

BROTHERS, FATHERS AND SONS, COUSINS, UNCLES AND NEPHEWS, EVEN A grandfather-and-grandson combination—there have been numerous combinations of relatives who played for the team over the years. Sometimes they played at the same time—like Tony and Billy Conigliaro at one point, or Pedro and Ramón Martínez—and sometimes they were generations apart. We'll look at some firsts here, another way to look at the history of the team and some of the remarkable moments that it embraces.

**Who were the first two brothers to play for the team?**

Their surname was Hughes.

Right-handed pitcher Tom Hughes was 23 months older than his brother Ed. Both were right-handed pitchers, but Ed was also a catcher. "Long Tom" Hughes was a 20-game winner for the first World Series winners ever, the 1903 Boston Americans. He had begun his career in 1900 with the Chicago Cubs (then known as the Chicago Orphans). He jumped to the new American League in 1902, signing with Baltimore, and was dealt to Boston in mid-July 1902. He was 3–3 for Boston that year but blossomed in 1903 (20–7, with a 2.52 ERA). He threw five shutouts during the season.

He only got one start in the World Series against Pittsburgh, though, losing Game Three, 4–2, and only lasting two-plus innings. There have been suggestions that manager Jimmy Collins may have believed gamblers had gotten to Hughes and thus chose not to use his 20-game winner, relying more on Cy Young and Bill Dinneen, each of whom worked four games. Hughes was not in uniform after Game Three and was traded that December. Tom Hughes did pitch in 1904 for the New York High-landers and then for nine seasons with Washington.

Ed Hughes was from Chicago, too, and he had begun his career there in 1902—for an American League team, the White Sox. He played in just one game, against the Philadelphia Athletics on August 29—as a catcher, filling in when even the backup for the team's regular catcher was unable to play. Ed was 1-for-4, a single. As a catcher, though, he perhaps lacked some of the requisite skills. In nine fielding chances, he committed two errors. He threw out two baserunners, but the Athletics stole 10 bases on him during the game—Topsy Hartsel stole four of the 10.

Wes Ferrell and Rick Ferrell at Fenway Park, 1935. Pitcher Wes was 62–40 for the Red Sox and hit 38 career homers. Catcher Rick—a Hall of Famer—hit 28 and never pitched. The two shared three-plus years with the Red Sox (1933–1937) and were both traded together, to Washington on June 11, 1937.
COURTESY OF THE BOSTON PUBLIC LIBRARY, LESLIE JONES COLLECTION

In 1905, he joined the Boston Americans as a pitcher. He got into six games, losing the first two but then winning three of the next four. He was 3–2 (4.59) and was 3-for-14 at the plate. In 1906, he was only used twice, in May, working 10 innings in relief with a 5.40 ERA. There might have been a time when the two brothers faced each other in either 1905 or 1906, but they never did.

Some other brother combinations on the Red Sox include Johnnie Heving and Joe Heving, Roy Carlyle and Cleo Carlyle, Alex Gaston and Milt Gaston, Rick Ferrell and Wes Ferrell, Roy Johnson and Bob Johnson, Ed Sadowski and Bob Sadowski, Tony Conigliaro and Billy Conigliaro, Marty Barrett and Tommy Barrett, and Pedro Martínez and Ramón Martínez.

**Who were the first two brothers to be on the team at the same time?**

Alex Gaston and Milt Gaston did face each other in 1926, with Alex catching for the Boston Red Sox and younger brother Milt pitching for the St. Louis Browns. It was Alex's first year with Boston. He had previously played four seasons for the New York Giants, batting .196 in 62 games as a backup. Milt had begun pitching for the New York Yankees in 1924, then traded to the Browns that December.

In Alex's first year with the Red Sox, he hit .223 in 301 at-bats. Did he ever face Milt when the Red Sox played the Browns? The two teams did play each other 23 times that year, with a record of 11–11–1. But it wasn't until August 16, in the second game of a doubleheader at Fenway Park, that they faced each other. The Browns won the first game, 6–1. When Alex came to bat, Milt was on the mound, and it was the bottom of the second inning, still early in a scoreless game. With two singles, a sacrifice bunt, and a walk, Milt was in trouble. The bases were loaded with just the one out. The *Boston Globe* said some fan called out, "No brotherly love stuff now!" Alex tripled to left-center field, clearing the bases. It proved the game-winning hit. The Red Sox won, 7–1. They faced each other once more that year, and Milt threw a two-hitter on September 12, for a 1–0 win. One of the two hits was a single by brother Alex.

Alex was in St. Paul in 1927 and 1928, but in 1929, the two brothers were on the same team—the Boston Red Sox. Milt was 12–19 (a winning percentage of .387, on a Red Sox team that was 58–96, or .377). Alex hit .224 with a couple of home runs. Were they ever batterymates in the same game? Yes, on May 1, with vastly different results: Alex was 3-for-5 at the plate, but as for calling the game? Milt, in his first start of the year, lasted just 1⅓ innings and gave up eight runs—all earned. He started again five days later and gave up five runs. He lost his first four decisions, though Alex didn't play in the latter two.

Alex was in a game Milt won on June 13. That was the only one in which they both played that Milt won. Alex was 0-for-1 in the game. There was an impressive pitching performance on September 8. Milt pitched 10 shutout innings against the visiting Browns, but the entire Red Sox team only mustered three base hits (two of them by Alex Gaston), and it ended in a scoreless 0–0 10-inning tie.

**Which were the first two brothers on the Red Sox to homer in the very same game?**

They actually did it twice. On the Fourth of July 1970, left fielder Billy Conigliaro led off the fourth inning with a home run over the left-field fence, breaking a scoreless tie and giving Boston a 1–0 lead over the visiting Cleveland Indians. Cleveland tied the game in the top of the seventh. With one out in the bottom of the seventh, Mike Andrews homered. Then Reggie Smith homered. Mike Fiore pinch-hit for Carl Yastrzemski and singled. The Indians brought on a reliever, and Tony Conigliaro hit a two-run homer over everything in left field. Boston won, 5–1.

And, yes, they did it again, on September 19, 1970, in the second game of a doubleheader. Boston beat the visiting Senators 7–3 in the first game. In the second, Washington took a 3–0 lead in the top of the third, and the Red Sox scored each and every inning for the rest of the game, winning 11–3. In the fourth, with two on and nobody out, Boston down 3–1, Billy Conigliaro hit a three-run homer over the left-field screen into one of the light towers, the game-winning hit, as things played out. Again, the homers were in the fourth and then the seventh. It was 6–3 Red Sox in the bottom of the seventh when Tony homered into the straightaway center-field seats, making it 7–3.

## Who were the first two brothers on a team to combine for the record of most home runs by siblings on the same team?

In 1962, Hank Aaron hit 45 homers for the Milwaukee Braves. His brother, Tommie Aaron, hit eight. Add the two together, and you have 53 home runs by a pair of brothers for one given year. In the year 2000, Jason Giambi hit 43 homers for the Oakland Athletics. His brother, Jeremy Giambi, hit 10. Add the two together, and you have 53 home runs.

The 1970 Red Sox featured one brother who hit 18 (Billy Conigliaro) and another who hit nearly twice as many (Tony Conigliaro, who hit 34). Add the two together, and you have 54 home runs.

As a side note, we see that Lee May hit 38 homers for the 1969 Cincinnati Reds, while brother Carlos hit 18, but they were on different teams and even in different leagues, years before interleague play. Lee May hit his for the White Sox.

## Who was the first Red Sox player whose father had previously played for the team?

It was Joe Wood, son of Smoky Joe Wood. There were two Joe Woods who played during the World War II years. One was the infielder from Houston who played in 60 games for the 1943 Detroit Tigers, batting .323. He did not play in 1944 and 1945—one guesses it was due to military service obligations. When he tried to come back in 1946 and 1947, his stats (such as we can see) appeared respectable, but he never got the call. The one who interests us was Joe Frank Wood from Pennsylvania. He was not Joe Junior but was often called that in the press. For that matter, Smoky Joe Wood's actual name was Howard Ellsworth Wood.

Smoky Joe was one of the greatest pitchers in Red Sox history. He was a member of the world-champion 1912 Red Sox and a member of the world-champion 1915 Red Sox. In 1912, he led the majors with 34 wins (and only five losses). He pitched 35 complete games that year and had 10 shutouts, with a 1.91 earned run average. In many fewer starts in 1915, he still compiled a 15–5 record with an even better 1.49 ERA. He was 3–1 in the 1912 World Series. Unable to pitch as effectively as he once had, he reinvented himself as an outfielder and hit .297 in six seasons with the Cleveland Indians.

Joe Junior pitched professionally from 1941 to 1947, but his stay in the big leagues was brief. It was indeed with the Red Sox, and he debuted on May 1, 1944. He worked in relief, coming into a game the Washington Senators led 6–1. He worked the first through the seventh innings, allowing one run. Four days later, he pitched against the Yankees in New York, giving up two runs in two innings of relief. The third assignment was a start at Fenway Park on May 14 against the Tigers in the first game of a Sunday doubleheader. In 4⅔ innings, he gave up six runs, four of them earned, and was replaced. The game was a 6–1 loss for the Red Sox. Wood developed a sore arm with what years later he realized was probably a then-untreatable rotator cuff injury.

Other father/son combinations on the Red Sox are Ed Connolly Sr. and Ed Connolly Jr., Walt Ripley and Allen Ripley, Dolph Camilli and Doug Camilli, Haywood Sullivan and Marc Sullivan, and Dick Ellsworth and Steve Ellsworth.

**Who were the first relatives to both play on a Red Sox world championship team?**

The year was 2004. The cousins were both named Martínez. One was a pitcher, and one was a catcher. There was yet another Martínez on that 2004 team, a pitcher named Pedro—and he was from the Dominican Republic as well but not related.

Pitcher Anastacio Euclides Martínez worked relief in 11 games for the 2004 Red Sox. A right-handed pitcher, this was his only time in the majors. He was 2–1 with an ERA of 8.32. Born in 1978, he was a native of Villa Mella, Distrito Nacional, in the Dominican Republic. His time on the team was from May 22 to July 2.

Catcher Ángel "Sandy" Martínez was born in 1970, in Villa Mella, Distrito Nacional. Was there a connection? Yes, according to a response from Jorge Sainz, the player agent who represented them both. They were cousins. Sandy Martínez had broken in with the Blue Jays back in 1995. He was in the minors, in the Cleveland system, when the Red Sox purchased his contract on August 31, 2004. So Anastacio was gone before Sandy arrived—they never had the opportunity to serve as a battery for Boston. One wonders if Sandy may have taken Anastacio's locker in the clubhouse, but there was enough coming and going on that team that it would be unlikely. They did both get rings later, though!

Sandy played in just three games—September 8 and then October 2 and 3. He was 0-for-4 at the plate with two strikeouts. He was error-free with three fielding chances, so he had a fielding percent of 1.000 to go with his batting average of .000.

Neither of them played in the majors again, but they do each have that ring.

There were two other pairs of relatives who each played for the Red Sox, with (in these two cases) one of them on a world championship Red Sox team. In both cases, it was the 2018 Red Sox.

Mookie Betts was the American League MVP in 2018, leading both leagues with a .346 batting average. He hit 32 homers and drove in 80 runs. Betts played in Boston from 2014 through 2019, four times an All-Star and an exceptionally popular player.

In addition to being AL MVP in 2018, and a world champion, Mookie Betts was presented both a Silver Slugger and Gold Glove award in April 2019 ceremonies.
BILL NOWLIN PHOTO

His uncle had played with the Red Sox, too. Infielder Terry Shumpert spent 14 seasons in the big leagues; he played with the Red Sox in 1995, appearing in 21 games from April through June.

Right-hander Rick Porcello played with the Red Sox from 2015 through 2019 and had won the American League's Cy Young Award for his work in 2016 when he was 22–4 with a 3.16 ERA. He was 17–7 with the 2018 Red Sox and the starter in Game Five of the World Series against the Los Angeles Dodgers. He allowed one run in 4⅔ innings, in a game the Red Sox finally lost in the 18th inning, 4–3.

Porcello's grandfather was infielder Sam Dente, who had broken into the big leagues with the Red Sox back in 1947. He hit .232 in 46 games, then went on to play for four other ballclubs in a nine-year career.

# RED SOX PLAYERS WHO ALSO PLAYED IN OTHER SPORTS

As talented and successful athletes, it should not be surprising that a number of Red Sox players also excelled in other sports—both in collegiate play but also professionally. Some—like right-hander Gene Conley, who pitched three seasons for the Red Sox—even won titles in other sports, something that may have eluded them in their time in baseball. In Conley's first year with the Red Sox, he pitched for the sixth-place team but also won his third consecutive NBA championship with the Boston Celtics.

There were other Red Sox players who played for other pro teams. Let's look at some of them and see who were the first.

**Who was the first (and only) Red Sox player to have played for a world championship team not only in baseball but in one of these other professional sports: basketball, football, hockey?**

Many Red Sox players excelled in more than one sport. We have seen earlier that John Reder played pro soccer as well as infield for the 1932 Red Sox. Sam Dente also played pro soccer, in the American Soccer League for the Kearny Americans. Some, like Harry Agganis, were recruited by both football and baseball teams. Jimmy Piersall had been drafted by the Boston Celtics but signed with the Red Sox instead.

Perhaps the way the question is phrased is a little misleading, in that Gene Conley was never with a world championship Red Sox team. Born in 1930, he never saw the Red Sox win a World Series until a couple of weeks before he turned 74. He was 9–9 for the 1957 Milwaukee Braves, who beat the New York Yankees in a seven-game World Series. As it happens, he pitched to eight batters in Game Three.

There was a strong Boston connection. He began his big-league pitching career with the Boston Braves in 1952. He pitched for the Milwaukee Braves when the team relocated there, after taking a year off to play basketball as a power forward for the Boston Celtics, for whom he played in 1952–1953. For the next five seasons, he left the NBA for a second stint in major-league baseball and was on the 1957 world champion Braves. He was traded to the Phillies in March 1959. After two seasons in Philadelphia, Conley was traded in December 1960. He was traded to the Red Sox for pitcher Frank Sullivan. He played in 1960 and 1961 for the Red Sox. Some called the Sullivan/Conley trade "the biggest trade in history"—Sullivan was 6' 6½", and Conley was 6'8".

In basketball, Conley was a member of the 1959, 1960, and 1961 world-champion Boston Celtics.

Not only was he the only professional sports player on champion teams in two different major sports, but because he had played for the Boston Braves, Boston Celtics, and Boston Red Sox, he is the only pro player on three different professional teams from the same major-league city—Braves, Red Sox, Celtics.

As noted in *Red Sox Threads*, on April 27, 1963, for at least a moment in the fourth inning, two NBA players (Gene Conley of the Celtics and Dave DeBusschere of the New York Knicks) each pitched for their respective Sox (Conley for the Red, and DeBusschere for the White). It was a 9–5 game, and Boston won it.

Not that long ago, on October 8, 2010, the Boston Celtics played a softball game at Fenway Park. There was no opponent—and it was indeed softball, not basketball. The goal was simply to build team *esprit de corps*. "It was a dream come true, man," said Kevin Garnett. "I felt like I was 10 years old."

There have been at least six members of the Red Sox who also played in the National Football League. They are, in chronological order:

Jack Perrin—right fielder, four games for the 1921 Red Sox and six NFL games for the 1926 Hartford Blues.

Dick Reichle—center fielder, 128 games for the Red Sox in 1922–1923, and offensive end for the 1923 Milwaukee Badgers.

Hoge Workman—pitcher in 11 games for the 1924 Red Sox and, later that year, 18 games for the Cleveland Bulldogs. He was 0–0 (8.00) for the Red Sox but threw nine touchdowns in nine games for Cleveland. Years later, he played football briefly with the 1931 Cleveland Indians and in one game for football's 1932 New York Giants.

Charlie Berry—catcher for the Red Sox 1928–1932 (366 games). He had previously played as offensive end for the NFL's Pottsville Maroons in 1925 and 1926. Later in his career, he worked as an official in both the American League (as an umpire from 1942 to 1962) and for 24 seasons as a referee in the NFL.

Bill McWilliams—he pinch-hit in two games for the 1931 Red Sox (without a hit) and, in 1934, played in five NFL games as a back for the Detroit Lions.

Carroll Hardy—the only man to ever pinch-hit for Ted Williams played outfield for the Sox from 1960 to 1962. In 1955, he had played in 10 games as halfback with the San Francisco 49ers, with four touchdowns. For Boston, he also pinch-hit for Carl Yastrzemski, too. For 20 years after baseball, he was director of player personnel and assistant GM for football's Denver Broncos.

**Which Red Sox MVP has also twice thrown a 300—a perfect game—in championship bowling?**

Mookie Betts, once in November 2017 in the qualifying rounds for the World Series of Bowling in Reno, Nevada, and again in January 2022 leading up to the West Region qualifier for the 2022 PBA Players Championship. He was, of course, American League MVP in the 2018 baseball season and a member of that year's world champion Boston Red Sox.

In other news from the bowling alleys, pitcher John Burkett became a pro bowler after 15 years of major-league baseball. He had hoped to become a pro bowler out of high school, but then he got drafted to play baseball and went that route. Even before he had quit left baseball, he started working again with a 22-pound ball—and finished in 32nd place in 2000 in the Brunswick Pro Source Don Carter Classic. He fell short of the first cut at the American Bowling Congress Masters in 2004. Wikipedia says he has 32 perfect games in bowling and finished 15th in the 2015 Suncoast PBA Senior US Open and fourth at the PBA50 Northern California Classic. In 2019, he won his first PBA title, a PBA Regional Tour event at the PBA Houston Emerald Bowl Southwest Challenge.

**Other items of note**

At one point, two players on the 1929 Red Sox both applied to become professional boxers—Bill Barrett and Ed Morris. Barrett primarily played outfield, appearing in 111 games in 1929 and batting .270. Teammate Morris was a right-handed pitcher who won 14 games for Boston that year, the winningest pitcher (he was 14–14) on a team that only won 58 games all year long. White Sox infielder Art Shires had made some extra money boxing, and the two Red Sox decided it might be a way to earn a bit more money. A match at the Boston Garden, Shires against one of the two, was discussed, but baseball commissioner Kenesaw Mountain Landis stepped in and said that a baseball player turning to pro boxing would be considered retired.

Ken Harrelson spent three years in professional golf, even competing once in the British Open. Many say that, in 1964, when he wore a pair of golf gloves as he stepped into the batter's box, he initiated the now-common custom of wearing batting gloves.

On August 10, 1929, Boston beat New Bedford, 3–2, in the opening game of the American Soccer League season. In 1968, the Boston Beacons of the North American Soccer League had Fenway as their home park. The team lasted just one year but drew 18,000 to see a match against a visiting club featuring Brazil's Pele.

**When was the first professional wrestling heavyweight title match held at Fenway Park?**

On July 9, 1929, some 25,000 professional wrestling fans crowded into Fenway Park to see wrestler Gus Sonnenberg—known for the "famous flying tackle"—defend his National Wrestling Association world heavyweight title against challenger Ed "Strangler" Lewis, himself famous for his headlocks. There were other bouts leading up to the main event. Fans were surprised that Sonnenberg took the first fall, but he recovered, and in a flurry of tackles, he pinned Lewis, enabling him to retain his heavyweight title.

## What was the first professional boxing match held at Fenway Park?

On September 2, 1930: a heavyweight boxing match drew 15,000 to a night bout at Fenway. Babe Hunt of Ponca City, Florida, outpointed Ernie Schaaf in 10 rounds. In February 1933, less than three years later, Schaaf died after a bout with Primo Carnera at Madison Square Garden. There were at least two other bouts at Fenway Park, both in September 1932: on September 2, junior lightweight boxing champion Kid Chocolate retained his title against challenger Steve Smith, taking every round of the 10-round event; and on September 13, a boxer named Unknown Winston (described as "Negro heavyweight from Waterbury, Connecticut") knocked out Walter Cobb of Baltimore in the second round of a scheduled 10-round fight.

## What was the first National Football League game played at Fenway Park?

There have been many other sporting events at Fenway Park—a large number of high school football games, for instance. In November 1919, B.C. High beat Boston English High 10–0, drawing 6,000 fans. On November 15, 15,000 saw Boston College beat Holy Cross 9–7. On November 29, BC beat Georgetown 10–7 and thus won the Catholic collegiate conference. Then years later, a November 1929 game drew 30,000 that saw B.C. beat Holy Cross, 12–0.

There has actually never been an NFL game played at Fenway, but the team now known as the New England Patriots—at the time in the American Football League—played there for five seasons. The AFL and NFL merged in 1971. The AFL's Boston Patriots hosted the Oakland Raiders on October 11, 1963, winning 20–14. The last game at Fenway Park was also a Patriots victory, a December 1, 1968, win against the Cincinnati Bengals, 33–14. Red Sox outfielder Dom DiMaggio was one of the original owners of the Patriots.

There had been pro football played previously at Fenway Park, dating back to 1933: the Boston Redskins, the Boston Shamrocks, the Boston Bears, and—starting in 1944—the Boston Yanks. One of the players on the Boston Yanks was Ted Williams—Theodore P. Williams, from Boston College, not the Red Sox outfielder. Williams later played for the NFL Philadelphia Eagles and the Washington Redskins.

**When was the first National Hockey League game played at Fenway Park?**

The answer is January 1, 2010, the first day of the year. More than 300,000 applied for tickets, but only 38,112 were able to get one. The Boston Bruins game against the Philadelphia Flyers went into overtime, tied 1–1. The Bruins had tied it with just 2:18 remaining in regulation time. In just one minute and 57 seconds of overtime, the Bruins won. Another NHL game was played at Fenway Park on January 2, 2023 between the Boston Bruins and the Pittsburgh Penguins. The Bruins rallied with two third-period goals to defeat the Penguins 2–1.

# ALL-STAR GAME FIRSTS

Every year, baseball holds an All-Star Game. From 1959 through 1962, there were two All-Star Games held each year. In the days before free agency, when player movement was far more restricted, players (and umpires, too) used to strongly identify with their respective leagues, and the All-Star Games were often a truly competitive event in which all played with more than simply personal pride in individual performance. Ted Williams always said that the home run that meant the most to him in his career was the walk-off homer he hit in the 1941 All-Star Game, a three-run homer in the bottom of the ninth that catapulted the AL team from a 5–4 deficit to victory. Here we look at some of the team's milestone firsts in All-Star Game history.

**Who was the first Red Sox player to appear in an All-Star Game?**
The first All-Star Game was held at Comiskey Park on July 6, 1933. It featured players such as Babe Ruth and Lou Gehrig, as well as some future Red Sox players such as Joe Cronin and Lefty Grove, but the sole representative of the Red Sox who played in the game was catcher Rick Ferrell. He apparently caught a good game, being kept in for the full game by manager Connie Mack, a 4–2 win for the American League, catching three innings each from two Leftys and a General—Lefty Gomez, General Crowder, and Lefty Grove. Former Red Sox player Babe Ruth hit a two-run homer in the third inning to give the AL a 3–0 lead. Ruth also made a spectacular catch in right field, pulling down an eighth-inning drive that might have led to a tie. Ferrell was 0-for-4 at the plate but laid down a sacrifice bunt in the sixth that put Cronin into scoring position for the fourth run, plated on Earl Averill's pinch-hit single.

Representing the Boston Braves in the game was center fielder Wally Berger, likewise 0-for-4 at the plate but making three putouts.

**Who was the first Red Sox player to get a hit in an All-Star Game?**

It took a while. It was Joe Cronin, in his first year with the Red Sox, in 1937—the fifth All-Star Game staged, played in his former home ballpark, Griffith Stadium, Washington. The game was 8–3, an American League win. Both teams had 13 base hits. Cronin was 1-for-4, a double to right field in the bottom of the fifth inning. The next batter, Bill Dickey, doubled, and Cronin scored, giving the AL a 6–2 lead at that point. Cronin had previously had hits in both the 1933 and 1934 games but had been a Senator at the time.

**Who was the first Red Sox player to homer in an All-Star Game?**

It was Ted Williams, in 1941, and the homer was, he wrote in *My Turn At Bat*, "the most thrilling hit of my life." Among the players in particular, the All-Star Game was in some ways more exciting than the World Series; they were the best players in the game, not just members of the best team. There was a true rivalry between the leagues, much more so in the years before free agency saw players routinely leaving one team for another. It was a real honor for the young Williams to play on the same team as, say, Joe DiMaggio and Bob Feller.

The game was on July 8 at Detroit's Briggs Stadium. It was 2–1, the AL on top, after the first six innings, but the National League scored two runs in the seventh and two more in the top of the eighth. In the bottom of the eighth, Joe DiMaggio doubled, but Williams struck out. Dom DiMaggio singled in brother Joe, and the score was 5–3, the NL still on top.

In the bottom of the ninth, after one out, pinch-hitter Ken Keltner reached on an infield single. Joe Gordon singled to right field, and Cecil Travis walked. That loaded the bases for Joe DiMaggio. He hit into a force play for the second out, Keltner scoring. Ted Williams stepped in, facing Claude Passeau. With a count of 2–1, "The Kid" homered into the right-field stands.

His three-run homer had won the game, 7–5. In his autobiography, Williams wrote, "Well, it was the kind of thing a kid dreams about and imagines himself doing when he's playing those little playground games we used to play . . . Halfway down to first, seeing that ball going out, I stopped running and started leaping and jumping and clapping my hand and I was just so happy I laughed out loud. I've never been so happy and I've never seen so many happy guys. They carried me off the field."

Later in the year, Williams finished with a 6-for-8 game, bringing his batting average for the season to .406. In the 81 seasons that have followed 1941, no other player has hit .400.

**Who was the first Red Sox pitcher to win an All-Star Game?**

It was a long time before a Red Sox pitcher was the winning pitcher in an All-Star Game. Part of the reason was that the National League often dominated in All-Star competition. Through 1985, the totals were NL 36 wins and the AL 19. Of those 19, not one was won by a Red Sox pitcher. That changed in 1986.

The game was played in the Astrodome on July 15. The starting pitchers were Dwight Gooden of the New York Mets and Roger Clemens of the Boston Red Sox, two teams that later faced each other in the 1986 World Series. Each pitched the first three innings. In the top of the second, Gooden gave up a two-out double to Yankees right fielder Dave Winfield and a home run to Detroit Tigers second baseman Lou Whitaker. Clemens threw three perfect innings—no runs, no hits, no walks. In the fourth and fifth innings, Fernando Valenzuela struck out five consecutive AL batters, tying an All-Star record set in 1934 by Carl Hubbell. Kansas City's Frank White (batting for Whitaker) homered in the top of the seventh. The National Leaguers scored twice in the bottom of the eighth off the Rangers' Charlie Hough, but the NL came up one run short and lost 3–2. Clemens was awarded the win.

Clemens was also named the game's Most Valuable Player.

**Who was the first Red Sox player to win the All-Star Game MVP award?**

The award began in 1962. The first Red Sox player to win it was Carl Yastrzemski in 1970. The game was held at Riverfront Stadium in Cincinnati. In the bottom of the ninth inning, the National League scored three times to even the score at 4–4. The game ran to 12 innings when Pete Rose hit a two-out single off the Angels' Clyde Wright. The next batter singled, and so did the one after that, Rose scoring at home plate while colliding with catcher Ray Fosse, hard enough to knock the glove off his hand (and to fracture his shoulder). The NL won, 5–4. Yaz was 4-for-6 in the game, with one run scored and one run batted in.

The next Red Sox All-Star MVP was Roger Clemens in 1986, and the story of the game appears just above.

Third to be named ASG MVP was Pedro Martínez in 1999. This game was at Fenway Park. The final score was American League 4, National League 1, but during the course of the game, the NL used nine pitchers (starting was Curt Schilling of the Philadelphia Phillies), and the AL used seven. Martínez started for the American League. He struck out the first batter, Barry Larkin of the Reds. He struck out the second batter, Larry Walker of the Rockies. He struck out the third batter, Sammy Sosa of the Cubs.

The American League got two runs in the bottom of the first.

In the bottom of the second inning, Martínez struck out the fourth batter he had faced in the game, Mark McGwire of the Cardinals. Fifth up was Matt Williams of the Diamondbacks. He reached on a fielding error by AL second baseman Robby Alomar. Jeff Bagwell of the Astros came to bat, and Martínez struck him out, too—a strike-'em-out/throw-'em-out double play with Williams caught attempting to steal second base. Pedro Martínez had faced six batters, not given up a hit, and struck out five of the six, in just two innings, tying an All-Star Game record.

There had been one other Red Sox MVP in All-Star play. It was J. D. Drew in the 2008 All-Star Game at Yankee Stadium, the last year the Yankees played in the original Yankee Stadium, which was first opened in 1923—the year the Yankees first won the World Series. Through six, the NL led 2–0. Edison Vólquez was pitching for the Nationals. The AL tied it in the seventh; with two outs and the Twins' Justin Morneau on third base, Drew entered the game, batting in place of Ichiro Suzuki. He had replaced Ichiro before the bottom of the sixth. It was Drew's first All-Star at-bat, and he homered into the first row of the right-field seats to tie the game, 2–2.

Neither team scored in the ninth, or the 10th, or any inning through the 14th. Drew did single to center in the 11th but didn't get any further than third base. In the 13th he reached on an error and stole second base but was left stranded.

In the bottom of the 15th, Brad Lidge was pitching for the National League. Morneau singled. After one out, Tampa Bay's Dioner Navarro singled. There were runners on first and second, and Drew came to bat again. He drew a walk, loading the bases—and thus advancing both base-runners, with Morneau on third. When the Rangers' Michael Young hit a fly ball to right field, Morneau was able to tag and score the go-ahead run.

### When was the first All-Star Game at Fenway Park?

There had been 12 All-Star Games played since it was first intro-duced in 1933. Fenway Park was supposed to have hosted the 1945 game, but there was none held that year, the final year of the Second World War. The 1936 game had been held at Braves Field, the first one in the City of Boston.

Rescheduled to 1946, it was quite a game, particularly from a Red Sox perspective. It wasn't due to the game being a 12–0 win for the American League. It was, from the start, something of a Red Sox extravaganza, not just due to being festooned by flags and all the attendant hoopla. The Sox dominated in 1946, particularly in the first half of the season. After the first two dozen games, they were 21–3. Of the 25 members of the All-Star squad, eight of them were members of the Red Sox. (The National League pennant-winning St. Louis Cardinals had six on the NL team.)

Representing the Red Sox were the first three batters in the lineup: center fielder Dom DiMaggio, shortstop Johnny Pesky, and left fielder Ted Williams. Batting fifth was second baseman Bobby Doerr. The other Red Sox on the team were pitchers Dave "Boo" Ferriss and Mickey Har-ris, catcher Hal Wagner, and first baseman Rudy York. Neither pitcher saw duty, but the other six Sox did.

In the first inning, Williams walked, and the Yankees' Charlie Keller homered. Given that the combined pitching efforts of Bob Feller, Hal Newhouser, and Jack Kramer allowed just three hits and no runs, that was enough, but it didn't stop the American League batters from pouring it on.

Ted Williams led off the fourth inning with a solo home run. In the fifth, St. Louis' Vern Stephens doubled in two. Williams singled and drove in a third run. In the seventh inning, Williams hit a two-out single and soon scored the first of two runs on a Joe Gordon double.

And in the bottom of the eighth, after one run had scored, Ted Williams came up again with two outs and runners on first and second. Swinging at Rip Sewell's famous "eephus" pitch (a high arcing pitch that sometimes went as high as 25 feet before dropping over home plate), he homered—his second of the game—into the American League bullpen in right field, the bullpen normally used by the Red Sox. In five years of pitching in the majors, no one had ever homered off Sewell's eephus. The Yankees' Bill Dickey had told Williams beforehand that the only way to really power it was not to stand still but instead to step into the swing with power. That gave Williams five RBIs; he scored four times.

**Which Red Sox player ranks first in RBIs among all those who have played in All-Star Games?**

The answer is Ted Williams, with 12. He played in 18 All-Star Games, from 1940 to 1960. Losing five years to military service in World War II and the Korean War almost certainly cost him some additional All-Star action, given that he otherwise missed no years during that stretch. His runs batted in were: four in the 1941 game, five in the 1946 game, one in the 1950 game (before breaking his elbow), and two in the 1956 game. Williams hit .304, with 10 runs scored and four homers.

Second in All-Star RBIs by Red Sox players, with five each, are Fred Lynn and Carl Yastrzemski.

**Which Red Sox player has drawn more walks than anyone else in All-Star Game history?**

When he wasn't busy driving in runs with homers and otherwise, Williams took bases on balls. His 11 walks in All-Star Games are the record, which still stands more than 60 years later. None of the walks were with the bases loaded, so he didn't pick up any RBIs that way.

## Who is the only former Red Sox player to hit a grand slam in an All-Star Game?

We might as well end this section with a bang. There's actually only one player who has ever hit a grand slam in an All-Star Game. It happened during the 50th game, in 1983, at Chicago's Comiskey Park. Representing the Red Sox at the game in the starting lineup was Jim Rice, and Bob Stanley was there as a relief pitcher. The National League scored once in the first. So did the American League. Former Red Sox star Fred Lynn was there in an Angels uniform. He walked in the first inning; Rice reached on an error. In the second inning, the AL added one more run, but Lynn struck out to end the inning. In the bottom of the third, Jim Rice led off with a homer. That was nice, but it wasn't a grand slam. In the third, both Lynn and Rice got a chance to bat again. With two runs added, runners on second and third, and with two outs, Robin Yount was walked intentionally by San Francisco's Atlee Hammaker. This brought up Lynn again; he'd struck out at the end of the second, but this time, he hit a grand slam—a "bullet into the lower stand" in right field, wrote Jerome Holtzman of the *Chicago Tribune*.

Rice popped out, but the score in the Golden Anniversary game was 9–1, and the NL never recovered. The final was 13–3. The 13 runs set a new record for most runs scored by one team. More significantly, the win broke a streak of National League wins—from 1963 through 1982, the NL had lost only once and had been riding a streak of 11 consecutive wins.

Lynn remains, even into the 2022 season, very popular in Boston and is a frequent guest in the Legends Suite at Fenway Park.

# PLAYER AWARDS

In addition to being named to an All-Star squad, there are other honors accorded players—typically after the season. For pitchers, there is the Cy Young Award. For all, there is the Rookie of the Year Award, the MVP, and awards such as the Gold Glove, Silver Slugger, and so on. There are also other honors, for overcoming adversity and for exceptional public service—awards like the Tony Conigliaro Award and the Roberto Clemente Award.

First, let's look at the rookies and move ahead from there.

**Who was the first Red Sox player named Rookie of the Year?**

The first Red Sox player named Rookie of the Year was "the Moose from Moosup"—Walt Dropo, of Moosup, Connecticut. The year was 1950. How did he do?

Ted Williams set a rookie record that still stands with 145 RBIs in 1939. Why was he not named Rookie of the Year in 1939? Because there was no Rookie of the Year designated before 1947. In that first year— 1947—there was one Rookie of the Year. It was Jackie Robinson. In 1948, it was Alvin Dark of the Boston Braves. From 1949 on, there have been separate Rookie of the Year winners in each league. The first Red Sox ROY was, as noted, Walt Dropo. Boston swept ROY honors in 1950, with Sam Jethroe winning the National League ROY with the Braves.

Dropo had played in 11 games in 1949, not enough to qualify, batting just .146. He might have, at that point, seemed an unlikely candidate to earn the honor the following year. He played in 136 Red Sox games in 1950 and hit for a .322 batting average (eighth-best in the league). He led the American League with 328 total bases and all of baseball with

144 runs batted in (perhaps tying Ted Williams for the all-time rookie record—see note elsewhere in this book). Teammate Gene Stephens also had 144 RBIs in 1950, but Stephens was in his tenth year in the majors. Dropo's first game in 1950 was not until May 2. He'd not played at all in April, missing 13 games. Had he driven runs at the same pace in April, he would have had 156 RBIs.

Other Red Sox players who have won Rookie of the Year honors are Don Schwall (1961), Carlton Fisk (1972), Fred Lynn (1975), Nomar Garciaparra (1997), and Dustin Pedroia (2007).

Dropo had a 13-year career (the first three-plus years with Boston), batting .270 with 152 home runs and 704 runs batted in.

### Who was the first Red Sox player named American League Most Valuable Player?

The Most Valuable Player in each league has been voted on since 1911. The first Red Sox player to win was Tris Speaker in 1912, the team's center fielder. Any year in which a batter hits .383 is an exceptionally good year.

Speaker hit that in 1912 and, in large part due to working 82 bases on balls, he led both leagues with an on-base percentage of .464. His 10 homers led the American League. His 53 doubles led both leagues. Speaker also starred on defense; he had 35 outfield assists that year, matching his career-high set in 1909. His 59 votes from the writers who used to determine the MVP almost doubled the number two candidate, Ed Walsh of the White Sox, who had pitched to a record of 27–17 and earned 30 votes. When the National Baseball Hall of Fame opened in 1936, they inducted five players. Speaker joined Cy Young, John McGraw, Connie Mack, and four others named in 1937.

### Who was the first Red Sox player to twice be named the league's MVP?

Ted Williams was voted the AL MVP both in 1946 and in 1949. It remains a travesty that he was not named MVP in 1942. His .356 batting average led the American League. His 137 RBIs led both leagues. His 36 home runs led both leagues. In other words, he won the Triple Crown—and was still not named MVP. Now let's see what else—he led both leagues in on-base percentage with .499. He led both leagues in slugging with .648. He led both leagues in total bases with 338. He led both leagues in runs scored with 141. He drew more walks (145) than anyone in either league. Admittedly, he wasn't a 20-game winner, but neither was the man who beat him out for MVP in 1942.

Who beat him? Joe Gordon. Of the New York Yankees. The Yankees did win the pennant, doing so by nine games over the second-place Red Sox. But if Williams led in all those categories, in what areas did Gordon lead? Let's look it up. Two. He struck out more than anyone in either league—95 times. That is seven more Ks than anyone else in the AL. Okay, he beat Ted Williams there; Williams only struck out 51 times. And Gordon grounded into 22 double plays, more than anyone else in the entire American League. Williams grounded into 12.

Maybe it was his defense? Gordon also committed more errors than any other second baseman in the league—28 of them. He ranked fifth in fielding percentage at his position.

If you're one of those who follows WAR (wins above replacement), Gordon did well. His WAR on Baseball-Reference.com was 7.7. But Ted Williams was 10.5.

### Who was the first Red Sox MVP after Tris Speaker?

Jimmie Foxx was the next Red Sox player named MVP, and it was in 1938. Ted Williams followed in 1946 and 1949, as we have just seen. Jackie Jensen won the award in 1958, Carl Yastrzemski in 1967, Fred Lynn in 1975, Jim Rice in 1978, Roger Clemens in 1986, Mo Vaughn in 1995, Dustin Pedroia in 2008, and Mookie Betts in 2018.

### Who was the first player named Rookie of the Year and Most Valuable Player in the same year?

Anyone reading the preceding paragraphs attentively will have noticed that Fred Lynn won the Rookie of the Year Award and the Most Valuable Player Award in 1975. He was an All-Star and won a Gold Glove, too. Lynn hit .331 in 1975, second only to Rod Carew's .359. His 103 runs scored led the league. His 47 doubles led both leagues. He homered 21 times and drove in 105 runs, four RBIs behind league-leader George

Scott of the Milwaukee Brewers. Lynn's slugging percentage of .566 led both leagues. Lynn was an All-Star each of the next eight seasons.

## Who was the first Red Sox pitcher to win the Cy Young Award?

This award was first initiated in 1956. For the first 11 years, there was one award winner for both leagues. Starting with 1967, there was a separate award for each league. That year, Red Sox pitcher Jim Lonborg won the Cy Young Award. He had helped lead the Red Sox to the American League pennant for the first time since 1946, winning a league-leading 22 games (a full 10 more than anyone else on the 1967 team), including a complete game 5–3 win over the Twins on the final day, in a year when the Sox only clinched the pennant with that final win. He got 18 of the 20 votes.

The most recent winner was Rick Porcello in 2016. The Red Sox finished first in the AL East in 2016, and a good part of the reason was Porcello's 22–4 record pitching. It was a relatively close vote, with Detroit's Justin Verlander (16–9) getting 132 votes to Porcello's 137, but it was Porcello who prevailed.

The Red Sox have had two other Cy Young winners; they are both included in the next section.

## Who was the first Red Sox pitcher to win a Cy Young Award two years in a row?

It was Roger Clemens; he won it both in 1986 and 1987. Baltimore's Jim Palmer (1975 and 1976) was the first AL pitcher to win in back-to-back years. Palmer also won it in 1973. In the earlier years, when there was just one Cy Young winner; Sandy Koufax won it in 1963, 1965, and 1966.

Clemens won the Cy Young again for the Red Sox in 1991. Then he won it for "other teams"—back-to-back in 1997 and 1998 for the Toronto Blue Jays and in 2001 for the American League team in New York. He even won it in the National League, with the Houston Astros in 2004—but Red Sox fans had their minds on other things that year. Interrupting Clemens, by winning in 1999 and 2000, was Pedro Martínez, winning two more Cys for the Red Sox.

In the National League, there have been two pitchers who both won four consecutive Cy Young Awards: Greg Maddux (1992–1995) and Randy Johnson (1999–2002).

### Who was the first Red Sox pitcher to have a major-league baseball award named after him?

Cy Young. Nothing wrong with a really easy question once in a while, is there? Young pitched from 1890 to 1909, including eight seasons for Boston, during which he was 192–112 with an overall earned run average of 2.00 (that is not a typographical error). His total of 192 victories for the team was tied by Roger Clemens. For Boston, he threw complete games in 275 of his 297 starts. In his first two years for the Boston Americans, he won 33 games and then 32. Over the course of his 22-year career, Young won 511 games, an average of more than 23 per season.

### Who was the first Red Sox player to win a Gold Glove?

This award was first initiated in 1957. Red Sox third baseman Frank Malzone won the Gold Glove that year, as well as in 1958 and 1959. The year 1957 was his first full season in the big leagues. He was named to the All-Star team, as he was each of the next three years. Malzone played 11 years for the Red Sox, batting .279 over that stretch. Playing the "hot corner" was never an easy task, but Malzone excelled, as witnessed by the three consecutive Gold Gloves he was awarded. Center fielder Jimmy Piersall won the award in 1958. Piersall had already been named an All-Star in 1954 and again in 1956. In 1958, the final year of his eight with the Red Sox, Piersall was also awarded the Gold Glove. He won it a second time, with Cleveland, in 1961.

### Who was the first Red Sox player to win the Silver Slugger?

This award was first presented in 1980. No Red Sox players won it that year, but two of them did in 1981: Carney Lansford as a third baseman and Dwight Evans as a right fielder. Lansford led the American League in batting with a .336 average. He also placed sixth in league MVP voting. Evans placed third. (Milwaukee's Rollie Fingers ranked first.) Evans led the league in home runs, with 22 in the strike-abbreviated season. He also led in OPS (on-base percentage plus slugging). He won the fourth of his eight career Gold Gloves in 1981 and was named to the second of three All-Star squads.

## Who was the first Red Sox player to win the Comeback Player of the Year award?

This award was only started in 2005, but already, three Red Sox players have won it—Jacoby Ellsbury in 2011, Rick Porcello in 2016, and David Price in 2018.

Ellsbury had placed third in Rookie of the Year voting in 2008 and hit for a solid .301 in 2009, leading the majors (and setting a new Red Sox record) with 70 stolen bases. His 10 triples led the AL. But in 2010, due to multiple rib fractures in an April collision, he only got into 18 games and hit just .192. In 2011, Ellsbury was back and healthy, appearing in 158 games and batting .321 with 32 homers and 105 RBIs. He led the majors with 364 total bases. If that's not a comeback, what is?

Porcello had started his career with Detroit and had won 15 games in 2014 with a 3.43 ERA. He came to the Red Sox in 2015 and struggled, going 9–15 with a 4.92 ERA. But in 2016, he bounced back—big time. He was 22–4 (3.15) with a majors-leading strikeout-to-walks ratio of 5.91. Porcello had gone from winning nine games to becoming the Cy Young Award winner in 2016.

Left-handed pitcher David Price signed with the Red Sox as a free agent in December 2015. He was a workhorse in 2016, leading the majors with 35 starts and was 17–9 (3.99), but he had a tough year in 2017 when elbow issues cropped up a couple of times, limiting him to just 11 starts (he was 6–3). However, he had a comeback year in 2018, going 16–7 (3.58), just one win behind Rick Porcello for most on the team. He won Game Two of the World Series and the decisive Game Five.

They may have come back, but they didn't always stay all that long with the Red Sox after their comeback. By 2014, Ellsbury was with the Yankees; by 2020, Porcello was with the Mets; and for Price, 2019 was his last year with the Red Sox. He sat out 2020, not wishing to take unnecessary chances with the COVID-19 pandemic. He joined the Dodgers in 2021.

**Which Red Sox manager was the first to be voted American League Manager of the Year?**

John McNamara in 1986. The Red Sox won the AL East (one might suspect that at least winning your division was something of a prerequisite) by 5½ games over the second-place Yankees. They had finished fifth the year before (also under McNamara.) The 1986 Red Sox went on to win the American League Championship Series over the Angels, in seven games. We won't revisit here what happened in the 1986 World Series.

The only other Red Sox manager to win the honor was Jimy Williams in 1999. The Yankees were a tough team to beat in 1999. They finished in first place in the East, and in the second round of the playoffs, they beat the Red Sox four games to one.

**Who was the first Red Sox player to win the MLB Defensive Player of the Year Award?**

This award was initiated very recently, in 2014, but the Red Sox soon had a winner. Right fielder Mookie Betts won the award in 2016. By position that year, Betts also won it for work in right field and Dustin Pedroia for his work at second base.

**Who was the first Red Sox player to win the Hank Aaron Award?**

This is awarded annually to the best overall offensive performer, beginning in 1999. In the 23 years through 2021 that the award has been presented, five Red Sox players have won it: the first was Manny Ramirez in 2004. In 2005, it went to David Ortiz. In 2008, Kevin Youkilis won the award. David Ortiz won it a second time, in 2016, his final year. And J. D. Martinez won it in 2018.

**When was the last time the Red Sox played an Opening Day game—and neither team won?**

It was Opening Day in 1910—playing the New York Highlanders at Hilltop Park in New York. Hippo Vaughn pitched for New York and threw 14 innings, giving up four runs on 11 hits. He walked two and struck out seven. Eddie Cicotte worked the first seven innings for the Red Sox. He allowed two runs on nine hits. Smoky Joe Wood took over from

Cicotte and pitched the eighth through the 14th, allowing two runs in the eighth and no more on just two hits.

### What was the first game the Red Sox played in which neither team ever scored even once?

In days gone by, there were tie games. In both 1907 and 1914, the team had six tie games—the 1907 team's record was 59–90–6, and the 1914 team's record was 91–62–6. The first year in which they did NOT have at least one time game was 1911. The next was 1918.

The most recent tie game was on July 31, 1985, at Fenway Park against the White Sox. It is the only tie game they have played since 1961. Both the 1961 and 1985 games were ended by rain. The June 8, 1961, game was a 4–4 tie against the visiting Los Angeles Angels. It was itself a makeup game for the April 16 game that had been called due to rain. It went into extra innings, the Angels taking a 4–3 tie in the top of the 11th on a home run by Gene Leek. Chuck Schilling singled to lead off the bottom of the 11th, then scored the re-tying run on a triple by Gary Geiger, but Geiger was thrown out after rounding third base, and the Red Sox were unable to score further. At 12:30 AM, the game was finally called.

Rather than attempt to play the game a third time, it went into the books as a tie. The teams played two on June 9, each team winning one.

The 1985 game was played over, from the start, the next night as one game of a doubleheader (each team won once). They ended up playing 163 games that year. Chicago scored their run before starter Bobby Ojeda even recorded an out. Boston scored its run in the bottom of the seventh. The score stood 1–1 after seven innings, when it was finally called after a 78-minute rain delay (the start had been postponed for 21 minutes).

All individual records counted, and Ojeda received credit for a complete game.

But there was another game in which two teams squared off and played 17 scoreless innings. It was on July 14, 1916—the year in which the Red Sox won their second consecutive pennant (and World Series). The St. Louis Browns were at Fenway Park.

Carl Mays started for the Red Sox, and he threw 15 innings without allowing a run. There were 20 Browns who reached base. Mays gave up nine hits and walked seven, but no one scored. Two reached on errors. Dutch Leonard relieved Mays and threw the 16th and 17th, allowing one hit and walking one. The Browns left 14 runners on base.

Ernie Koob was the Browns pitcher, and he worked 17 innings. He gave up 14 base hits and walked three. The Red Sox left 18 men on base.

The game had to be called due to darkness. It was 0–0, in 17 innings. Leonard had come into the game in the 15th when the St. Louis pitcher Koob rounded third base and headed for home, colliding with Mays, who was protecting the plate. Mays dropped the ball. But it turned out that Koob had failed to touch third base and was tagged out when third baseman Mike McNally picked up the ball that had been jarred out of Mays's grasp and tagged out Koob. Mays was not seriously hurt, but manager Bill Carrigan had Leonard take over at that point.

**Who was the first Red Sox player to win the Tony Conigliaro Award?**

It was an award instituted by the Red Sox in 1990 and given each year to a major-league player who "overcomes an obstacle and adversity through the attributes of spirit, determination, and courage that were trademarks of [Tony] Conigliaro."

It was only in the award's ninth year that a Red Sox player was so honored. It was Bret Saberhagen who had triumphed over a number of maladies over the years but had missed the entire 1996 season with rotator cuff surgery that required installing a titanium anchor to hold it together. He had previously been off and on the DL with more than one bout of tendonitis, undergone elbow surgery in two different years, and suffered a torn MCL in his right knee. In short, the wear and tear on his body was considerable, yet he kept on battling. Saberhagen was named the Tony C Award recipient in 1997.

Another Red Sox pitcher was the recipient in 2007—Jon Lester, who had been diagnosed with cancer—non-Hodgkin's lymphoma—just the year before. Lester was able to return in late July 2007 and was 4–0 in limited action. He pitched and won the final Game Four of the 2007 World Series as the Red Sox swept the Colorado Rockies, working 5⅔ innings in a game the Red Sox won, 4–3.

A third Boston Red Sox pitcher, Jon Lackey, was the recipient in 2013, after coming back from Tommy John surgery that cost him the entire 2012 season. He contributed big-time in 2013 postseason play, winning Game Two of the Division Series, with a 1–0 win in Game Three of the League Championship Series, and the final Game Six of the World Series against the Cardinals, allowing just one run in 6⅔ innings.

**Who was the first Red Sox player to be honored with the Roberto Clemente Award?**

Originally named the Commissioner's Trophy, the award was first given in 1971 to Willie Mays and then Brooks Robinson the following year. After the death of Roberto Clemente on a humanitarian mission to bring supplies to earthquake victims in Nicaragua on the last day of 1972, it was renamed in honor of Clemente and is "bestowed annually to the player who best represents the game of Baseball through extraordinary character, community involvement, philanthropy, and positive

Knuckleballer Tim Wakefield pitching at Fenway.
BILL NOWLIN PHOTO

156

contributions both on and off the field." Two Red Sox players have been recognized by the award, in back-to-back seasons—Tim Wakefield in 2010 and David Ortiz in 2011.

Mike Andrews, chairman of Boston's Jimmy Fund, which funds research and treatment of childhood cancer, said of Wakefield, "I would have to say in my years of baseball playing and then my 31 years with the Jimmy Fund, I have never seen anybody exceed his charitable generosity. Giving his time, giving his money, and really caring, he's one of those very, very unique people that come along every now and then. You always know with Tim that it's heartfelt. It isn't something that he feels an obligation to do it, he really gets into it."

Ortiz founded the David Ortiz Children's Fund, which provides medical care for children in the Dominican Republic and the United States, in partnership with Massachusetts General Hospital. Commissioner Bud Selig said, "David's remarkable commitment to helping children receive essential pediatric care in the United States and the Dominican Republic makes him a wonderful choice for this honor. The legacy of the great Roberto Clemente lives on through the selfless actions of players like David and so many of his peers."

# SOME OTHER FIRSTS ON THE FIELD OF PLAY

LET'S NOW TURN TO PLAY ON THE FIELD AND LOOK AT A NUMBER OF RED Sox firsts. We have already looked at the first win, the first shutout, and will try not to repeat too much here (though the occasional memory isn't necessarily a bad thing). We'll look at some other elements of play we have not covered.

### A Few Oddball Items
*What was the first "walk-off" win in team history?*
There were notable games, such as the June 14, 1901, game at the Huntington Avenue Grounds when the team broke a 7–7 tie in the bottom of the eighth (scoring nine runs), but the first true walk-off game was on June 20. The opponents were the Chicago White Sox, who beat Boston to first place in the 1901 season. The starters were Cy Young for Boston and left-hander Zaza Harvey for Chicago. The White Sox scored twice in the second inning on a two-run homer by catcher Billy Sullivan. They scored once more in the third. The Boston Americans scored twice in the bottom of the fourth. Charlie Hemphill was thrown out at the plate attempting to score what would have been the tying run.

With no more scoring as the innings progressed, Boston was still trailing 3–2, heading into the bottom of the ninth. Catcher Ossee Schrecongost ("Schreck" in both the *Herald* newspaper coverage and box score) singled to lead off. Cy Young drew a base on balls. Left fielder Tommy Dowd singled in Schreck, which tied it. Center fielder Chick Stahl hit one back to Harvey, who threw to third base and forced Young. Jimmy Collins walked, and the bases were loaded. One could imagine most of the 3,782 fans were keyed up. Buck Freeman came to bat. All the outfielders pulled in since even a deep enough fly out could allow Dowd to tag and score. Freeman singles to deep right-center, and the game was over, 4–3 Boston.

### When was the first time the Red Sox opened a season with three extra-inning games?

In 1969, the Red Sox opened the season on the road, playing the first two in Cleveland and then moving on to Baltimore. The first game was at Memorial Stadium on April 8, with Dave McNally against Boston's Jim Lonborg. Both starters left the game early (in Lonborg's case, a precaution for a sore arm), though the score was only 2–2 at the end of nine innings. By the time the game was over, both teams had used six pitchers. In the top of the 10th, Tony Conigliaro (in his first major-league game since being beaned in 1967) hit a two-run homer, giving Boston the lead—but the Orioles' Frank Robinson responded with a two-run homer of his own off Boston's Sparky Lyle. Neither team scored in the 11th, but the Red Sox got another run in the top of the 12th. A walk to Tony C (reaching base for the fourth time), a single, and a walk loaded the bases with nobody out. Russ Gibson flied out to right, but it was not deep enough for the runner on third to tag. Pinch-hitter Dalton Jones then flied out to right, too, this one deep enough for Tony C to tag and score. The Orioles were unable to match the run, and the Red Sox won, 5–4.

There was no game scheduled for April 9, but on April 10, it was Mike Cuellar for Baltimore and Ray Culp for Boston. Both of these starters went 10 innings. In the second inning, Tony C singled, then took second on a passed ball. George Scott hit the ball right back to Cuellar, but the O's committed two errors—by Cuellar and center fielder Paul Blair, and Conig scored on what went down as a fielder's choice. It was their only run of the game. In the bottom of the third, after Culp struck out the first two batters, Don Buford doubled, and Blair singled him home. The game ran longer than the previous game, into the bottom of the 13th inning, still 1–1. With Juan Pizarro pitching in relief, Baltimore's Frank Robinson doubled to right, and Boog Powell singled, driving him home. Baltimore 2, Boston 1 (13 innings).

The Red Sox traveled to Cleveland, where they played their third game of the new season at Cleveland Stadium, and this one lasted longer than the previous two. It was another low-scoring game, 1–1 after seven innings. The Indians had scored first on Tony Horton's second-inning leadoff homer off Dick Ellsworth. The Red Sox got their one run when Russ Gibson led off the seventh with a walk, Ellsworth sacrificed, bunting and moving Gibson to second, and Reggie Smith singled to drive in the run. Neither team scored in the 8th or 9th, or the 10th, 11th, 12th, 13th, 14th, or 15th. Finally, Boston eked out a run in the top of the 16th inning. With one out, Rico Petrocelli singled to left field. Gibson singled to right, and Rico went first to third. George Thomas pinch-hit and grounded out, second to first—but Petrocelli scored. Pizarro allowed a double but no runs.

The Red Sox had started the season with three extra-inning games, each one longer than the game before—12, 13, and 16 innings.

### *Who was the first female nuclear family relative of a Red Sox player to come to Fenway to play in a professional baseball game?*

It was pitcher Gina Satriano, later a deputy district attorney in Los Angeles. Satriano had been the first girl in California to play Little League baseball. She played with the Colorado Silver Bullets and appeared twice in games at Fenway Park, once in 1994 and once in 1995. Her father, Tom Satriano, had closed his 10-year major-league career as a catcher with the Red Sox with 47 games in 1960 and 59 games in 1970. She was not used in either game but had been in the bullpen for both games, ready to be called upon if the occasion warranted.

## Some Other Pitching Firsts
### *Who was the first pitcher to win the pitching Triple Crown for the Red Sox?*

That means to lead the league in wins, in strikeouts, and in earned run average. It didn't take long for a pitcher to win it—Cy Young did in 1901, for the Boston Americans. His 33 wins led both leagues. So did his 1.62 ERA. His 158 strikeouts led the American League. Cincinnati's Noodles Hahn struck out 239 National League batters.

No other pitcher won the Triple Crown for the Red Sox until the end of that century. Pedro Martínez won it in 1999. He won 33, posted a 2.07 ERA, and struck out 313.

*Who was the first pitcher to come anywhere close to Cy Young's 275 complete games for the team?*

It was his teammate Bill Dinneen, who threw 156 complete games from 1902 through 1907. Dinneen's win/loss record for the Boston Americans was exactly 85–85. He was three times a 20-game winner and won three games in the 1903 World Series. Yet another teammate ranks third on the list—George Winter, who had 141, from 1901 through 1908. The most complete games by anyone in the last 50 years is the 100 thrown by Roger Clemens. The most complete games by one in the last 30 years (as of 2022) is Pedro Martínez, with 22.

*Who is the first pitcher with more than 40 decisions to have a winning percentage of more than 75 percent?*

It is Pedro Martínez, who posted a record of 117–37 (.760) over the course of his seven seasons with the Red Sox. His earned run average in his time with Boston was 2.52. Smoky Joe Wood's .674 ranks second. He was 117–56. Babe Ruth (89–46, .659) is third.

*Who was the first team pitcher to throw a shutout in his big-league debut?*

The first pitcher on the team to do so was left-hander Rube Kroh of Friendship, New York. It was the only game he pitched in 1906, and the second game of the September 30 doubleheader on a Sunday afternoon at Sportsman's Park, St. Louis. The Browns won the first game, 7–1, dealing Joe Harris his twentieth loss of the season. The Boston Americans had lost six games in a row and 10 of their last 11 games. Kroh put a stop to that. He pitched the full nine innings, allowing two base hits—both singles—and walked four, but no one scored. Kroh won 2–0. In 1907, he was 1–4, though, with a good 2.62 ERA but then released in early 1908.

Six other pitchers have matched Kroh's feat—Larry Pape, Buck O'Brien, George Hockette, Dave Ferriss, Dave Morehead, and Billy Rohr. We've been waiting since 1967 for the next.

*Who threw the first no-hitter for the team?*

It was Cy Young who threw the first no-hitter in team history, in Boston on May 5, 1904. He did so beating the Philadelphia Athletics. He accomplished two other firsts in doing so. It was not just a no-hitter; it was a perfect game. So Young also holds the record of throwing the first perfect game in team history. And not only that—it was the first perfect game in American League history. And there's even one more thing—in 1893, the pitching distance from the rubber to home plate was fixed as the current 60 feet, 6 inches. Before that, it had been 45 or 50 feet, giving the batter considerably less time to adjust his swing. Young's perfect game was the first thrown from the current distance.

### *Who was the first pitcher to throw 24 consecutive no-hit innings?*

It was Cy Young, and his perfect game was in the middle of it. In the game that followed his perfecto, he threw a 15-inning shutout. The first six innings of that game were hitless.

Young himself was 3-for-5 at the plate and also showed some real fielding skills (among other things, handling three infield grounders in the 12th inning), but the winning run was knocked in by Patsy Dougherty in the bottom of the 15th. Young had previously thrown hitless ball in the final two innings of the April 25 game. He worked seven innings of hitless relief on April 30—the third through the ninth. That adds up to 24 hitless innings in a row. He pitched to 75 consecutive batters without any one of them getting a base hit.

### *Who was the first Red Sox pitcher to retire 37 consecutive opposing batters?*

Unlikely as it is that he would be retiring his own team's batters, the answer is Koji Uehara. That's equivalent to a perfect game plus 10 batters. It took him nearly a month to do so. On August 17, 2013, he came in to face the Yankees, struck out two, then gave up a double, but got the final out. That was a total of one batter. Working exclusively in relief, and never pitching to more than four batters in any one game, Uehara's sojourn took him from Boston to San Francisco, then Los Angeles (against the Dodgers), back to Boston, then to New York (against the Yankees) and to St. Petersburg to face the Rays, and back to Boston. In all, he pitched in 12 games, facing 37 batters in five different ballparks in four different states. The first batter who got a hit off him was 32 days after the last—the leadoff batter tripled in the September 17 game against the Orioles. Of the 37 batters he retired, almost half (17) were batters who struck out.

Later in 2013, he was the MVP in the American League Championship Series, appearing in five games without giving up a run. He pitched in five World Series games, allowing two base hits but, again, no runs.

### *Who ranks first for strikeouts in a game?*

Roger Clemens struck out 20 batters in the April 29, 1986, game against the Seattle Mariners at Fenway Park, winning 3–1. The lone Seattle run came on a seventh-inning homer by Gorman Thomas. It gave the Mariners the lead, 1–0, because though he only struck out four in the game, Mike Moore had pitched exceptionally well for Seattle. In the bottom of the seventh, though, Dwight Evans hit a three-run homer and gave Clemens and the Red Sox all the runs they needed.

Ten years later, Clemens tied his own record, on the road, striking out 20 Detroit Tigers on September 18, 1996. He didn't walk any. This time he didn't give up any runs at all—throwing a 4–0 shutout. The Red Sox got their runs on a fourth-inning two-run double by Rudy Pemberton, followed by an RBI single by Clemens's batterymate Bill Haselman, and then another RBI single in the eighth by Haselman.

### *Which pitcher ranks first on the Red Sox for the most strikeouts thrown in relief?*

On September 22, 1974, veteran right-hander Diego Seguí, wrapping up his first season with the Red Sox, was called on to relieve starter Reggie Cleveland in a game against the Orioles at Fenway. Cleveland had given up three runs in the top of the first and had just loaded the bases by hitting a batter. Manager Darrell Johnson summoned Seguí. He struck out the first batter he faced, getting out of the inning without further damage. Seguí pitched 7⅔ innings of long relief and struck out 12 batters in all. He also gave up four runs, but the 7–2 loss was Cleveland's.

### *Who was the first relief pitcher in team history?*

It might not have been surprising had it been 10 games into the 1901 season, given that pitchers often worked complete games way back when.

But it was actually in the second game ever played. Cy Young was the starting pitcher who was pulled. Boston was playing in Baltimore, and this was Cy Young's debut for the new team. He lasted 5⅔ innings, hit for 10 runs (eight of them earned). One could well agree he didn't have it that day. Manager Jimmy Collins had Fred Mitchell come on in relief. Mitchell threw the remaining 2⅓ innings, allowing two more runs. The final score (a complete-game win for Baltimore's Harry Howell) was 12–6.

Mr. Young finished the year with 33 wins and only nine other losses. In his 41 starts, he threw 38 complete games. In his eight years with the team, he started 297 games and threw 275 complete games, winning 192 games—still a franchise record (albeit tied with Roger Clemens in team wins). The team's second and third most-active starters in 1901 (George Winter and Ted Lewis) each won 16 games, together one less than Cy Young. Fred Mitchell's record was 6–6. After an 0–1 start in 1902, he was loaned to the Philadelphia Athletics and was 5–8 for them.

### *Who was the first Red Sox reliever to give up a homer to the first batter he faced?*

Interesting, it's only happened two other times in team history that an incoming pitcher was tagged for a home run by the first batter he faced—and it didn't happen at all for the team's first 83 years. The very first time was on August 9, 1984, at Arlington Stadium. The Rangers had a 6–3 lead when Charlie Mitchell came in to pitch the bottom of the eighth. The first batter he faced was first baseman Pete O'Brien. Home run. 7–3. Mitchell retired the next three batters. It was the only homer he gave up in 1984, and he only gave up one in 1985, but he only pitched a total of 18 innings in his career, without a win or a loss. His younger brother, Fred, was a pitcher, too, who broke in with the Mets in 1986. He had a career record of 9–14.

The other time was on Opening Day in 2007, on April 2, in Kansas City. The Red Sox were losing to the Royals, 5–1, after 5½ innings, with starter Curt Schilling responsible for all five. Hideki Okajima came in to pitch the sixth inning, and the very first pitch he threw was over the plate—but hit out of Kauffman Stadium by catcher John Buck.

*Who was the first Red Sox starting pitcher to give up a home run to the first batter he ever faced in the major leagues?*

At Fenway Park on July 17, 1995, the first batter that right-hander Jeff Suppan ever faced in the major leagues was second baseman Keith Lockhart of the Kansas City Royals. Lockhart was in his first full big-league season. He had three homers to his credit. Suppan was only 20 years old but had a couple of minor-league seasons under his belt. On a 3-2 count, on Suppan's sixth pitch of his first game, Lockhart homered into the visitors' bullpen. The Red Sox lost the game, 4–3, but Suppan survived and prospered, pitching in 447 more major-league games over 17 years, winning 140.

*Which pitcher ranks first in single-season batting average against?*

In the year 2000, Pedro Martínez held opposing batters to a batting average of .167, an American League record. It's not surprising, then, that he also holds the best single-season mark for the lowest on-base percentage achieved by opposing batters—.213. And the best WHIP (walks and hits per innings pitched), which kind of goes hand-in-hand. His WHIP that year was 0.74, a record among all major-league pitchers since 1900.

*Which Red Sox pitcher recorded the lowest single-season earned run average for left-handers?*

Still holding the major-league record (since 1900), it was Dutch Leonard, with an ERA of 0.96 in 1914. He was just 22 years old, in his second season with the team. His win/loss record was 19–5 that year. Holding this record for more than a century is quite an accomplishment. Over the course of his six seasons with the Red Sox, Leonard's ERA was 2.13.

*Which right-hander ranks first among team pitchers in single-season ERA?*

Cy Young, in 1908, recorded an ERA of 1.26. Like Leonard's, it's a record that has stood for more than 100 years. Pitching for a team that finished fifth in the league, Young was 21–11 that year, his last with the Red Sox.

### *Who was the first pitcher to start the most Opening Day games for the Red Sox?*

There are plenty who could get ruled out pretty quickly. This pitcher not only started eight Opening Day games for the Red Sox but had time enough in his career to win Cy Young Awards for three other teams. That's the clue that might have made the difference for many. Yes, it was The Rocket—Roger Clemens. He started each year from 1988 through 1995, then a final time in 1996. He was 5–2.

### *Who was the first Red Sox pitcher to win three consecutive Opening Day starts?*

It wasn't Roger Clemens. He never did win three in a row. The first was Babe Ruth. He won 2–1 (allowing four hits) in 1916, 10–3 (allowing three hits) in 1917, and 7–1 (allowing four hits) in 1918. He pitched 8⅓ innings in the first game and then two complete games. He was 3–0, with a total of 11 base hits allowed. Ruth was 2-for-9 at the plate in the three games. In 1919, he played left field on Opening Day and helped beat the Yankees in a 10–0 win. His two-run inside-the-park homer in the first inning was the game-winning hit.

The other two pitchers with three consecutive Opening Day wins are Wes Ferrell (1935–1937, with the first win a 1–0 two-hitter against the Yankees) and Pedro Martínez (1998–2000). In 1998 and 2000, Martínez worked seven innings each game without allowing a run and only gave up three hits in 1998 and two in 2000.

### *Who was the first pitcher to throw an "immaculate inning" to start off a game?*

An immaculate inning is defined as throwing nine pitches, each one a strike. Face three batters and strike all three out—with no balls, no foul third strikes, nothing other than nine strikes leading to three outs. The pitcher was Pedro Martinez. These were not Triple-A batters getting a look sometime later in the season with a team that was out of the hunt. This happened on May 18, 2002, and the batters were the first three for the Seattle Mariners. The team was in first place, already five games ahead of the second-place Angels. The Mariners were on their way to a 93-win season. The first three batters were Ichiro Suzuki (who had led the league in batting the year before and been the AL MVP), the veteran Mark McLemore (who'd hit .270 in 2001), and Ruben Sierra (who had hit .291 for the Rangers the prior season). Nine pitches, three outs. McLemore's was a called third strike; the other two were out swinging. The Red Sox won the game, 4–1, the one run coming on Sierra's homer in the fourth. Others have thrown immaculate innings, but this one was said to be the first one in league history that started off a game.

### Who was the first pitcher to strike out four batters in one inning?

In the bottom of the ninth inning of the August 10, 1999, game against the Royals, the Red Sox were leading, 5–2. Tim Wakefield struck out the side—but the Royals tied the game after his third strikeout. The game should have been over. Instead, catcher Jason Varitek let strike three get away from him—a passed ball—and the batter (Johnny Damon) reached first base safely. Next up was Carlos Febles, who homered and tied the game. Finally, Wakefield struck out his fourth batter of the inning, Carlos Beltran. In the 10th, the Royals scored one run—but the Red Sox had scored four and won the game. Varitek, who singled and scored, provided the run that proved to win it.

On May 25, 2017, Craig Kimbrel faced four batters and struck them all out. This was also in the ninth inning, at Fenway against the Rangers. The first batter reached base on a wild pitch, but Kimbrel just kept striking them out, and the game was over, a 6–2 win.

### What game ranks first (and worst) in terms of bases on balls doled out by Red Sox pitchers?

The game against the Indians at Cleveland Stadium on May 20, 1948. Mickey Harris started for Boston. He only lasted 1⅓ innings, in large part because he couldn't find home plate. He faced 16 batters and walked seven of them. He also gave up four hits. He was charged with seven runs. Mickey McDermott took over and threw the remaining 6⅔ innings (there was no need to pitch the bottom of the ninth, since the Indians led, 13–4). McDermott walked 11 of the 32 batters he faced. That's a total of 18 bases on balls.

*Who was the first team pitcher to go 2–21 in a season and get offered a contract for the following year?*

In 1906, Joe Harris did indeed end the season with a record of 2–21. He was brought back the following year, hoping to top that .087 winning percentage. He didn't. He was 0–7 in 1907.

*Who was the first Red Sox pitcher to start a season 14–0?*

He's the only one! It was Roger Clemens, and the year was 1986. One would not have predicted this after his 7–5 season in 1985, but 1986 was his first full year, and he started 1–0, then went to 2–0, and so on. There was one no-decision mixed in, but he won 14 of his first 15 starts and never lost a game until July 2. Had his teammates driven in three more runs, he might well have had that one, too. Clemens finished the year with a record of 24–4. He won not only the Cy Young Award but also the MVP in that year's pennant-winning season.

*Which Red Sox pitcher ranks first among American League left-handers for shutouts thrown in a single season?*

Grover Cleveland "Pete" Alexander of the 1916 Phillies threw 16 shoutouts that year—but he was a right-hander and in the "wrong league" for the purposes of this answer. The AL record holder for lefties set the record that same year—it was Babe Ruth, who threw nine shutouts in 1916. Unsurprisingly, his 1.75 ERA led the league that year. A full 39 percent of his 23 wins were shutouts.

*Which Red Sox pitcher ranks first in shutouts of the Yankees in one season of play?*

In 1953, Mel Parnell shut out the Yankees four times: July 1 (4–0, allowing four hits), July 9 (4–0, at Yankee Stadium, with eight hits), September 19 (3–0, with five hits), and September 25 (again at Yankee Stadium, 5–0, with four hits). Parnell finished the season with a record of 21–8 with a 3.06 ERA. He only faced the Yankees once without shutting them out. On September 7, he worked six innings and gave up four runs—but still won the game, 7–4.

Catcher Sammy White and left-hander Mel Parnell, 1951–1956.
LESLIE JONES COLLECTION, BOSTON PUBLIC LIBRARY

*Who was the first team pitcher to be a "20-game loser"?*

The same guy was a 21-game winner—in 1902, Bill Dinneen both won 21 and lost 21, despite a good 2.93 earned run average.

*There was a Red Sox pitcher—and it wasn't that long ago—whose debut saw him retire one particular batter. He then left the game, but the next day, he was back again—throwing to just one batter (the very same batter)—with the same result. In his third game, he faced two batters. He walked the first one but then faced the very same batter he had gotten out each of the two previous days and got him out again. He was the first to pull off such an unlikely stretch. Who was he?*

The pitcher was Tommy Hottovy, a reliever, of course. On June 3, 2011, he got Oakland's David DeJesus to ground out to second base, to end the top of the sixth at Fenway Park. On June 4, DeJesus came up again with one out and a runner on first in the top of the seventh.

Hottovy came in and got him to groundout to shortstop, kicking off an inning-ending double play. On June 5, in the top of the seventh, Hottovy faced Ryan Sweeney and walked him. Up came DeJesus, who grounded out to second base. Hottovy's night was over. He earned a hold in the latter two games. The Red Sox won all three. Because a walk does not count as an at-bat, three A's batters had a total of three at-bats against the rookie pitcher—but the batter was the same man each time, and each time he hit into an infield groundout. Hottovy never did get a win or a loss; he appeared in five other games for Boston and nine for Kansas City the next year but never faced Oakland again.

**Teams do get swept at times, but which was the first major-league team to lose more than 10 postseason games in a row?**

It was . . . the Boston Red Sox, who lost not just 10 but 13 consecutive postseason games. The first two in the streak were Game Six and Game Seven of the 1986 World Series, lost to the Mets. Then they followed by losing all four games of the best-of-seven ALCS to Oakland in 1988. The first two losses were one-run games but were losses nonetheless. In 1990, they made the playoffs again. It was something of a re-run: Oakland won all four games. After waiting five years for their next postseason appearance, there had been a new round added—the best-of-five Division Series. In their first shot at the ALDS, they were swept in three games by the Cleveland Indians. In 1998, they had a rematch with Cleveland and won Game One, snapping the postseason losing streak at 13. But then they lost the next three. And lost four of five in the 1999 ALDS against the Yankees, winning only Game Three. We'll stop there—even though we know they also lost the 2003 ALCS to the Yankees. From that Game Six loss in 1986 through 1999, the Red Sox were 2–20. Things got better.

Just as a side note, we'll observe that the Red Sox did have the Angels' number in postseason play—winning the final three games of the 1988 ALCS, all three games of the 2004 ALDS, all three games of the 2007 ALDS, and the first two games of the 2008 ALDS before the Angels won Game Three in 12 innings. That was 11 wins in a row—won despite the opponents craftily changing their geographic name from the California Angels to the Anaheim Angels to the Los Angeles Angels of Anaheim.

*Who was the first pitcher to win the deciding game in each round of one season's playoffs?*

This should be a relatively easy question—it was only in 1995 that there have been three rounds of postseason playoffs. And this was a Red Sox pitcher. That limits the possible years to 2004, 2007, 2013, and 2018. Derek Lowe pitched the final inning—the 10th—of the clinching Game Three of the 2004 ALDS, not allowing the Angels a run and becoming the beneficiary of a walk-off David Ortiz home run. Lowe won the final Game Seven of the 2004 ALCS against the New York Yankees, throwing the first six innings and allowing just one base hit and one run as the Red Sox rolled up an 8–1 lead they never came close to relinquishing. In the 2004 World Series against the Cardinals, Lowe allowed just three hits and no runs at all over the first seven innings.

In the 14 combined innings, he'd allowed just one run. He had one no-decision in that year's postseason. He'd been the starter in Game Four of the ACLS. The Red Sox had lost the first three games to the Yankees. In 5⅓ innings, he had allowed three runs. The Red Sox had a 3–2 lead after five innings, but Lowe was pulled after giving up a triple to Hideki Matsui in the top of the sixth. The Yankees took the lead in the game, but Boston tied it in the ninth (on "The Steal") and won it in the 12th on a two-run homer by Ortiz.

*With five or more decisions, who has the best win/loss record among postseason pitchers?*

Ranking first is Curt Schilling. With the Red Sox, he is 6–1, his only loss coming at the hands of the Yankees in the first game of the 2004 American League Championship Series. Schilling won Game Six of the 2004 ALCS (the "Bloody Sock" game) and, indeed, won one game each in the 2004 ALDS, ALCS, and World Series, and the same in 2007—one game each in the three rounds.

### Some More Hitting Firsts

*Who was the first Red Sox batter to have a home run as each one of his first three major-league hits?*

Over the course of his first seven games, Mike Greenwell was 0-for-5 at the plate with two strikeouts. On September 25, 1985, in Toronto,

Greenwell entered the game playing left field in the eighth inning. The game was tied, 2–2. He came to bat in the top of the 10th and popped up foul to the catcher for the last out of the inning. In the top of the 13th, Bill Buckner led off with a double. Greenwell then homered—his first big-league hit and a hit that led Boston to a 4–2 win.

The next day, Greenwell started. He struck out his first time up. In the fourth, he hit a two-run homer, giving the Sox a 2–1 lead in a game they won, 4–1. He now had two hits, both homers and both homers that were the game-winning hit. He made outs in each of his next seven at-bats.

On October 1, still on the road, he entered the game before Baltimore came to bat in the bottom of the seventh. The Red Sox already had a 9–3 lead. In the eighth, he hit a solo homer in his only at-bat of the game. On October 3, Greenwell had a 3-for-5 game but spoiled his building record by singling (and then doing it twice more).

***Who was the first Red Sox batter to amass more than 400 total bases in a season?***

To date, the only Red Sox player to complete a season with more than 400 total bases is Jim Rice, in 1978. He had an MVP season with 406 total bases, leading both leagues in hits (213), triples (15), homers (46), RBIs (139), and slugging percentage (.600). His OPS was .970, leading the American League.

The closest Ted Williams got was 368 TB in his 1949 MVP season. David Ortiz had 363 in the year 2005.

***Speaking of 406, most readers will know that Ted Williams hit .406 in 1941, the last man to hit .400 in a major-league season. He batted left-handed. Who ranks first all-time for the highest batting average among Red Sox right-handed hitters?***

Ted Williams also ranks second, with a .388 average in 1957. And Tris Speaker hit .383 in 1912. Tops among right-handed hitters is Nomar Garciaparra, who hit .372 in the year 2000. There's an oddity worth noting. Dale Alexander hit .372 for the Red Sox in 1932, but he had come to Boston in a June 13 trade, so he only appeared in 101 games for the Red Sox. His season average was .367, brought down by the .250 he hit in earlier limited action for the Tigers. If you wanted to quibble (which we do), Alexander's average with the Red Sox was .3723404 and Garciaparra's was .3724007.

### Who was the first batter in team history to hit a grand slam in his first at-bat?

Not only was it his first at-bat, but it was also on the first pitch he was thrown in a major-league game. It was Daniel Nava. The date was Saturday, June 12, 2010. Nava debuted at Fenway Park in an interleague game against the Philadelphia Phillies, World Series contenders in both 2008 (which they won) and 2009 (which they did not). Joe Blanton was the pitcher. Nava was ninth in the Red Sox lineup. Blanton allowed a double in the first, but no more. In the bottom of the second, with the Phillies having taken a 2–0 lead, right fielder J. D. Drew swung at the first pitch he saw and homered. Taking a total of just six more pitches, the next three Red Sox singled, loading the bases. That brought Nava to the plate. He had not been a bonus baby presented a huge signing bonus. He was signed for one dollar. That's all, signed out of independent baseball by Red Sox scout Jared Porter. Apparently Red Sox broadcaster Joe Castiglione had been talking with Nava before the game and, for some reason, said something along the lines of being sure to swing at the first pitch you see because you will never get that chance again. Nava swung and hit the pitch into the Red Sox bullpen for a grand slam.

Nava came to the plate again the very next inning. There was one out, but a single, a walk, and a single had presented Nava with the opportunity to do something truly legendary. Blanton was still pitching, and the bases were loaded. But . . . Nava struck out. Swinging. Thanks to Marco Scutaro batting behind him, and Dustin Pedroia after that, all three baserunners scored. The Red Sox won the game, 10–2. Nava doubled later in the game.

The grand slam was the only home run Nava hit all year, despite playing in 60 games.

### It wasn't on the first pitch, but before Daniel Nava, there was another Red Sox player who had made a good impression by hitting a grand slam on his first day as a Red Sox player. Who was he?

On June 14, 1947, first baseman Jake Jones changed Sox. He was traded to Boston by the Chicago White Sox for Rudy York. His first game was the next day, June 15. The White Sox were in Boston for a doubleheader. Through 6½ innings, the Red Sox had a 6–3 lead. Jones hit a solo home run to make it 7–3. That was the final score. In the second game, the score was 4–4 after six innings. In the bottom of the ninth, looking for the one run to give them a win, Johnny Pesky started with a single to right field. He advanced to second on a sacrifice bunt. With first base open, there was no way Chicago was going to pitch to Ted Williams, so he was walked intentionally. And Bobby Doerr was a major RBI threat, too, so he was walked intentionally, too, even though it moved Pesky to third base with just the one out. Manager Ted Lyons figured he'd have starter Orval Grove—still in the game—pitch to Jake Jones, who'd been a .240 hitter that year with Chicago. They knew Jones and figured he'd perhaps already used up his quota of power with the first-game homer and two RBIs in the second game. The White Sox, asserted the *Boston Globe*, had said they were "glad to get rid of him. They said he wasn't there in the clutch." Jones hit the first pitch into the left-field screen—a grand slam.

### *Who was the first team player to hit four grand slams in one season?*

This happened in 1919. In 1914, his first year, Babe Ruth hit zero home runs. He only had 10 at-bats. In this first full season, 1915, he won 18 games as a pitcher but only hit four homers. In 1916, he hit three (all in a five-day stretch in June). In 1917, he hit two. This was the man later dubbed "the Sultan of Swat" or "The Colossus of Clout"? In 1918, Ruth hit two more than the previous four seasons added together—but that was only a total of 11 homers. Keep in mind that this was the Deadball Era. Those 11 homers were enough to lead both leagues. Oddly, there was a stretch in May when he homered three days in a row and another in June where he homered four games in a row. Not one of his homers was a grand slam.

His first grand slam was on May 20, 1919, against the Browns in St. Louis. He hit three more—on June 30 in the first game of a doubleheader at the Polo Grounds against the Yankees, on July 18 in Cleveland, and on August 3, in Detroit. All told, Ruth hit 29 homers in 1919 and drove in

113 runs. Both figures led the two leagues. The next year, Ruth was playing for the New York Yankees.

Ruth finished his career was 16 grand slams. Not one of them was
ever hit at Fenway Park. Nine of them were hit in Yankee Stadium.

### When was the first time the Red Sox hit two grand slams in the same game?

The hitters were Bucky Walters and Ed Morgan, on May 13, 1934.
The White Sox were in Boston. In the bottom of the second, the first
three batters all drew walks off Chicago starter (and former Red Sox
pitcher) Milt Gaston. Red Sox third baseman Bucky Walters then homered. In the third inning, the first three batters all got on base again—with
a single, a single, and a walk. Ed Morgan, the first baseman, homered, over
the fence in left-center—another grand slam. Walters hit another home
run, a two-run homer (again, with nobody out, again over the left-field
wall, near the corner) in the bottom of the seventh. The Red Sox won,
14–2. Walters also hit a single and a triple and could have had a cycle if
he'd been able to cash in one of the homers for a double.

### Who was the first Red Sox player to hit two grand slams in the same game?

Needless to say, this doesn't happen very often. It's only been done 13
times. But four of those 13 times, the hitter was a Red Sox player. The first
one to do it was 22-year-old third baseman Jim Tabor, in the second game
of a July 4, 1939, doubleheader in Philadelphia.

The first game had seen Ted Williams hit a three-run homer, Joe
Cronin hit a two-run homer, Bobby Doerr hit a two-run homer, and then
Tabor lead off the eighth with a solo home run to make it 17–7, Red Sox.
The A's had three homers of their own, but obviously, they didn't quite
match up.

In the second game, the A's scored 12 runs without the benefit of a
home run. But that wasn't enough. In the third inning, Jimmie Foxx had
doubled in two runs. He was on third base with Williams and Lou Finney
on second and first. Starter George Caster threw a pitch that Tabor hit
high into the upper deck of Shibe Park's left-field stands—a grand slam.

That made it 8–3 Red Sox, but the Athletics responded with seven runs to take a 10–8 lead. After five innings, the score was 11–11. In the top of the sixth, Chubby Dean walked Foxx, and then gave up a double to Williams. Lynn Nelson relieved Dean. He walked Joe Cronin, got Finney to fly out to shallow center, but Tabor took him deep, too. This one was an inside-the-park home run that banged off the fence in left-center and bounced "halfway back to the infield" (*Boston Herald*). Tabor scored standing up. It became 15–11, Red Sox. Just for good measure, Tabor homered a third time, too, a solo home run—also to left field off Nelson—in the top of the eighth. The final score was 18–12 Red Sox, and Tabor had four homers and 11 runs batted in on the day. The Red Sox had scored 35 runs in the doubleheader.

The only prior batter to have hit two grand slams in one game was Tony Lazzeri of the Yankees, in 1936 (also at Shibe Park). Only two batters could previously have boasted of four homers in a doubleheader— Earl Averill (1930) and Jimmie Foxx (1933, with the Athletics).

There were three other Sox stars who later accomplished this feat. The first was Rudy York on July 27, 1946, in St. Louis against the Browns. In the first inning, York hit a two-run double. In the second inning, he hit a grand slam off reliever Tex Shirley, some eight rows deep into the left-field bleachers. His third time up, he walked. When he came up in the fifth inning, still facing Shirley, he hit another grand slam—to the same place but much, much deeper—maybe as far as 50 feet further than the first. He had 10 RBIs and could have added on, but he struck out to end the seventh and was the last batter of the day for the Red Sox, grounding into a double play in the top of the ninth.

Nomar Garciaparra also had a 10-RBI game at Fenway Park on May 10, 1999, against the visiting Seattle Mariners. Brett Hinchliffe was the Seattle starter. In the very first inning, he was welcomed with a leadoff single by Jeff Frye, a single by John Valentin, and then hit Brian Daubach with a pitch. Bases loaded, nobody out, and Nomar at the plate. On a 2-0 count, it was a grand slam into the visitor's bullpen in right field. It was 4–0 Red Sox, still nobody out. That was all they got, and Hinchliffe retired the side in order in the second. Come the third inning, Daubach led off with a double. Garciaparra hit a two-run homer, also to right, near

Nomar Garciaparra in the dugout before a game.
BILL NOWLIN PHOTO

the Pesky Pole. Nomar led off the fourth, popping up foul, fielded by the second baseman. He walked in the sixth, loading the bases with one out for Troy O'Leary, but a double play followed. Boston still had a comfortable 8–2 lead. In the bottom of the eighth, with Eric Weaver pitching, after a single, an out, and two walks, he faced Garciaparra with the bases loaded once more. This time Nomar hit it into the left-field screen for his second grand slam of the day. The final score was 12–4.

That's three Red Sox players with a pair of grand slams, but for the fourth one, we need to introduce a twist. The question is the next entry.

***Who is the only Red Sox player to hit two grand slams in a game, one while batting right-handed and one while batting left-handed?***

Bill Mueller was a switch-hitter. The July 29, 2003, Red Sox game was in Arlington, Texas, against the Rangers. Mueller led off the third inning with a solo home run to right field. It was Rangers 2, Red Sox 1. Through six innings, the Rangers led 4–2. In the top of the seventh, Boston took a 5–4 lead on an RBI single by Gabe Kapler and two-run double by David Ortiz. Two walks loaded the bases, left-handed reliever Aaron Fultz doling out the second of the two. Mueller batted right-handed against Fultz and hit a grand slam to left field. 9–4. Red Sox. Nomar Garciaparra hit a solo homer off Fultz in the top of the eighth. Jay Powell relieved Fultz, with two outs and a runner on first. Powell allowed a single to Kevin Millar and then walked Trot Nixon. This brought up Mueller again, and with a right-hander on the mound, he batted from the left side. He hit another grand slam, to right-center. It was the first time in major-league history that anyone had hit grand slams from both sides of the plate. Mueller had nine RBIs on the day. The Red Sox won, 14–7. At the end of the year, Mueller's .326 batting average earned him the AL batting title.

### Who was the first Red Sox player to hit two pinch-hit grand slams?

Vic Wertz—once on the road and once at home. The one on the road was at Yankee Stadium, off Ryne Duren on August 14, 1959, one of seven homers he hit that year. It came in the top of the eighth and erased a 6–4 Yankees lead. The Red Sox got five more runs before the inning was done and won the game, 11–6. Wertz's second pinch-hit slam was on August 25, 1960, at Fenway Park. The Indians had just taken a 4–3 lead in the top of the fourth; Cleveland pitcher Don Newcombe's double drove in that fourth run. A Willie Tasby double gave Boston a fourth run. With the bases loaded, Wertz pinch-hit for pitcher Bill Monbouquette and slammed Newcombe's pitch out of the park.

Wertz hit 266 homers in this career, mostly for the Tigers. He was with the Red Sox in 1959, 1960, and most of 1961, and hit 37 of his home runs for Boston.

### When was the first time the Standells' "Dirty Water" became a Fenway Park staple—played after every Red Sox win? It was prompted by a grand slam.

It was Opening Day 1998—the April 10 home opener. The team was off to a 3–5 start but now were home. The starters were Brian Rose, a Bay

State native, and Randy Johnson for the Seattle Mariners. The score was 7–2, Seattle, and seemingly all but locked up heading in the bottom of the ninth. It was approaching 6:00 PM, and most of the fans had departed. It was Good Friday, and Passover, and the Red Sox had decided not to serve alcohol at the ballpark. Heathcliff Slocumb took over from Johnson, who had only allowed two hits and struck out 15 Red Sox. Troy O'Leary singled, and Mark Lemke drew a walk. After Darren Bragg doubled in O'Leary, manager Lou Piniella had Tony Fossas relieve Slocumb. On eight pitches, he walked Boston's Mike Benjamin. Piniella waved in the third pitcher of the inning, Mike Timlin. (Both Slocumb and Fossas were former Red Sox pitchers; Timlin was a future one.) Garciaparra singled in Lemke. The bases remained loaded. Timlin hit John Valentin with a pitch. Now it was 7–5, Seattle, and the bases remained loaded—with nobody out. Due up was "The Hit Dog"—Mo Vaughn. A double might tie up the game. A fourth pitcher was brought in—left-hander Paul Spoljaric.

Peter Gammons estimated about 13,000 of the 32,805 fans had remained. Those who had were rewarded. On an 0–2 count, Vaughn homered "several rows deep into the red seats" of the right-field grandstand.

Red Sox 9, Mariners 7. The game had been turned around, and the Sox had won Opening Day with a walk-off grand slam.

And a new Red Sox tradition had begun. Kevin Friend of BCN Productions had played "Dirty Water" often at the Boston Garden, and it went over well with Bruins fans. He had wanted to try it out on the crowd at Fenway, and his company had just received the contract to provide recorded sound at Fenway Park. He and Amy (Sill) Tobey were working the booth and were inspired. The moment was perfect. The song blared out, and a new tradition was born; GM Dan Duquette said that manager Jimy Williams liked the idea of celebrating home wins with a victory anthem. The book *Love That Dirty Water* tells the full story of the Standells and the song, in about 220 pages.

### Who ranks first among Red Sox batters in walk-off grand slams?

There have been 21 of them in team history. Eleven were in extra innings; the other 10 were in the bottom of the ninth. Only one player has hit more than one. It was Vern Stephens. His four-run homer beat the Washington Senators, 5–1, on August 13, 1949. Just a bit more than a year later, he repeated the feat on August 24, 1950, breaking a 2–2 tie with a walk-off grand slam off the St. Louis Browns' Ned Garver.

### What was the first time that two grand slams accounted for all the runs in a game?

The slams were hit by two college teammates—John Valentin and Mo Vaughn, both of whom had attended Seton Hall, Valentin drafted by the Red Sox in 1988 and Vaughn in 1989. The date was May 2, 1995. The opponent? The New York Yankees. The place? Yankee Stadium. The starting pitchers? Sterling Hitchcock for the Yankees and, pitching in his major-league debut, Vaughn Eshelman for the Red Sox. In the top of the third inning, Tim Naehring singled, Lee Tinsley singled, and Luis Alicea drew a base on balls. On a 1-0 count, shortstop Valentin hit a grand slam into Yankee Stadium's left-field seats. The bases got loaded again before the inning was done, but reliever Brian Boehringer got an inning-ending fly out from Naehring.

The next inning, the first three batters got on again, without an out, off Boehringer—a double by Tinsley, another walk to Alicea, and then Valentin got hit by a pitch. Mo Vaughn swung at the first pitch and hit a grand slam into the third deck in right field. Not a single other run scored in the game—for either team. Red Sox 8, Yankees 0. Mo helped the other Vaughn (Eshelman) to his first major-league win. Eshelman had never even pitched at Triple-A but threw six innings and allowed just three hits.

### Who was the first Red Sox player to hit an inside-the-park grand slam at Fenway Park?

Don Lenhardt, on April 19, 1952. It was hit in the fourth inning of the morning game of a dual admission Patriots Day doubleheader off Dick Fowler of the Philadelphia Athletics. The bases were loaded—always a prerequisite for a grand slam—when Lenhardt swung at a 3-2 pitch. The ball caromed off the wall in left-center, about halfway up, then bounced and skittered toward right field. As the fielders chased it down, Lenhardt kept chugging around the bases and was waved home. The Red Sox won both games, 11–2 and 6–1.

Gary Geiger also hit an inside-the-park grand slam, on August 8, 1961, against the Minnesota Twins.

There had been earlier inside-the-park slams hit by team batters: Jimmy Collins (July 25, 1902), Freddy Parent (July 8, 1904), Jake Stahl (April 21, 1910, in New York), Duffy Lewis (October 3, 1912, in Philadelphia), and Shano Collins (August 18, 1921, in Detroit). The Collins and Parent homers were hit at Boston's Huntington Avenue Grounds.

### Who was the first Red Sox batter to hit two inside-the-park homers at Fenway Park, with the second one being a grand slam?

On July 7, 1989, Red Sox left fielder Mike Greenwell hit an inside-the-park home run off New York Yankees left-hander Greg Cadaret. The score was 4–4 after the top of the sixth inning. Greenwell was the leadoff batter in the bottom of the sixth. He hit a ball to center field that became an inside-the-park home run as center fielder Roberto Kelly "played it like a man experiencing his first game of racquetball . . . watched it hit at the base of the wall and bounce 100 feet away" (*Boston Globe*). There was a close play at the plate and a jarring collision that knocked the ball out of catcher Don Slaught's grip. The Sox scored another run later in the inning and won the game, 6–4.

On September 1, 1990, the Yankees were back at Fenway Park again. Andy Hawkins was the starting pitcher for the Yankees, but he didn't make it through the first inning. Ellis Burks hit a three-run homer. Greenwell doubled, and then Tom Brunansky hit a two-run homer. Hawkins was pulled, and who replaced him? Greg Cadaret. He got out of the inning and pitched a scoreless second, third, and fourth. In the fifth, a leadoff walk, a double, and another walk loaded the bases with nobody out. Greenwell versus Cadaret again. Greenwell hit a grand slam—an inside-the-park grand slam. It was a ground ball—not a line drive—hit down the first-base line and into the right-field corner. This one was without a collision. The ball got away from right fielder Jesse Barfield who "had an adventure trying to field it, looking like someone attempting to trap a rolling coin" (*Globe*). Barfield fell down and bruised his knee. He had to leave the game. The grand slam made the score 9–1; the Red Sox won, 15–1.

*Who was the first Red Sox player to enter a game as a pinch-runner, get thrown out at the plate, and then hit a grand slam that very same inning?*

The Red Sox were playing the Yankees at Fenway Park on July 13, 1959. After five innings, Boston led 4–2. In the sixth, Jackie Jensen doubled and Ted Williams singled him in. Gene Stephens came into the game as a pinch-runner for Williams, who was still recovering from a neck problem in spring training that cost him the first month of the season and saw him hitting only .201 as recently as July 3. Frank Malzone singled, and Stephens ran to third. Yankees reliever Jim Bronstad entered the game, and Stephens was thrown out at home plate when trying to score on Sammy White's grounder to third. He did eventually score a run, though—that very same inning. There followed two singles, a double, and a hit by pitch. It was now 8–2, Red Sox. Bronstad got the second out of the inning on a fielder's choice, again on a runner thrown out at the plate. Jensen, up for the second time, walked. Williams's spot in the lineup was due up, and Stephens had subbed for him, so it was Stephens who came to bat. He hit a grand slam into the right-field seats, and it became 13–2, with Stephens, of course, scoring on the homer that capped a nine-run inning.

*Who was the first Red Sox player to hit into a triple play in one inning, then two innings later hit a grand slam to win the game?*

On Monday night, August 6, 2001, the Texas Rangers were in Boston. The Red Sox were ahead 4–2 heading into the bottom of the fourth. They had Chris Stynes on first and Brian Daubach on second and nobody out. Catcher Scott Hatteberg came to bat, in a position to help out his pitcher, Hideo Nomo. Hatteberg lined out to shortstop Alex Rodriguez, who flipped the ball to second baseman Randy Velarde, who stepped on the bag to double off Daubach and tagged the oncoming Stynes. Triple play. Inning over.

The Rangers scored five runs in the top of the fifth and took a 7–4 lead. With reliever Juan Moreno on the mound and the score 7–5 thanks to a solo home run by Nomar Garciaparra, Daubach walked, loading the bases. Stynes singled, driving in the sixth Sox run. There was still nobody out, so Hatteberg could have hit into another triple play. Instead, he hit a grand slam into the Red Sox bullpen in center field, and the Red Sox took a 10–7 lead, which held.

### When was the first time a grand slam supplied all the runs in a 4–0 Red Sox extra-innings victory?

There was some stellar pitching in the April 11, 1962, game against the visiting Cleveland Indians. It was the second game of the season. There were a couple of other firsts in the game. It was the debut game for Cleveland right-hander Ron Taylor, and he pitched a scoreless gem for the first 11 innings. Bill Monbouquette was the Red Sox pitcher, and he gave up a total of one hit over the first nine innings (a single by Taylor). In the bottom of the 12th, Carl Yastrzemski led off with a triple. Manager Mel McGaha ordered intentional walks given to Frank Malzone and Russ Nixon, setting up better possibilities to get out of the inning unscathed. Right fielder Carroll Hardy was due up. He was far from the most potent hitter on the team (at the end of 1962, he'd appeared in 115 games but only hit for a .215 batting average). Hardy contributed another first—his first Fenway Park home run. It was a grand slam, which cleared the left-field wall by about a foot. A ball off the wall, or even caught on the warning track, would have won the game—but this was better. Except for Ron Taylor. He went on to win 45 major-league games, mostly in relief.

Settling down from grand slams but never forgetting Mo Vaughn's Opening Day winner, let's look at a few other walk-offs.

### Who was the first batter to hit four game-ending home runs in one season?

In 1940, Jimmie Foxx won games with homers on June 2, June 6, July 3, and August 16. He hit some game-winning homers on the road, too—see, for instance, May 14. Fred Lynn hit three walk-off home runs in 1985. So did David Ortiz in 2004—one in the regular season and two in the postseason. Ted Williams hit four in the course of his career. Bobby Doerr hit seven. David Ortiz hit eight. Foxx hit 12 in all, as did Babe Ruth, but in both cases, not all the homers were for the Red Sox. Foxx's most dramatic game-winner was perhaps the grand slam he hit in the bottom of the ninth inning on August 23, 1938, giving the Red Sox a 12–10 win.

### Who was the first Red Sox pitcher to hit walk-off home runs two days in a row?

The days were July 21 and July 22 in the year 1935. The pitcher was Wes Ferrell. As one might surmise, Ferrell was a good-hitting pitcher. He had a career .280 batting average and a .351 on-base percentage in 1,345 plate appearances. He hit 38 homers, hitting seven in 1933 (for Cleveland) and seven again for the Red Sox in 1935. Manager Joe Cronin used him 35 times (!) as a pinch-hitter in the course of the 1935 season.

On July 21, the visiting Detroit Tigers held a 6–4 lead heading into the bottom of the ninth. Cronin led off with a single, and Billy Werber singled. They were sacrificed to second and third. Pitcher Lefty Grove was due up (when completed, his career batting average was .148). Cronin had Ferrell pinch-hit and—as the Associated Press put it—he cranked a Tommy Bridges pitch "far over the left field wall." Grove got the win.

Ferrell was the starting pitcher the next afternoon. Through 8½, it was a tight 1–1 pitcher's duel against the St. Louis Browns' Dick Coffman. With one out in the bottom of the ninth, on a count of 0–2, Ferrell did it again—homered to win the game over the left-field fence.

### They weren't all walk-off home runs but the home runs provided the run(s) needed to win the game. Who ranks first among Red Sox batters for game-deciding home runs?

Among the 521 home runs Ted Williams hit over the course of his career, a full 110 (21.11 percent) of his homers provided the margin of victory in a Red Sox game. The book *"The Kid" Blasts A Winner* details each and every one of those 110 home runs.

### Who was the first (and only) Red Sox batter to homer 30 or more times in at least 10 different seasons?

From 2003 through 2016, David Ortiz homered 30 or more times exactly 10 times, only falling short in the years 2008, 2009, 2011, and 2012. Ortiz, of course, holds iconic (and well-deserved) status in Red

Sox history. Just the one stretch alone, winning the clinching game of the 2004 Division Series and then Games Four and Five of the League Championship Series, would be enough to make anyone an icon. But, of course, he kept going. The Red Sox honored him in September 2005, naming him the "Greatest Clutch Hitter in the History of the Boston Red Sox." In 14 seasons for the Red Sox, Ortiz hit homers 483 times and drove in 1,530 runs, in regular season play, and 17 more home runs in the postseason.

### Who was the first Red Sox player to hit two home runs in the same inning?

The major-league record is two. It would be truly stunning if it were more. Ellis Burks hit two in the fourth inning on August 27, 1990, leading off with a solo home run off Cleveland's Tom Candiotti, watching his teammates bat around and score four more runs, then be due to bat again with runners on second and third. A new pitcher was brought in to face Burks—Colby Ward. Burks homered again, producing three more runs.

A dozen years later, the Red Sox came into the bottom of the fourth inning down 4–0 to Tampa Bay on July 23, 2002. Johnny Damon led off with a homer off Tanyon Sturtze. Lou Merloni singled, and Nomar Garciaparra hit a two-run homer. Manny Ramirez homered right after Nomar. The team kept hitting. Eight runs had crossed the plate when Nomar came up again, facing a new pitcher, Brandon Backe, with Damon on first base. He homered again, giving him five RBIs on two home runs. The final score was 22–4.

The first Red Sox player to hit two home runs in the same inning, however, had been second baseman Bill Regan. It was in Chicago on June 16, 1928. The White Sox had a 3–0 lead when Regan homered into the left-field stands off Ted Blankenship to lead off the top of the fourth. After a double, two walks, and a single, the score was tied, and Sarge Connally took over pitching. He secured two outs, but then back-to-back doubles produced three more runs. Regan was up again. He hit a grounder into right-center that rolled all the way to the wall as the center fielder tried to chase it down. It went for an inside-the-park home run. That made it 8–3. The final score was 10–5.

*Who was the first player to hit two inside-the-park home runs in the same game?*

Believe it or not, it's been done four times. The first was Hobe Ferris back on May 4, 1903, at the spacious Huntington Avenue Grounds. The first was to left field in the third, the second to right-center in the sixth, the game-winner over Washington. Ferris hit nine IPHR in 1903; every homer he hit that year was one hit inside the park. Primarily a second baseman, Ferris played seven seasons, the first seven seasons in team history. He hit 34 home runs in his time with the Boston Americans.

*Who was the first Red Sox batter whose last home run for the team (at age 41) was an inside-the-park home run?*

He hit 174 homers, with 48 of them in his Red Sox years. Facing Kirk McCaskill at Fenway Park on April 25, 1990, Bill Buckner smashed a drive to right field. Angels right fielder Claude Washington crashed into the low wall and fell into the seats. He had to leave the game. Taking advantage of the ball shooting away from Washington, Buckner kept running, and even on legendarily gimpy legs, he made it all the way around the bases.

*Who hit the most extra-inning homers for the Red Sox?*

Ted Williams hit 13 extra-inning home runs for the Red Sox. David Ortiz is second, with 11. Interestingly, of his 13 extra-inning homers, only three of them were walk-off home runs. There was a ninth-inning one on May 19, 1957, a 10th inning one on May 2, 1946, and a 12th inning one on July 19. 1958.

The team record for extra-inning homers in a single season is three, held by Mookie Betts (2019), David Ortiz (2003 and again in 2014), and Ted Williams (1946.)

*Who was the first Red Sox player to hit three home runs on his birthday?*

It wasn't Carlton Fisk. He played in 1,078 games for the Red Sox and even more for the White Sox, but he was born on the day after Christmas (in 1947), and the Red Sox have yet to play a game on December

26. It wasn't Bob Stanley; he appeared in more games for the Red Sox (637) than any other pitcher, but he didn't bat that often. In fact, he never batted—except once in Game Two of the 1986 World Series. He struck out on three pitches, the third being a foul bunt.

It was Nomar Garciaparra. He not only hit two home runs in the third inning of the July 23, 2002, game. He hit a grand slam in the fourth inning.

### Who was the first Red Sox slugger to end a season with more home runs than strikeouts?

Ted Williams, and he did it four times. In 1941, he homered 37 times and struck out 27 times. In 1950, when he missed most of the second half of the season after breaking his elbow in the All-Star Game, he homered 28 times and struck out 21 times. In 1953, in a partial season after return from combat in the Korean War, the no-longer-a-kid hit 13 homers and struck out 10 times. In 1955, he hit 28 homers and struck out 24 times.

The two top single-season homer hitters for the Red Sox are David Ortiz (54 homers in 2006, with 117 strikeouts) and Jimmie Foxx (50 homers in 1938, with 76 Ks).

### There was a time when a Red Sox batter hit the very first pitch of the entire major-league season for a home run. When was that, and who hit the homer?

It was Opening Day (obviously) in 1986. The first game of the new season was at Tiger Stadium in Detroit on April 7. Traditionally, the Cincinnati Reds always hosted the season's first game, but the first pitch in Detroit was at 1:37 PM while in Cincinnati it was at 2:05. People in Cincinnati were miffed. Jack Morris was the Tigers' pitcher. Dwight Evans swung at his first pitch and homered to left-center. It was the first of five runs the Red Sox scored (and the first of four home runs they hit)—but the Tigers scored six runs, and Morris got the win. Evans recalled after the game that he had done the same thing in 1962, hit the first pitch of his local Little League season—also for a home run.

*Who was the first team player to hit for the cycle—hitting a single, double, triple, and home run all in the same game?*

Buck Freeman on June 21, 1903, in a game at Cleveland. His six RBIs were half of the team's 12 that beat the Naps, 12–7. He played either first base or right field in most of the team's games. Freeman's 12 homers had led the Boston Americans in homers in the team's first season, 1901. He hit twice as many as anyone else on the team. He led the team again in 1902 and led both leagues in 1903. That year, he homered 13 times, hit 39 doubles, and had 20 triples.

After the team changed its name to the Red Sox, who was the first Red Sox player to hit for the cycle at a home game?

The name was changed before the 1908 season. It was 36 years before a Sox player hit for a cycle in Boston. The batter was Bobby Doerr. The date was May 17, 1944.

Jimmie Foxx and Bobby Doerr at Fenway Park 1937.
COURTESY OF THE BOSTON PUBLIC LIBRARY, LESLIE JONES COLLECTION

Home or away, Doerr was the first—and remains the only—team batter to hit for the cycle in two regular-season games. His second cycle was on May 13, 1947. Both Doerr's cycles were hit at Fenway.

There have been 22 regular-season cycles hit by Red Sox batters over time. There has only been one hit in postseason play.

***Who is the only Red Sox batter to hit a cycle in a postseason game?***

On June 16, 2015, Brock Holt hit for a cycle in a regular-season game in Boston. Holt is the only major-league player to ever hit for a cycle in a postseason game.

It was Game Three of the 2018 American League Division Series. The game was in Yankee Stadium on October 8. The Red Sox won Game One. The Yankees won Game Two. In Game Three, Holt played second base. He grounded out his first time up. He led off the fourth inning with a single. The team batted around, and Holt came up again and tripled, driving in the sixth and seventh Red Sox runs of the inning. The Red Sox led, 10–0.

In the sixth, Holt grounded out to first base, unassisted. Before the Yankees came to bat in the seventh, Holt was asked to play first base, and Ian Kinsler came in at second. In the top of the eighth, Holt hit a ground-rule double and collected another RBI. He came up for the last time in the top of the ninth. There were two outs, and Kinsler was on first base after a walk. The Red Sox were leading 14–1. He acknowledged afterward that he was aware all he lacked for a cycle was the home run. He also acknowledged that he was going for it—and, after all, why not? It's not as though it was a one-run game. It worked. Holt homered to right field, and it was 16–1. Each of Holt's hits were hit off a different pitcher: Luis Severino, Chad Green, Stephen Tarpley, and Austin Romine.

***Who was the first Red Sox player to hit for a "natural cycle"? That means to collect the four hits in the sequence of single, double, triple, and home run.***

It's only been done twice, first by Leon Culberson on July 3, 1943, in Cleveland. And 36 years later, Bob Watson did so on September 15, 1979, in Baltimore. Let's remember Johnny Damon hitting for a triple, a single, and a double all in the first inning of the June 27, 2003, game. That was the inning when the Red Sox scored 14 runs in the first inning of the game against the Marlins. If only the team had scored another nine or so runs, Damon could have come up a fourth time. They did eventually score another 11 runs in the game, but not all in the first inning.

### Who still ranks first in doubles, holding the major-league record for a season?

Earl Webb, with the 1931 Red Sox. Right fielder Webb hit 67 doubles that year. The number of doubles was more than double any other year in his career. He hit 30 in 1930 and 28 in 1932. Webb simply had a tremendous year in 1931. The worst that was said about him was that—as he approached the record—he sometimes may have held back from going for a triple so he could add to his two-base hit totals. He hit .333 that year and drove in 103 runs for a team that only played 152 games that season.

### Who holds the team record for the most extra-base hits in a season?

In 1938, Jimmie Foxx hit 33 doubles, 9 triples, and 50 home runs for a total of 92 extra-base hits. The very next year, 1939, Ted Williams put together 86 extra-base hits in his rookie season—44 doubles, 11 triples, and 31 homers. In the year he set the team home-run record, David Ortiz had 85 XBH—29 doubles, two triples, and 54 homers. In 1978, when Jim Rice set the team record for total bases, he hit 25 doubles, 15 triples, and 46 homers—86 XBH. Mr. Foxx still prevails.

### Who ranks first among Red Sox players for total bases in a single game?

Fred Lynn. On June 18, 1975, at Tiger Stadium, Lynn hit three home runs and two doubles for 16 total bases. In the process, he drove in 10 runs. (The Red Sox won, 15–1.) Lynn is tied for the most RBIs in a Red Sox game, a record he shares with Rudy York (July 27, 1947), Norm Zauchin (May 27, 1955), and Nomar Garciaparra (May 10, 1999).

### Who was the first player to drive in more than 100 runs, in one season, at Fenway Park?

To be precise, counting only home games played at Fenway Park, and not runs batted in during games on the road, this player amassed more than 100 RBIs at Fenway in just one year. It was Jimmie Foxx, in 1938. Foxx led both leagues with 175 RBIs—well ahead of second-place Hank Greenberg, who had 147. It's a still-standing Red Sox record. Second of the Sox are two players, tied: Vern Stephens, with 159 in 1949, and Ted Williams, also with 159 and also in 1949. Next on the list is David Ortiz, with 148 in 2005.

Foxx drove in 104 runs at Fenway Park and 71 on the road. It was quite a year.

### When was the first time the Red Sox scored 10 runs in the first inning?

At Fenway Park, on June 27, 2003, the Red Sox hosted the Florida Marlins. The visitors scored one run off Boston's Byung-Hyun Kim. The Red Sox paid them paid for such effrontery and scored 10 runs before even making the first out. Then they kept on going. By the time the third Marlins pitcher of the inning recorded the third out, the Red Sox had scored 14 times. And they didn't stop there. They added 11 more runs before the game was done—and since they were leading after 8½ (25–8), they didn't even get to bat in the bottom of the ninth. Leadoff batter Johnny Damon tripled to kick things off. Before the inning was done, he was 75 percent of the way to a cycle, adding a double and a single in his next two times up. The major-league record was 15, set by the Dodgers on May 21, 1952.

The *Boston Globe* reported that it was the twenty-ninth time the team had scored 10 or more runs in an inning. The first seven batters all reached on base hits. Then there was a walk, followed by three more hits, making it 10 consecutive at-bats with a hit. The half-inning lasted 50 minutes, from 7:16 to 8:06 PM.

### Who was the first Red Sox batter to get three hits in one inning?

Almost exactly half a century before Damon, it was Gene Stephens on June 18, 1953. He hit two singles and a double in the seventh inning. The Red Sox won that game, too. Stephens was an outfielder who first broke in with Boston while Ted Williams was serving most of 1952 and

1953 as a Marine Corps aviator. Despite the three hits, his average for the year was .204 in 78 games. After spending 1954 with Triple-A Louisville, he had his best big-league season in 1955, when he hit .293.

### When was the first time the Red Sox scored more than 15 runs in one inning?

It came the day after they had beaten the visiting Tigers, 17–1. They apparently weren't prepared to show mercy. The Red Sox were leading 5–3, entering the seventh inning of the aforementioned June 18, 1953 game when Gene Stephens got three hits. There were 11 other base hits that half-inning, too, and six walks. The team scored 17 runs in the one inning. George Kell made two of the outs, both on fly balls to left, including the third out with the bases loaded. The final score was 23–3. One player who was not involved at all was Ted Williams. His first game in 1953 was on August 6, after returning from combat in the Korean War.

### Listing all the games in which the Red Sox scored lots and lots of runs, what game ranks first?

June 8, 1950, when the Red Sox beat the St. Louis Browns, 29–4. The game also ranks first in terms of the largest margin of victory—25 runs. Fenway Park fans were sated after back-to-back Wednesday and Thursday afternoon wins of 20–4 on June 7 and then 29–4 on June 8. Bobby Doerr had eight RBIs in the June 8 game, and Walt Dropo had seven. Ted Williams had five. Appreciative of the run support, no doubt, was Boston pitcher Chuck Stobbs. The winning pitcher the day before was Joe Dobson.

### What ranks first among the worst?

In other words, what's the worst drubbing the Red Sox ever suffered? We won't devote quite as much space to this one. You can look it up if you want to know more and remember what it was sometimes like to be a Red Sox fan. It was a 27–3 loss in the first game of the July 7, 1923, doubleheader, which was mercifully on the road in Cleveland. The Indians won the second game, too, 8–5. The only home run of the day was in the second game.

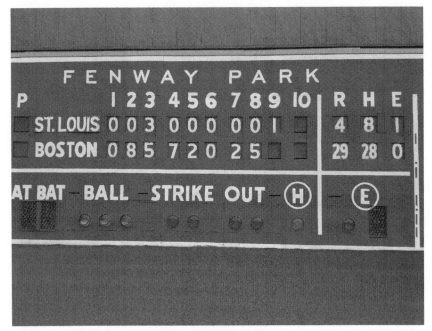

June 8, 1950: The Red Sox won by 25 runs.
BILL NOWLIN PHOTO, WITH THANKS TO THE FENWAY PARK GROUNDS CREW FOR SETTING UP THE SCOREBOARD

*Who ranks first among Red Sox batters for base hits in a single season?*
Wade Boggs hit safely 240 times in 1985. His .368 average led both leagues. He had eight homers, three triples, 24 doubles, and 187 singles. His 1985 season was one of seven consecutive seasons in which he hit 200 or more hits, ranging from 1983 through 1989. In five of those seasons, he won the league batting championship.

*What Red Sox batter won the American League batting title the very first year he was eligible to do so?*
Wade Boggs, batting .361 in 1983. He'd hit .349 in his rookie year, but even though 1982 qualified as his rookie year, he didn't have enough plate appearances to qualify for the batting title. Willie Wilson won the batting title, despite coming in significantly behind Boggs with a .332 batting average. To win the title, though, you have to have 3.1 plate appearances

per game, or at least 502 in a 162-game season. Boggs played in 104 games and only had 381 plate appearances. When he did first qualify, in 1983, he won the title and then won it four more times.

*The book* **Moneyball** *brought the on-base percentage stat to public attention. Who ranks first among all major-league players in career on-base percentage?*

Okay, that was an easy one—Ted Williams, with a lifetime on-base percentage of .482. No matter how many times one contemplates the meaning of that, it remains remarkable. In a career that touched on four decades (1939–1960, with most of five seasons lost to military service). Williams reached base nearly 50 percent of the times he came up to bat.

*Who holds the record for reaching base in consecutive plate appearances?*

Ranking first among all major-league batters is Ted Williams, who reached base 16 times in a row, from September 17 through September 23, 1957—seven days in a row—his plate appearances included two pinch-hit homers, one other homer, and just one other hit, which was a single. He had nine walks and was hit by a pitch, all adding up to 16 times in a row.

*Many dedicated baseball fans know that the Yankees' Joe DiMaggio once had a 56-game hitting streak—collecting at least one base hit in 56 consecutive games in 1941. Who ranks first among Red Sox batters, with the longest hitting streak for a Red Sox batter?*

Joe's brother, Dom DiMaggio, set the team record in 1949, hitting safely in 34 consecutive games.

Ranking second on the Sox are Tris Speaker in 1912 and Nomar Garciaparra in 1997. Both had 30-game streaks. Two recent players had 29-gamers: Johnny Damon in 2005 and Jackie Bradley Jr. in 2016.

Dom DiMaggio was an excellent center fielder and a consistent and good hitter. Though he never won a batting title, his average over his full career (losing three years to military service in World War II) was .298. He was a seven-time All-Star.

*Reaching base safely in consecutive games, such as by a hit or walk, definitely shows consistency. Who holds both the team and major-league record for reaching base in consecutive games?*

Ted Williams reached base in 84 consecutive games. After going 0-for-5 on June 30, he started his CGOBS (consecutive games on base safely) streak on July 1, 1949, and he had a single and a walk. He reached base safely in every game he played in July—31 games. He reached base safely in every game he played in August—31 more games. And he reached base safely in the first 24 games he played in September, through September 27. On September 28, in Washington, Ray Scarborough struck him out twice and got him to fly out to the shortstop. Williams was in the on-deck circle when his teammates went down 1–2–3 in the top of the ninth. In all of 1949, there were only five games in which he did not reach base safely. And in a true mark of consistency, there were never two games in a row when Ted Williams failed to reach base for more than 10 years—from July 14, 1940, until September 26, 1950—if one tosses out games in which he pinch-hit and had just that one shot.

## Additional Fielding Firsts

Looking at fielding, let's start with some team records and some individual records.

*Which Red Sox team ranks first in fielding—and had the fewest errors in a full season?*

The 2006 Red Sox played a full 162-game season and committed only 66 errors. The most errors were committed by Kevin Youkilis—with eight, five of them at first base and three at third base. Álex González committed seven at shortstop. Alex Cora also made seven: six at shortstop and one at second. Mike Lowell committed six at third base. There were only seven by all outfielders combined. The pitching staff collectively committed 11 errors, and the catchers committed seven. The team as a whole had a .98910 fielding percentage.

Back when fields were not as well-manicured and considerably rougher, and gloves not as well-made, fielding percentages were lower. The 1901 team was the worst, with a .943 fielding percentage.

The 2020 Red Sox only committed 45 errors, but that was a pandemic-shortened season in which they only played 60 games.

### Which Red Sox player ranks first in terms of the number of consecutive games played without an error?

The answer is 290 games in a row by center fielder Jacoby Ellsbury, from July 29, 2009, and all the way through 2010 and 2011 through September 1, 2012—more than three years. On September 2, he committed an error and two more before the month was done. He had not committed any errors in his first two seasons with Boston, in 411 chances. Over the course of his time with the Red Sox, Ellsbury had 1,734 fielding chances but only committed 8 errors, a fielding percentage of more than 99 percent—.9954.

### Which Red Sox player ranks first in terms of the number of consecutive chances handled without an error?

Kevin Youkilis started his streak in 2006. After an error on July 4, he didn't commit another error the rest of the season in any of his next 69 games that year. He played the entire 2007 season without an error, despite being given 1,080 opportunities (fielding chances) in which to do so. On June 7, 2009, he played third base almost the full game, but with the Red Sox up, 11–2 over Seattle, having moved to first base for the last two innings, he dropped a ball thrown to him. The Red Sox won. Youkilis had handled a league-record 2,379 chances at first base without an error.

In 1921, another first baseman—Stuffy McInnis—handled 1,300 consecutive chances all in that one year, without an error.

Catcher Jason Varitek handled 1,053 consecutive chances without an error in a streak that ran from July 24, 2009, through September 14, 2011.

### There have been numerous times that a position player pitched for the Red Sox. These have included Ted Williams and Jimmie Foxx, once each. Who was the first Red Sox player to do it three years in a row?

Outfielders Harry Hooper and Duffy Lewis both once did it in the same game—October 3, 1913. Tris Speaker did it in 1914. Shortstop Eddie Lake did it six times in 1944. Dave McCarty did it three times in the 2004 world championship season. In 2020, 2021, and 2022, catcher Kevin Plawecki thrice took a turn on the mound, totaling 2⅓ innings of hitless pitching.

### Who was the first Red Sox position player to both pitch and catch parts of a game in the same year?

On August 13, 2020, Tzu-Wei Lin caught the final inning of the game while Kevin Plawecki moved from catcher to the mound and worked a scoreless ninth against Tampa Bay. The Rays won off runs scored against the usual pitching staff, 16–5. The Plawecki/Lin combo didn't allow them a single run. Almost six weeks later, in another Fenway Park game, the Baltimore Orioles were leading 10–1. It seemed like another likely lost cause. Lin became pitcher for the top of the ninth. Leadoff batter Austin Hays swung at Lin's first pitch and homered. Lin allowed two more runs before the inning was over, and his teammates failed to score the dozen runs it would have taken to tie. Lin did close out the inning and still stands as the only Red Sox infielder or outfielder to both pitch and catch in the same season.

It is much rarer for a position player to catch than to pitch. Aside from Lin, there have only been three other position players to catch in a Red Sox game: Mike Greenwell (July 17, 1987), Randy Kutcher (June 8, 1989), and Steve Lyons (September 8, 1993). In Lyons's case, it was his final year with the Red Sox, and he had played every position on the field except catcher—so manager Butch Hobson gave him a shot, catching Tony Fossas in the ninth inning of a game the Red Sox were losing, 8–0. Apparently, he called a good enough game. No one got past second base, and no runs were scored.

### Who was the first, apparently versatile, Red Sox player to play a different position on Opening Day each year for five years in a row?

He didn't commit an error at any one of them. Jack Rothrock played infield his first three seasons. On Opening Day 1928, he led off and was the starting shortstop. In 1929, still batting leadoff, he was the Red Sox center fielder. In 1930, he was the right fielder. In 1932, dropped to fifth in the order, he was Boston's third baseman. In 1933, leading off once more,

Rothrock played left field. Near the end of April, he was traded to the White Sox. His versatility was noted early on. In 1928, he even pitched a perfect inning of relief during the September 24 game in Detroit. Five days later, he caught an inning, thereby having played all nine positions in the one season.

***Who was the first Red Sox player to pull off a triple play in the very last fielding chance he had in the big leagues?***

It could almost have been anybody. He wasn't in a lot of games, though. He was a pitcher, Pete Smith, who worked in one game in 1962 and six in 1963. He worked a total of 18⅔ innings, with a record of 0–1 and a career 6.75 earned run average. He was 0-for-3 as a batter. He had a total of four fielding chances, with one putout and three assists. In the September 28, 1963, game against the visiting Los Angeles Angels, Bill Monbouquette started. The Red Sox were losing 3–2, after six innings. Smith pitched the seventh and eighth. It was in the seventh he got his fielding chance. After giving up a double to the leadoff batter, he walked the next man. Félix Torres bunted to advance the baserunners, and he popped up back to the pitcher. Shortstop Eddie Bressoud alertly shouted, "Let it drop!" Smith did, pounced on the ball, and threw it to Frank Malzone at third. Malzone threw it to Bressoud, who fired it to second baseman Félix Mantilla, covering first base, and the Red Sox had a triple play.

Smith got two groundouts and a strikeout in the eighth, saw Bressoud single to tie it, and then gave way to Dick Radatz, who kept the Angels scoreless in the ninth and picked up the win when Lou Clinton singled in Gary Geiger with the winning run.

***Who was the first team player to have a career fielding percentage of 0.00? This is someone who truly fielded a ball, not someone who played in a game but was never presented with a fielding chance.***

One might guess that the number of fielding chances was small. If someone had had 10 chances and committed errors all 10 times, he wouldn't have lasted long. This man played center field for the first seven innings in Chicago on June 8, 1910. He took Tris Speaker's place in the Red Sox lineup, batting cleanup, and was 1-for-4 at the plate, with a single in the sixth inning. He stole second, thus adding a stolen base to his credits. Ralph Pond wasn't the only Red Sox player to commit an error this day—Hack Engle, Larry Gardner, and Charlie Smith each committed one, too, and shortstop Harry Lord committed three. With seven errors, it's perhaps not surprising that Boston lost, 5–4.

*We saw that Kevin Youkilis was superb defensively at first base. His fielding percentage of .997 ranks tops among all position players. Through the 2021 season, which catcher who has worked at least 400 Red Sox games ranks first in fielding percentage?*

It's quite a competition, with three catchers all finishing with .994. Christian Vázquez first played with the Red Sox in 2014 and played through the first half of the 2022 season. Tony Peña ranks first with a .9942807 fielding percentage. Christian Vázquez is second with .9941696113, and third is Jason Varitek with .9935969.

*Among infielders, aside from first base, who ranks first in fielding percentage?*

Both played the "keystone sack." Second baseman Dustin Pedroia (2006 into 2019) had a career fielding percentage of .991 (57 errors, in 6,635 chances). Marty Barrett ranks second among second basemen with .986 (he played for the Red Sox from 1982 into 1990). Pedroia had an errorless streak of 436 chances from July 29, 2009–May 20, 2010.

*Which shortstop ranks first in career fielding percentage?*

It is Xander Bogaerts, who broke in with the Red Sox late in 2013. His .978 tops John Valentin (.972) and Vern Stephens (.971). The longest streak of error-free chances is held by Rico Petrocelli—227 from August 20, 1968, to May 30, 1969.

*That leaves third base. Who ranks first among Red Sox third basemen?*

Mike Lowell (in 612 Red Sox games from 2006–2010) finished with .972, edging Rico Petrocelli (727 games, from 1966 through 1976) at .970. Just as he does with shortstop, Rico holds the lengthiest errorfree streak at third base—232 chances from June 8 to August 31, 1971.

*What about outfielders? Who ranks first?*

The outfielder with the best fielding percentage is Jacoby Ellsbury, noted a few questions previously, at .995. He is followed closely by three others who are very tightly bunched—Darren Lewis (.9917696), Mookie Betts (.9917173), and Johnny Damon (.9912927).

*While we're at it, who was the best-fielding Red Sox pitcher?*

Bill Monbouquette. His career fielding percentage with the Red Sox was .985. He had 344 fielding chances in his seasons with Boston, 1958 through 1965. He won 254 games. Joe Dobson's second-place mark was .980.

*Helping turn double plays, which Red Sox player ranks first—well above any competition?*

Second baseman Bobby Doerr, who helped turn 1,507 double plays over the course of his 14 seasons with the Red Sox. Second place is held by second baseman Dustin Pedroia, with 940. Third is first baseman George Scott, with 815.

Assists see Doerr's 5,710 top Pedroia's 4,004. Shortstop Everett Scott is third with 3,394.

*Which Red Sox player recorded the most putouts?*

Catcher Jason Varitek ranged into five digits—recording 10,166 putouts in the course of his career. Second, though, was a first baseman—Phil Todt, who played seven years for the Red Sox from 1924 to 1930. Though it was the worst stretch for the team itself, games only typically end after nine innings, and the outs still have to get recorded, even if the final score is 15–2. Todt had 8,676 putouts at first base for Boston.

*Which Sox player recorded the most putouts in nine innings of work?*

Christian Vázquez recorded 23 putouts in the 10-inning game against the Rays at Tropicana Field on September 25, 2016. He actually had 21 putouts through nine innings, accumulated while catching four different Red Sox pitchers, all on strikeouts, and then caught two more in the bottom of the 10th. During the course of the game, pitchers Eduardo

Rodríguez and Heath Hembree combined to strike out 11 Rays in a row. Since neither a hit-by-pitch nor a walk counts as an at-bat (E-Rod hit a batter in the third and walked a batter in the fourth), one could accurately say that in 16 consecutive at-bats, Tampa Bay batters struck out.

Rich Gedman caught Roger Clemens's 20-strikeout game on April 29, 1986, so he earned 20 putouts.

Why didn't catcher Bill Haselman get 20 putouts for Clemens's other 20-K game, on September 18, 1996, in Detroit? He got 19 but failed to catch the ball cleanly when Travis Fryman struck out swinging, the first batter up in the bottom of the second. As Fryman ran to first, Haselman had to throw to first base where Mo Vaughn got the putout. It was a K for Clemens but not a PO for Haselman.

There are two players who recorded 21 putouts in a game. Who were they? They were both first basemen. The first was Stuffy McInnis on July 19, 1918, when Carl Mays pitched a 5–1 shutout at Fenway against the Detroit Tigers. Mays struck out two, depriving McInnis of a shot at two more putouts. Matching McInnis in PO was Bill Sweeney on June 24, 1931. The game was in Cleveland. Wilcy Moore was Boston's pitcher, and he apparently kept the ball down, too. He struck out one, and the Red Sox won, 7–3.

### Who was the first Red Sox player to wear #1 as his uniform number?

It was the same Bill Sweeney, noted in the previous entry, in 1931—the first year the Red Sox wore numbers on their uniforms. Twenty-nine different players have worn the number, but it has been retired since 1988 in honor of Bobby Doerr. Sweeney was a first baseman who only played two years for the Red Sox, 1931 and 1932, but he hit well, batting .309 and then .295.

### Who was the first Red Sox player to wear #9?

There were actually nine players to wear it before the player who, for more or less the past eight decades has been known as "Number Nine"—Ted Williams. Someone different wore it every year until "The Kid" debuted with the team in 1939. The first was catcher Charlie Berry, in 1931 and 1932. And John Smith wore it in 1931 as well, though not at the same time. Berry's last game that year was September 7, Smith played in four games, two on September 17 and two on September 18. Berry returned for part of 1932 but, in late April, was dealt away in a trade that brought Smead Jolley to Boston. In 1933, the number was worn by Merv Shea and then Rick Ferrell. In 1934, Gordie Hinkle wore #9. In 1935 and 1936, Dusty Cooke was assigned the number. In 1937, it was Bobby Doerr's, and in 1938, it was Ben Chapman's.

It may seem like sacrilege, but while Ted Williams was in military service during World War II, both Johnny Peacock and then Lou Finney wore #9 for a while.

Boston Red Sox Ted Williams (#9) with back to the camera chatting with two unknown Red Sox near the batting cage at Fenway Park, late 1950s.
COURTESY OF THE BOSTON PUBLIC LIBRARY, LESLIE JONES COLLECTION

*When was the first time two players wore #9 in the same game at the same time? The Red Sox had two players on the field wearing the name number.*

It was on August 28, 1955, in Kansas City. Ted Williams was 4-for-5 with a home run and two RBIs. Pitching for the Red Sox was Frank Sullivan. It was a hot day, Sullivan explained. "I had to change shirts every inning, and wound up the game in one of Ted Williams's uniforms." The Red Sox beat the Athletics, 14–2.

### Some Baserunning Firsts

We've seen the first stolen base (Tommy Dowd, who had four stolen bases in the team's first four games), the first caught stealing, and so on.

*Who is the first Red Sox player to successfully steal 25 bases before ever being caught?*

Jacoby Ellsbury. He stole nine bases in 2007 and never got caught. Perhaps emboldened, he kept stealing and stealing until May 9, 2008, when he finally got caught. Catcher Jason Kendall of the Brewers threw to second base, and Ellsbury was out. By the end of the 2008 season, he had 50 stolen bases—but had been caught 11 times. The Red Sox record at the time was 54, set by Tommy Harper in 1973 (Harper had stolen 73 bases in 1969 for the Seattle Pilots).

*Who ranks first among Red Sox players for stolen bases in one season?*

It was Harper. With his 50 in 2008, Jacoby Ellsbury had gotten really, really close. In 2009, Ellsbury went for it and stole 70. It remains the Red Sox record. He stole 411 in his seven years with the Sox.

*Who holds the team record for most stolen bases in one game? It was not Ellsbury in 2008 or 2009.*

It was Jacoby Ellsbury in 2013—in the May 30 game against the Phillies in Philadelphia. He stole five bases—in the second, the fourth, twice in the sixth, and once in the eighth.

*In terms of stolen bases, Ted Williams was the first (and only) member of the Red Sox to pull off this feat. What was it?*

Williams stole two bases in his rookie season, 1939. He stole 14 in the 1940s, despite losing three full seasons to military service. He stole seven in the 1950s, the decade in which he turned 40 (and despite missing most of two seasons to additional military service). He stole one in 1960—making him the only Red Sox player to steal a base in four different decades.

*When was the first time a BoSox baserunner was hit by two different batted balls in the same game?*

If hit by a batted ball, the baserunner is out. On June 28, 1917, just five weeks after this "perfect game," Ernie Shore, the pitcher, was hit by a batted ball in the third inning of a home game against the visiting St. Louis Browns. It was the second game of a doubleheader. Shore had singled but was struck by a ball hit by Sox center fielder Jimmy Walsh. In the fifth inning, he bunted and was struck by—or ran into—his own batted ball. And he was out again, this time scored as interference by the batter. The Red Sox won both games by the same 3–2 score.

*Who was the first "ghost runner" in Red Sox history?*

During the pandemic-shortened 2020 season, Major League Baseball implemented a rule to try to enable extra-inning games to come to a quicker conclusion. In each extra inning, the team at bat would start off with a runner placed at second base rather than with the bases empty. That runner was usually the player who had made the final out in the previous innings, but with some exceptions we won't go into here. During the 2020 season, there were four extra-inning games in which the Red Sox played. The first was in Baltimore on August 22. Left fielder Alex Verdugo had made the final out in the ninth, so with the score tied 3–3 after Baltimore's at-bats in the bottom of the ninth, Verdugo was stationed at second base to start the top of the 10th.

The first in the Red Sox 10th struck out, but reliever Cole Suiser walked the next two, and the bases were loaded. Then the third batter walked, and Verdugo was forced home with the go-ahead run. A new pitcher was brought in and got out of the inning. Baltimore's ghost runner in the bottom of the 10th also scored, after a sacrifice bunt (for a base hit) and a wild pitch. The score was tied again, now 4–4. Another single put runners on first and third, so an intentional walk was ordered to load the bases and create more opportunities for outs. After a strikeout, a single drove in the winning run for the Orioles.

There were three other Red Sox games with ghost runners in 2020. On September 3, the Blue Jays scored four runs in the top of the 10th, and the Red Sox never did score. On September 18, neither the Yankees nor Red Sox scored in the 10th, but both teams scored once in the 11th. In the 12th, New York scored again, and the Red Sox failed to match it. In Atlanta on September 25, the Red Sox broke a 4–4 tie with two in the 10th, but the Braves matched that. The Sox scored again in the 11th, but Freddie Freeman hit a two-run homer to give the Braves the walk-off win.

### When was the first time the Red Sox actually won a game, thanks to the ghost runner scoring?

After four fruitless efforts in 2020, it didn't take too long in 2021 for the Red Sox to win such a game. The "ghost runner" rule was continued in 2021 and 2022. On April 6, 2021, at Fenway Park, the Red Sox scored once in the bottom of the eighth and once again in the ninth, creating a 3–3 tie against Tampa Bay. In the 10th, the Rays couldn't advance the runner to third base. The Red Sox did but couldn't get him home. In the top of the 11th, a Willy Adames double scored their ghost runner. In the bottom of the 11th, a Rafael Devers single re-tied the game. In the 12th, the Rays once again got their runner home and held a 5–4 lead.

Hunter Renfroe had made the final out in the 11th so was the ghost runner in the 12th. Ryan Thompson was pitching for Tampa Bay. He got the first batter to ground out and the second to line out. There was no opportunity for Renfroe to advance either time. A wild pitch, though, let both runners to move up 90 feet. J. D. Martinez then doubled deep to right field, both tying the game again and winning it, 6–5.

Rafael Devers's single re-tied the game in the 11th. His 2021 season was his first as an All-Star.
BILL NOWLIN PHOTO

# A FURTHER LOOK AT OTHER POSTSEASON FIRSTS

THERE HAVE BEEN A LOT OF POSTSEASON FIRSTS TOUCHED ON IN PREVIous chapters, particularly the last one, and here are some others.

**What was the first postseason walk-off game?**
In Game Eight of the 1912 World Series, the Red Sox walked off with a win—and the world championship. We touched on this previously when talking about the contributions of the first and only native of Denmark to play in major-league baseball. It's a big enough story to revisit. There had been a tie in Game Two, so Game Eight began with both the Red Sox and New York Giants tied with three wins apiece. The deciding game was at Fenway Park, in the first year the park was open. The starters were Hugh Bedient for the Red Sox and Christy Mathewson for the Giants. Bedient had bested Mathewson in Game Five, 2–1, allowing just three hits to the five off Mathewson.

Game Eight was on October 16. The Giants scored once in the top of the fourth. The Red Sox didn't match that until the bottom of the seventh, when Olaf Henriksen pinch-hit for Bedient and doubled in player/manager Jake Stahl. Smoky Joe Wood relieved Bedient. The game was still tied at the end of nine innings. In the top of the 10th, the Giants got a second run on Red Murray's second double (his first had driven in the earlier run). This time he hit a ground-rule double, then scored on a single to center by Fred Merkle.

Hack Engle pinch-hit for Joe Wood. He reached when center fielder Fred Snodgrass dropped the fly ball hit his way, a ball considered a pretty routine catch. Harry Hooper fielded out to deep center, and Snodgrass caught that one. Mathewson walked Steve Yerkes. Tris Speaker singled to right, scoring Engle and tying the game, 2–2. On the throw to the plate, Speaker took second and Yerkes took third. Duffy Lewis was walked intentionally to increase the possibilities of getting the final two outs while the score was still tied. Third baseman Larry Gardner hit a fly ball to right field, easily deep enough for Yerkes to score the winning run.

### Other Postseason Walk-Offs

There have been 13 other postseason walk-offs for the Red Sox. With more rounds, there are more opportunities for walk-offs—if your team can make the postseason to begin with. The Red Sox won with walk-offs in Game Three of the 1915 World Series and Game Two of the 1916 World Series.

### What was the first walk-off home run in Red Sox postseason history?

It's one that staved off defeat and was, like the 1912 walk-off, in extra innings. On October 21, 1975, Fred Lynn hit a three-run homer in the bottom of the first inning. The Cincinnati Reds tied it in the top of the fifth, then added two more runs in the seventh and another in the eighth. They led 6–3. With two out in the bottom of the eighth, Bernie Carbo pinch-hit and banged a three-run homer into the center-field bleachers, tying the game and giving the Red Sox fresh life. Though the Red Sox got the bases loaded in the bottom of the ninth, with nobody out, the Reds got three outs. In the bottom of the 12th, the score still tied, Carlton Fisk homered right down the left-field line, the ball just staying fair, and the Red Sox won. Red Sox fans only wish they had won Game Seven the next night, but they did not. The team had gone 57 years without a World Series win. Fans would have to wait longer.

### What was the first walk-off home run that clinched a postseason series for the Red Sox?

Red Sox fans were still waiting in 2004. There had been some real opportunities, particularly in 1986 and 2003, but fans were still waiting. Starting in 1981, there were three rounds in the playoffs—the Division Series, the League Championship Series, and the World Series. In 2003, Trot Nixon had won Game Three of the Division Series with an

11th-inning home run. That win prevented the Oakland Athletics from clinching. Boston went on to win the next two games and advance. They battled the Yankees to Game Seven of the 2003 ALCS, but Red Sox fans only wish . . . it didn't happen.

In 2004, the Red Sox won the first two games of the ALDS, beating the Angels 9–3 and 8–3. Game Three, the first one in Boston, saw the Red Sox with a 6–1 lead through five innings, but the Angels scored five runs (four on a Vladimir Guerrero grand slam) in the top of the seventh. The game went into extra innings. Two outs in the bottom of the 10th, with one on, the Angels brought on a new pitcher to face David Ortiz (we will spare him by not mentioning his name). First pitch, home run. A walk-off 8–6 win. The team advanced to the ALCS. The name Ortiz crops up again.

### When was the first time a Red Sox player had three postseason walk-offs all in the same year?

He's in the Hall of Fame. It was David Ortiz. Not only did he hit the walk-off in Game Three of the 2004 ALDS, but he also had two more walk-offs in store for the second round of the playoffs, the ALCS against the Yankees. Most baseball fans know the story. We don't feel the need to go into it deeply here—though it's always a pleasure for a partisan writer to chronicle.

There was Game Three of the ALDS. Then there was Game Four of the 2004 ALCS. With the Red Sox facing elimination, having lost the first three games to the same team that beat them (as they always seemed to do) in Game Seven of the 2003 ALCS. The Yankees had won the first two games in Yankee Stadium, 10–7 and 3–1. Then they slaughtered the Red Sox at Fenway Park, 19–8, in Game Three. In Game Four, though, the Red Sox hung tough, tying the game in the bottom of the ninth on "The Steal" and Bill Mueller's game-tying hit. In the bottom of the 12th, Manny Ramirez led off with a single and David Ortiz hit a walk-off home run.

And in Game Five, the very next night, the Red Sox again came from behind, scoring twice in the bottom of the eighth on a leadoff home run by Ortiz and a second run that scored on a sacrifice fly by Jason Varitek. This game went into extras, too, past the 12th, the 13th, and into the 14th. Johnny Damon had walked in between two strikeouts. Manny Ramirez worked a walk on seven pitches, and now there were runners on first and second. Ortiz singled into right-center, and Damon scored. It was Ortiz's third walk-off hit in an 11-day stretch.

The Red Sox still clung to life. This time they didn't squander it, winning each of their next six postseason games, too—Games Six and Seven of the ALCS in Yankee Stadium and all four of the World Series games against the Cardinals.

**When was the first time a Red Sox rookie clinched a postseason series with a walk-off?**

The Red Sox won the World Series again in 2007. There was one walk-off early in that postseason—in Game Two of the ALDS, Manny Ramirez hit a three-run homer over the Green Monster for a bottom-of-the-ninth 6–3 win.

The Red Sox finally won it all in 2004, after 86 years.
BILL NOWLIN PHOTO

In the best-of-five 2008 ALDS, the Red Sox won the first two games over the Angels in Anaheim, then came back and dropped Game Three at Fenway, losing in the 12th inning, 5–4. In Game Four, the Red Sox took a 2–0 lead on back-to-back RBI at-bats from Jacoby Ellsbury and Dustin Pedroia. In the top of the eighth, the Angels struck back and tied it on a two-run single by Torii Hunter. They led off the top of the ninth with a double. A sacrifice bunt set up a possible go-ahead run, but an attempted steal of home led to an out at the plate. The Red Sox came to bat in the bottom of the ninth. J. D. Drew struck out, and Jason Bay hit a ground-rule double. Mark Kotsay lined out to the first baseman. Rookie shortstop Jed Lowrie stepped into the box. On the first pitch, he singled between first and second, and Bay ran home and scored. It was on to the League Championship Series.

As it happens, J. D. Drew drove in the winning run in a walk-off game in the ALCS. The Rays won three of the first four games, so the Red Sox had their backs to the wall. In Game Five at Fenway, the Red Sox were losing, 7–0, heading into the bottom of the seventh. It looked like all was lost. The Red Sox were reigning world champions, but hopes of another crown were pretty dim. Jed Lowrie led off with a double. After a couple of outs, Coco Crisp singled, Dustin Pedroia singled in Lowrie, and David Ortiz hit a three-run homer. In the eighth, Drew hit a two-run homer, and after Kotsay doubled, Crisp singled in a third run, creating a 7–7 tie. It remained tied in the bottom of the ninth until Drew singled to win it.

**Who was the first Red Sox batter whose last name is 14 letters long to chalk up a postseason walk-off hit?**

Before 2013, the most letters any walk-off hitter had in his last name was seven—a tie between Gardner and Ramirez. David Ortiz already had three walk-offs, all in 2004. In 2013, the Detroit Tigers took on the Red Sox in the League Championship Series. They won Game One on Saturday night at Fenway, winning 1–0, with Aníbal Sánchez only granting the Red Sox one base hit, and spoiling a strong start by Jon Lester. In Game Two, the Tigers led 5–0 after 5½ innings. Pedroia doubled in one run in the bottom of the sixth, and then David Ortiz hit a grand slam in the seventh to tie the game, 5–5. Koji Uehara sent down the Tigers in order in the top of the ninth. Rick Porcello, pitching for Detroit, gave up a leadoff single to Jonny Gomes, who took second base on a throwing error by the shortstop. On a wild pitch, Gomes took third base, from where he scored easily on a single hit by the only player the Red Sox had ever had whose last name was 14 letters long—catcher Jarrod Saltalamacchia. The Red Sox did go on to win the ALCS and the World Series.

As something of a postscript here, we will note that, in 2021, the Red Sox again had back-to-back walk-off hits against Tampa Bay. In Game Three of the ALDS, catcher Christian Vázquez won it with a two-run homer in the bottom of the thirteenth, and in Game Four, Kike Hernández won the clinching game with a sacrifice fly in the bottom of the ninth. The Sox advanced to the ALCS but lost it in six to the Astros.

# A FEW PARTING ITEMS—
# SOME OTHER ODDBALL THINGS

THERE ARE, OF COURSE, SOME OTHER "FIRSTS" THAT ONE MIGHT NOT wish to remember. When did the team first lose more than 100 games and other things like that. We wouldn't want to dwell on the negative but will mention a few such items—briefly.

We've already answered the 100-loss team, in passing. The first time was 1906 (49–105). There were three years in a row—1925 through 1927—and then 1932 and the all-time record 111 losses in 1932. Tom Yawkey bought the team early in 1933 and began to pump more money into player acquisition and building a stronger farm system. Only once did the team ever lose 100 again—right on the nose, 100 losses in 1965.

**Who ranks first among major-league batters for grounding into double plays?**

Jim Rice set the major-league record, grounding into 36 double plays in 1984. It was part of a four-year stretch (1982–1985) when he led the majors four years in a row. The same year he set the record, though, he drove in 122 runs, second in RBIs only to teammate Tony Armas, who drove in one more—123. Rice's 35 GIDP was almost twice as many as anyone else on the team.

**Which pitcher ranks first (worst) in terms of the number of runs surrendered in just one inning?**

It's perhaps unfair, in that Lefty O'Doul was more noted as a left fielder, who played in 970 big-league games. He did pitch in 34 games, however. His fifteenth appearance for the 1923 Red Sox was a game not to remember. He was 1–1 on the season at that point, the first game of a July 7 doubleheader in Cleveland. And he didn't lose the game. When he took over from starter Curt Fullerton, the Red Sox were already losing 8–2. He'd entered the game as a pinch-hitter and made the third out of the fourth. The Indians got one run off him in the bottom of the fourth and two in the fifth. In the bottom of the sixth, he faced 17 batters. After the first four batters, there were two outs and runners on first and second. The next 12 batters all reached base—on six walks and six hits (four singles and two doubles). The team might have kept on batting, but Riggs Stephens got greedy and tried to steal third. O'Doul threw him out.

Thirteen runs scored off O'Doul in just the one inning and another three before the game was over. Manager Frank Chance left O'Doul in. The Red Sox lost, 27–3. They lost the second game, too, 8–5.

**Who was the first team manager to commit suicide?**

It was Chick Stahl, who had the misfortune to play for the 1906 team (and manage the last 40 games of the season, with a record of 14–26). The team finished with 105 losses. But it wasn't the play on the field that drove him to swallow four ounces of carbolic acid during spring training in March 1907. He had resigned as manager two days earlier. He said that having to be in a position to release players "grated on my nerves" and "made me sick at heart." Dennis Auger has said Stahl was said by some to have suffered chronic depression and had perhaps been haunted by a pregnancy of someone other than his wife, or even a homosexual relationship.

**Who was the first former Red Sox manager to be convicted of a crime involving a death?**

Aside from a perhaps tasteless joke that Grady Little killed the chance for the Red Sox to reach the World Series in 2003, or for Joe McCarthy to have done the same starting Denny Galehouse in the 1948 single-game playoff, there actually was a Red Sox manager who killed a man—a Louisiana state highway worker in 1958. It was Mike "Pinky" Higgins, and he was convicted of driving while intoxicated. He was sentenced to four years of hard labor in the Louisiana State Penitentiary but was paroled after two months and died of a heart attack less than 48 hours later.

### Who was the first Red Sox player named "John Smith"?

No, it was not one of those foreign-born players like Aloysius Szymanski, who changed his name to Al Simmons. Or Jack Quinn (1922–1925), who was born Joannes Pajkos. It was . . . John Smith. The only player named John Smith in either the AL or NL after 1900.

Smith didn't have a long major-league career—four games with the 1931 Red Sox. Four games in two days: back-to-back doubleheaders on September 17 and 18. He was a first baseman and a switch hitter. He handled 46 chances in the field without a single error. At the plate, he got a couple of singles and drove in one run, the only run in a 2–1 loss. He wore #9 for the Red Sox, but he is not the man in whose honor the number was retired. After baseball, John Smith worked as a legal adviser with the Internal Revenue Service.

### When was the first time a three-pound fish fell out of the sky during a Red Sox game and landed on the pitching mound?

On May 17, 1947, Ellis Kinder was pitching for the St. Louis Browns, and in the bottom of the third inning, the game had to be interrupted. A six-inch three-pound smelt had fallen from the sky—dropped by a passing seagull—and landed right on the mound. Plate umpire Bill Summers handled the removal himself. The game continued. The Red Sox lost the game, 4–2.

### When was the first time Ted Williams was ejected from a game?

He was sometimes called "Tempestuous Ted." He was known to make rude gestures toward the press box and to expectorate toward the stands. We saw that the first player for the team was ejected in the thirteenth game in team history, back in 1901. When was the first time Ted Williams was ejected, and what for?

You may have known the answer. He was never ejected. He never got in a heated argument with an umpire. If he had words, it was quietly, looking at the ground and saying something along the lines of, "You can do better than that" regarding a strike call with which he disagreed. He never showed up an umpire. And he was one of the few players who, on the last day of the season, stopped by the umpires' room to wish them well for the winter.

Strategic? There's no way to know if he might have had a close call go his way once in a while. There's the famous quote of an umpire telling a catcher who squawked about not getting a strike call on a close pitch, "If Mr. Williams did not swing, it's not a strike."

Jim Rice was another longtime Red Sox player who was never ejected from a game. In just eight years with the Red Sox, however, manager Terry Francona was ejected 25 times.

Among Red Sox players, in part reflecting his 23 years on the Red Sox, the career leader in ejections is Carl Yastrzemski, with 11.

**What was the first time the Red Sox had four managers in one game?**
This story has an ejection connection, to say the least. It was May 30, 2014, a Friday night at Fenway Park. Tampa Bay was in town. The Red Sox had won in a walk-off the night before, beating the Atlanta Braves, 4–3. Rays pitcher David Price hit David Ortiz in the back with a pitch in the first inning. There was some history; the benches had emptied the previous Sunday when the two teams were in Florida. Words were exchanged. Price may still have been upset at Ortiz hitting two homers off him in the 2013 ALDS and maybe had admired the second one a bit too long for Price's liking. In any event, plate umpire Dan Bellino promptly issued warnings. Red Sox manager John Farrell was ejected "after a few seconds and a few loud curses" (*Globe*). In the fourth inning, after Mike Carp was hit by a pitch, bench coach Torey Lovullo angrily threw his hat on the ground, and he, too, was ejected. Third-base coach Brian Butterfield moved into the dugout to manage, but in the sixth inning, he, too, was ejected when a Brandon Workman pitch went behind Evan Longoria's head. Because the benches had been warned, both Workman and Butterfield were tossed. Someone took over as the fourth manager, but newspaper stories don't say who.

Not a single Ray was ejected, despite three Red Sox batters being hit by pitches and no Rays batters. The Red Sox won the game, in 10 innings,

3–2. Perhaps ironically, the winning run was scored by Jonny Gomes, the third batter hit by a Tampa Bay pitch, when the next batter, catcher A. J. Pierzynski, tripled him home.

### What was the first time the Red Sox were involved in a forfeit?

They weren't the Red Sox the first time, but they were the next two or three times. Only twice did the forfeit stand. Boston came out on top each time.

June 28, 1902: The first forfeit came early on and involved John McGraw—the same McGraw who, in 1940, managed the New York Giants and refused to play in a World Series against Boston. In 1902, he was manager of the Baltimore Orioles. The game was in Baltimore. McGraw was a player/manager (and a future Hall of Famer) who played third base in the game. Boston was in second place, 3½ games behind the White Sox. Baltimore was in seventh place, nine games behind. McGraw had a history of disputes with umpires, particularly those in the new American League, and was quite often at odds with league leader Ban Johnson.

Boston scored first, one run in the first, and Baltimore answered with one, then took a 3–1 lead through five. Boston leaped ahead with four runs in the sixth, three more in the seventh, and were ahead 8–4—enough to put McGraw in a bad mood. Cy Young wasn't pitching poorly but had been victim of four errors (one his own). In the bottom of the eighth, the Orioles had runners on first and second with nobody out. On a ball hit by Roger Bresnahan to Jimmy Collins at third, Collins threw to the plate, hoping to get Dan McGann, who had already rounded third and headed for home. Caught in a rundown, McGann managed to get back to third safely—but Cy Seymour had been equally aggressive and had himself rounded third. For a moment, it had looked like all the runners were safe, but umpire Tommy Connolly (a Hall of Famer himself) ruled that Seymour hadn't re-touched third base on his way back to second and was tagged out. McGraw exploded, and Connolly later said that McGraw had called him a "robber and a thief." He may have used other words, too. He was ejected—but refused to leave, so Connolly forfeited the game to Boston.

McGraw managed one more game for Baltimore but was then suspended by Ban Johnson, who had any number of other issues with McGraw. Wilbert Robinson took over as Orioles manager—and McGraw jumped back to the senior league, becoming manager of the Giants.

September 3, 1939: This time, the villains were Red Sox fans at Fenway who were trying to prevent what might have become a Red Sox loss to the Yankees. Given that New York held a 12½-game lead over second-place Boston, it wasn't as though the pennant was on the line, but the Red Sox had beaten the Yankees seven times in a row and maybe the fans were just feeling rambunctious. It was a Sunday doubleheader, and the Red Sox had won the first game, 12–11.

There was a Sunday curfew time on games back then—6:29 PM. They had to get the game in before it was called. Both teams scored once in the first. The Sox led 3–1 heading into the fourth. The Yankees held a 4–3 lead after the top of the sixth, but the Red Sox scored two in the bottom of the sixth. The Yankees tied it, 5–5, in the top of the seventh. Young rookie right fielder Ted Williams had two home runs in the game. In the course of the two games, the Red Sox had come from behind five times—but now time was running out.

The Yankees scored twice in the top of the eighth inning and had runners on second and third. Red Sox manager Joe Cronin began to slow down play, in hopes of the curfew kicking in and the score reverting to the 5–5 tie after the last completed inning. Joe Heving took a *l-o-n-g* time intentionally walking Babe Dahlgren. But the Yankees wanted to get the game in, and Dahlgren started swinging wildly at the intentional pitchouts. Cronin killed some more time objecting to the tactics and said he would play the game under protest. George Selkirk faked a steal of home and was easily tagged out. Then Joe Gordon did the same thing—a pretend steal of home intending to get an out. The fans expressed their feeling and "from almost every sector of the enclosure, articles ranging from Summer skimmers to undevoured hot dog rolls were thrown until the park was beyond playing condition. The barrage lasted for fully three minutes." Plate umpire Cal Hubbard forfeited the game to New York. The forfeit was later overruled, and the game was declared a 5–5 seven-inning tie game. The New York players were reportedly fined.

August 15, 1941: Newspaper readers the next day read about a 6–3 home victory for the Washington Senators—but look at the box score today. There was no winning pitcher and no losing pitcher. The game was called off due to rain. The Red Sox had been leading 3–0 after three innings but then (as rain fell and the grounds got wetter and wetter) gave up six runs over the next four innings. Joe Cronin protested the game because the Washington ground crew had failed to cover the field; Senators manager Bucky Harris said there weren't enough grounds crew members to pull out the tarp. And the fans weren't about to help. The Senators may have thought they were smart, but AL president Will Harridge later forfeited the game to the Red Sox, but rather than a 9–0 forfeit score, or the apparent 6–3 Senator win, it was made a 6–3 Red Sox win, and one can see it in the historical record today: Senators 6, Red Sox 3—a 6–3 win for the Red Sox. Ted Williams was 0-for-2 in the game, his batting average dropping to .405.

**Who was the first former Red Sox player and United States espionage agent to have been tasked to perhaps assassinate a German physicist?**

Whole books—and even movies (*The Catcher Was A Spy*)—have been written about Moe Berg. He was indeed a catcher, joining the Red Sox as a backup to future Hall of Famer Rick Ferrell in 1935 and 1936 at age 33. A lifetime .243 hitter, Berg did better than that for the Red Sox, hitting .262 in 148 games over five seasons. He became a coach in his last season (1939) and then coached the next two years as well.

He was a practicing attorney, a graduate of Columbia University Law School who was also noted for his ability to speak as many as a dozen languages. In August 1943, at age 41, he was recruited into the OSS (the Office of Strategic Services, today renamed the Central Intelligence Agency, or CIA) and contributed to WW2 intelligence work on three continents: Asia, North America, and South America. In addition to his other talents, Berg knew enough about physics to have been sent to a conference in Switzerland, where he met informally with German physicist Werner Heisenberg, but had purportedly been armed and instructed to assassinate Heisenberg if he concluded that Germany had advanced significantly in plans to develop an atomic bomb. Fortunately for both, the plans had not progressed to a dangerous degree.

**Who was the first player selected by the Red Sox when the current Player Draft began in 1965?**

Billy Conigliaro was a first-round selection in 1965, the fifth pick overall. Billy joined his brother, Tony, on the Red Sox in 1969. His best year was his first full year, 1970, when he hit 18 homers and drove in 58 runs. Combining two stats, the two brothers accounted for 54 homers and 174 runs batted in that year.

**What was the first player selected by the Red Sox in the Player Draft who later was inducted into the National Baseball Hall of Fame?**

Jim Rice was the team's first-round pick in 1971, the fifteenth overall selection in the draft. He was inducted into the Hall of Fame in 2009. The second was ... well, actually, we're still waiting on that. Many other draft picks did make major contributions to the ballclub.

**Which Red Sox pitcher ranks first among appearances in a single season?**

In 2005, Mike Timlin appeared in exactly 50 percent of the team's 162 regular-season games. For anyone who is mathematically challenged, that means that Timlin appeared in 81 games. He did well, too—finishing the year with a record of 7–3 with a 2.24 earned run average. He averaged almost—but not quite—one inning per outing, working a total of 80⅓ innings.

**Who was the first non-pitcher to "earn" a "Golden Sombrero" in a game?**

The term refers to striking out four times in a game. It's not a mark of prowess at the plate. It took six years for the first one, but Hobe Ferris did in on September 1, 1906—but, to be fair, it was a 24-inning game. (Pitcher Bill Dinneen had done this on July 9, 1902—in a 17-inning game, in which he went the distance.) First in a nine-inning game: center fielder Denny Sullivan on June 29, 1907—courtesy of Rube Waddell.

**Who was the first non-pitcher to earn a "Platinum Sombrero" in a nine-inning game?**

A Platinum Sombrero is awarded to someone who struck out five times in one game. Phil Plantier was the first, on October 1, 1991. He wasn't cheated by plate umpire Derryl Cousins; every one of the five Ks ended on a swinging strike.

Cecil Cooper once struck out six times in one game, a 15-inning affair on June 14, 1974.

**Who was the first Red Sox player to achieve what Herm Krabbenhoft calls a "Downtown Golden Sombrero"—four strikeouts and a home run?**

Jim Rice, in an 11-inning Red Sox win on July 31, 1979. In the first game of a doubleheader on July 20, 2000, Carl Everett managed it in just nine innings.

**What was the first time the Red Sox had a 10–5 victory taken from them and declared a "no-decision"—as though the game had not existed?**

On July 28, 1924. Here's the story. It was in St. Louis against the Browns. The Red Sox held a 5–4 lead going into the bottom of the ninth, but the Browns tied it up and had a runner on second. Plate umpire Brick Owens refused to let Norm McMillan bat and ordered the catcher to bat instead. He grounded out. Manager George Sisler protested the game, but it continued, and the Red Sox jumped on the Browns for five runs in the top of the 10th. The protest was upheld by the league, and the victory was taken away from the Red Sox. Why had Owens refused to let McMillan bat? He'd come into the game as an eighth-inning pinch-runner, and in the same inning, the Browns also had a pinch-hitter. Owens was a veteran umpire, in the twelfth year of a 25-year career, but he apparently became confused. The league declared the game a "no-decision," and the two teams squared off to re-play it from scratch on September 13. The Red Sox won that one, 13–11. Owens was again the plate umpire, but despite the 12 hits per side, seven errors in all, and all the scoring, there were no disputes of significance.

Let's return to some better memories.

**Who ranks first among Red Sox batters for leadoff home runs?**

Mookie Betts, with 20 of them—twice as many as the second-place batter, Jacoby Ellsbury, who had 10.

**Who ranks first among Red Sox leadoff homers in a single season?**

Nomar Garciaparra, who hit seven of them in 1997. His career total is also seven. The most Mookie hit in any one year is six, in 2016. In 2021, Kike Hernández hit six.

**Who was the first Red Sox player to hit a pinch-hit homer in both games of a doubleheader?**

It was player/manager Joe Cronin. The date was June 17, 1943. The park was Fenway Park. Cronin had pinch-hit on June 15 in the first game of a doubleheader and hit a three-run homer off Philadelphia's Lum Harris. The Sox still lost, 7–4. In the second game, he pinch-hit again, with one out and runners on first and second in the bottom of the ninth. That time he fouled out. He didn't play on June 16, but on June 17, he pinch-hit for pitcher Lou Lucier with two on in the bottom of the seventh and the Red Sox losing, 4–1. His three-run homer off Russ Christopher tied the game, and Skeeter Newsome won it for Boston in the ninth, 5–4, on a bases-loaded error. There was a second game on June 17. The Red Sox were losing 8–4, going into the bottom of the eighth. Again, there were two on base and again Cronin assigned himself to pinch-hit for the pitcher. Once more, he hit a three-run homer. This time the team came up short and lost, 8–7.

Cronin hit .312 in his 1943 season's 77 at-bats.

**Which Red Sox team ranks first for regular-season wins?**

After the first 122 years of franchise history, the 2018 Red Sox team ranks first in wins. There have only been four times the team won more than 99 games—in 1912, they were 105–47–2; in 1915, they were 101–50–4; in 1946, they were 104–50–2; and in 2018, the team finished 108–54.

**Which team ranks first in winning percentage?**

Ignoring the tie games, and working just with wins and losses, the winning percentages were 1912 (.691), 1915 (.669), 1946 (.675), and 2018 (.667).

**Adding in postseason wins and losses, which team ranks first in winning percentage?**

The totals are 1912 (.685), 1915 (.673), 1946 (.665), and 2018 (.660).

# SELECTED BIBLIOGRAPHY

Abrams, Roger, *The First World Series and the Baseball Fanatics of 1903* (Boston: Northeastern University Press, 2003)

Bradlee, Ben Jr., *The Kid: The Immortal Life of Ted Williams* (New York: Little, Brown, 2013)

Burgess, Chuck and Bill Nowlin, *Love That Dirty Water: The Standells and the Improbable Boston Red Sox Anthem* (Burlington, MA: Rounder Books, 2007)

Nowlin, Bill, *Day By Day with the Boston Red Sox* (Burlington, MA: Rounder Books, 2007)

Nowlin, Bill and Jim Prime, *Fenway Park at 100: Baseball's Hometown* (New York: Sports Publishing, 2012)

Nowlin, Bill, *Fenway Park Day by Day: The First Hundred Years* (Burlington, MA: Rounder Books, 2012)

Nowlin, Bill, *Fenway Park Trivia: Fact and Fancy From the First 100 Years* (Burlington, MA: Rounder Books, 2012)

Nowlin, Bill, *Pumpsie and Progress: The Red Sox, Race, and Redemption* (Burlington, MA: Rounder Books, 2010)

Nowlin, Bill, *Red Sox Threads: Odds and Ends from Red Sox History* (Burlington, MA: Rounder Books)

Nowlin, Bill, *Red Sox in 5's and 10's* (Cheltenham, UK: The History Press, 2010)

Nowlin, Bill and Jim Prime, *The Red Sox World Series Encyclopedia* (Burlington, MA: Rounder Books, 2008)

Prime, Jim and Bill Nowlin, *Ted Williams: The Pursuit of Perfection* (Champaign, IL: Sports Publishing, 2002)

Shaughnessy, Dan and Stan Grossfeld, *Fenway: A Biography in Words and Pictures* (Boston: Houghton Mifflin, 1999)

Smith, Curt, *Mercy!: A Celebration of Fenway Park's Centennial Told Through Red Sox Radio and TV* (Washington, DC: Potomac Books, 2012)

Stout, Glenn, *Fenway 1912: The Birth of a Ballpark, a Championship Season, and Fenway's Remarkable First Year* (Boston and New York: Houghton Mifflin Harcourt, 2012)

Stout, Glenn and Richard Johnson, *Red Sox Century* (Boston: Houghton Mifflin, 2004)

Tan, Cecilia, and Bill Nowlin, *The 50 Greatest Red Sox Games* (New York: John Wiley, 2006)

Wisnia, Saul, *Fenway Park: The Centennial /100 Years of Red Sox Baseball* (New York: St. Martin's, 2011